CONVERSATIONS

WITH

Milton H. Erickson, M.D.

VOLUME 1

Changing Individuals

Edited by

Jay Haley

TRIANGLE PRESS

Library of Congress Catalog Card Number 84-052027

ISBN 0-931513-18-9

Published by Triangle Press
Distributed by W. W. Norton & Co., Inc., 500 Fifth Avenue,
 New York, N. Y. 10110
W. W. Norton & Co., Ltd., 37 Great Russell Street, London,
 WC1B3NU

CONTENTS

v

CONVERSATIONS

WITH

Milton H. Erickson, M.D.

VOLUME 1

Changing Individuals

INTRODUCTION

Milton H. Erickson, M.D., was the first strategic therapist. He might even be called the first *therapist*, since he
was the first major clinician to concentrate on how to
change people. Previously, clinicians devoted themselves
to understanding the human mind; they were explorers of
the nature of man. Changing people was of secondary interest. In contrast, Erickson had one major concern in his
professional life – finding ways to influence people. Whether influencing people with hypnosis, persuasion, or direc-
tives, Erickson focused upon developing a variety of techniques to relieve psychological and physical distress. He
seems to have been the first major therapist to expect clinicians to innovate ways to solve a wide range of problems
and to say that the responsibility for therapeutic change
lies with the therapist, rather than with the patient.

In the conversations contained in this volume, Dr. Erickson expresses his basic ideas about the theory and practice of therapy. It is extraordinary to be able to present
interviews with a master therapist describing all aspects
of his work at a time when he was most productive. Many
readers who met Dr. Erickson in his later years, and who
thought of him as a physically infirm old guru with almost
magical hypnotic powers, will be surprised by what he has
to say about therapy. During these conversations he was
in his prime, conducting a busy practice while also traveling and teaching everywhere in the country. There is no
magic in his work: He was a man who trained carefully to
know his business and expected others to do the same.

The conversations, beginning in 1955, continued through 1968. This is Volume 1, containing Dr. Erickson's views on changing individuals. Volume 2 presents his therapy with married couples, and Volume 3 his ways of changing children and families. Discussions with him about hypnosis have been selected out and will, it is hoped, be presented in a later volume.

These conversations were the product of Gregory Bateson's research project on communication, which extended from 1952 to 1962.* John Weakland and I were research associates on that project, and Don D. Jackson and William F. Fry were psychiatric consultants. These conversations with Erickson were primarily about the nature of therapy, about hypnosis, and about ways of describing human interaction, because the project focused upon those topics. Bateson had introduced the cybernetic perspective of the self-correcting system into the field of psychology and psychiatry after attending the Macy Foundation meetings on that subject in the 1940s. By the mid-1950s our research project was attempting to explain schizophrenia as a product of a family system, and we were beginning to do therapy with whole families. We were also explaining other kinds of symptomatic behavior as systematic responses to intimates, partly as the result of observations in our private practices. In 1957 Jackson expressed this view in a paper, "The Question of Family Homeostasis."**

This volume begins with conversations I had with Dr. Erickson in 1957. In private practice, I was attempting to do brief therapy using hypnosis and I realized that I needed to know more about it. Although I had made use of hypnosis in research and taught it in psychiatric seminars, I was finding that knowing how to hypnotize people is quite

---

*Haley, J. "Development of a Theory: The History of a Research Project." In: *Reflections on Therapy*. Washington, D.C.: Family Therapy Institute, 1981.

**Jackson, D. D. "The Question of Family Homeostasis," *Psychiat. Quart. Suppl.*, 1957, 31, 79–90, Part 1.

different from knowing how to *change* them with hypnosis. To better understand hypnosis and brief therapy techniques I sought out Dr. Erickson as a consultant. At the same time the Bateson project was beginning to study different therapy techniques, and we also wished to include his special approach in that research.

Besides the brief therapy conversations, this volume includes many conversations John Weakland and I had with Erickson over the years as part of our investigation of the nature of communication in therapy. Gregory Bateson is involved in some of these conversations, particularly the ones on family issues. Also, to show Erickson at work, in the Appendix to this volume I have included two verbatim interviews of patients done by Erickson. One of them is a consultation at a seminar in 1963, where difficult patients were brought in for him to interview as a demonstration. The second is with Erickson and a patient he relieved of pain, who talks about the experience of therapy with Erickson. The identities of the patients have been disguised.

The conversations presented here were not conducted or recorded with any idea of publication. Gregory Bateson's research tradition was to film and record data. Audio recordings were an alternative to taking notes and allowed us to listen at our leisure and consider the more subtle aspects of Erickson's ideas. Since we did not anticipate publication, the conversations were not designed with an audience in mind. John Weakland and I usually prepared questions in advance that were relevant to our special research interests at that time; we went from topic to topic in a sequence which was important to us but would not interest a reader today. Therefore, I have organized and selected the conversations with today's reader in mind. When there is a break between sections of transcript, I have indicated it with three asterisks (* * *). That also may indicate an interruption of an hour, or a day, or more. At times the reader might find it disconcerting when a line of conversation is interrupted and not continued. In such instances we never resumed where we left off after a break.

I might mention in passing that interviewing Erickson required some skill. Not only did he have his own ideas about what should be discussed – not necessarily our research interests – but also the topics were complex. Our task was to gather specific information about therapy, as well as to stimulate him to free associate, so that what he had not presented previously in papers or lectures, or perhaps even said before, might be expressed. He was developing an approach to therapy which was new, and the premises of it had not been articulated. Therefore, we needed to interview him about ideas and theory, as well as about cases which expressed his basic ideas and theory implicitly. It might be said that we were attempting to question a revolutionary during a revolution, when all of us were unclear about the direction in which the ideas and techniques were leading.

Reading these conversations, it seems obvious that at times Dr. Erickson had to be patient with our obtuseness and our difficulty in understanding some of his premises. Many readers today will find a similar difficulty with Erickson's ideas. In the 1950s he was particularly difficult to understand because the therapy of that time was primarily oriented toward the development of insight and uncovering of psychodynamics. The therapist was expected to be only an explorer with a patient of the ideas behind his problems and their roots in childhood. There was no emphasis on changing people. Family therapy and behavior therapy were just beginning, and the idea of using a range of therapeutic techniques was unknown. Hypnosis had been essentially forbidden to the field for years, and so ideas based upon it were simply bewildering to the average therapist at the time. Although every major psychiatrist knew of Dr. Erickson, many of them thought he came from another planet. It seems odd now, but in the therapy mystique of that time it was Dr. Erickson's emphasis upon the real world and common sense that was particularly difficult to grasp.

Another problem for John Weakland and I at the time was the fact that we were developing a theory that symptoms were functional in a family system. We were concerned with elaborating the homeostatic idea that people governed each other's behavior by their responses to one another. Inevitably, this view suggests that a family member reacts against, or must adapt to, a change in another family member. When we brought up this idea, Dr. Erickson responded as if we were presenting ideas that would make therapy more difficult. He was interested in change, not in how situations remain stable, which is the systems view. That is, the homeostatic view is a way of explaining how change does not occur; it is not a way of thinking about how to induce change. Today, when students talk to me about resistance, I feel the same irritation that Dr. Erickson must have felt. Thinking about resistance is a handicap if one is seeking new ways to bring about change, which was Erickson's interest. Typically, too, we were seeking theoretical generalizations and Dr. Erickson was emphasizing the importance of recognizing the uniqueness of each person. It is hoped that the conversations that came out of our differences will be of value to a reader puzzling over these basic issues.

As we struggled in these conversations to understand Erickson's approach, his ideas and cases often startled and amazed us. They also delighted us because of their refreshing humor. The transcript does not fairly represent the laughter which so often took place as we enjoyed the absurdity of some human problems and the absurdity of some of the solutions.

The reader unfamiliar with Milton H. Erickson will find these conversations a lively presentation of his ideas and approach to therapy. The reader who has read everything written by and about Erickson will find the basic data on his views here in his own words. Many of the case reports will be familiar because I drew upon these conversations for my book, *Uncommon Therapy*.* Some of these cases Erickson told to other people, who then published them. The Erickson scholar will have the opportunity to examine these recordings of what Erickson actually said and compare them with the summaries of authors who considered themselves to be presenting his work.

Except for editorial corrections and the elimination of side issues, the conversations are verbatim. Nothing is changed in what Erickson or his interviewers said, although at times there are guesses because of the quality of the recordings. The research-minded will find a copy of the original tape recordings of these conversations on file with The Milton H. Erickson Foundation in Phoenix, Arizona.

---

*Haley, J. *Uncommon Therapy: The Psychiatric Techniques of Milton H. Erickson, M.D.* New York: Norton, 1973.

CHAPTER 1

The Body Image

1957. Present were Milton H. Erickson and Jay Haley.

Haley: I have two reasons for being here. Our research project is about to begin an investigation of psychotherapy; we're going to explain it. And I went into private practice a few months ago doing brief hypnotherapy on various kinds of symptoms. I find I don't know enough about what I'm doing, so I want to find out more about brief psychotherapy. I would like to present you a description of about nine or ten patients, which I think are typical, and have you tell me how you would handle them.

Erickson: All right.

H: I have a whole week, so I expect I can learn all about psychotherapy in that time. I wouldn't expect that anywhere else but here.

E: (Laughs) Well, we can have our dreams.

H: In my practice I get regular referrals of various kinds — physical symptoms and some behavioral problems. My difficulty is that I am referred to largely for hypnosis, and I get quite a few people who are not very good subjects. I'd like to help them even though they are not good subjects, and I don't know enough about how to do brief therapy. I've been doing the more traditional kind of therapy for three or four years. I know

1

how to handle patients if I sit back and listen to them and make comments once in a while. But when I have people come to me expecting something in a hurry, the hurry being anywhere from one or two to 20 sessions, I don't know enough about what sort of information I need from them or what I need to do when I get that information.

E: In brief therapy what are usually your problems?

H: Well, I have symptoms like headaches, menstrual pains, a youth with a speech block, a woman who lost her voice, insomnia, and so on. I would really like to go over some of them one by one. Mostly I get problems from doctors who think that hypnosis will cure like a miracle, you know, and they send them to me. In my area there is no one working with hypnosis, except the people John Weakland and I are teaching. The local medical folk are very reluctant to refer patients who have somatic symptoms to psychiatrists, even when there is no physiological basis for the symptom. They don't like the idea of long-term psychotherapy. So they send them to me expecting something quick. I know you often do very brief therapy, and I have a pretty good idea that this is the place I can learn more about it than anywhere else.

I am actually using some of the techniques I have heard you mention in our conferences on hypnosis and finding them useful. I'll give you an example, beginning with a simple kind of problem, or one that should be simple. This is a girl referred to me a couple of weeks ago for severe premenstrual cramps. About eight hours a day once a month she is incapacitated and must go to bed with Seconal and aspirin and such. She has been doing this since she was 14 years old. She is not a good hypnotic subject. I have seen her for two sessions. I don't think I can help her with hypnosis in a straight kind of direct suggestion. I don't

think that I can even persuade her that she is enough
in a trance so that other kinds of suggestions can carry
the aura of hypnosis. Yet I feel that her problem isn't
very complicated. She started to menstruate at 12 –
perfectly normal. At 13 she was in a city during a
bombing raid; she lived up on the hillside and saw the
raid but she wasn't injured in any way. For a year
after that she didn't menstruate. She returned to the
States with her mother, and at the age of 14 she began
to menstruate again. This was very painful. She has
menstruated painfully ever since.

E: Is she a pretty girl?

H: Yes.

E: Does she think so?

H: Yes, she does. She is not by any means fully confident
that she is pretty. She works a little too hard at it.

E: What do you think about that?

H: What do I think about it? Well I think she is 28 years
old and isn't married for reasons she doesn't understand.

E: Yet she is a pretty girl? And she works too hard at it.
You see, in brief psychotherapy one of the important
considerations is the body image. Did I ever discuss
that with you?

H: No, I don't think so.

E: By body image I mean how does the person look upon
herself? What sort of an image do they have of themselves? She's a pretty girl; she works too hard at it.
She is telling you she has a defective body image. It
is so tremendously important that she have a good
body image. A good body image implies not only the
physical self as such, but the functional self, and the
personality *within* the body. Does she know that it
is *all right* to know that she has very pretty eyes?
Does she know that it is *all right* to be aware of the
fact that her chin is too heavy? Is it *all right* for her

to have a pretty mouth, but to have her ears set unevenly? Does she know that the individuality of her face is the thing that gives her individual appeal?

H: Is that the way you would put it to her?

E: That's the way it should be put to her. You'll see these pretty girls that absolutely depreciate themselves. They are unaware of the fact that they are trying to classify their looks in terms of other people's looks. They usually think about some symptom of some sort that proves to them conclusively that they are not adequate people. The girl with the painful menstruation—exactly what does she think about her body? Are her hips too large? Or her ankles too large? Is her pubic hair too scarce, too straight, too curly? Or what about it? It may be too painful a thing for her ever to recognize consciously. Are her breasts too large? Too small? The nipples not the right color? In brief psychotherapy, one of the first things you do, whether it's a man or a woman, is try to find out what their body image is.

H: How do you find this out?

E: Sometimes, after a few minutes with a patient, with a girl in particular, I ask her what her best features are. And why. I make it a straightforward inquiry, in the same way that one would do a physical examination. You start to examine the scalp and you work down to the soles of the feet. It's purely an objective examination. You really want to know what the body image is, so you do a physical examination of the body image.

H: I see. What this girl does is work a little too hard at looking feminine. Her curls are placed just so, her makeup is just so, her earrings just so.

E: In other words, what does she lack in her body image that is feminine, so that she has to overdo, or overemphasize, the external evidence of femininity? What deficiency does she think she has in her genitals? In her breasts, in her hips, in her figure, in her face?

H: Well, how do the patients accept such an objective look at their genitals? Do they take your discussion so objectively?

E: They do for me.

H: I think that might be difficult for me, but it might not.

E: You see a girl come in with a very crooked part in her hair. The next time she comes in, her hair is combed slightly differently, but with a crooked mid-line part. And you ought to wonder about her attitude towards her genitals.

H: If the part is crooked you should go into that?

E: Yes. Because you should bear in mind that our own familiarity with ourselves, our physical selves, is so great that we never really appreciate that familiarity — consciously.

H: Hmm.

E: How do you recognize that a woman is wearing falsies?

H: I don't know how I would recognize it, except in terms of the proportion with the rest of her body.

E: I'll demonstrate to you. I ask a woman to sit up straight and pretend that she has a mosquito on her right shoulder, then I ask her to please swat it. First, I'll show you how I swat it (demonstrates swatting with arm not touching chest). Now I'll exaggerate as I show you how she swats it. You see, she detours her elbow in accord with the actual size of her breast.

H: Oh, I see, she brushes her breast with falsies.

E: Yes. If she's got very small breasts, practically no breasts, she tends to swat her shoulder in much the same way that I would. If she has got large breasts she makes a large detour.

H: That's a simple test.

E: A very simple test. When I see a patient with a defective body image, I usually say, "There are a number of things that you *don't* want me to know about, that you *don't* want to tell me. There are a lot of things about yourself that you don't want to discuss. Therefore, let's discuss those things that you feel free to discuss, and be sure that you don't discuss those that you are unwilling to discuss." She has blanket permission to withhold anything and everything. But she did come to discuss things. Therefore she starts discussing this, discussing that. It's always, "Well, *this* is all right to talk about." Before she's finished, she has mentioned everything.

H: You made it safe.

E: I made it safe. And each new item, 'Well, this really isn't so important that I have to withhold it. I can use the withholding permission for more important matters." Simply a hypnotic technique. To make them respond to the idea of withholding, and to respond to the idea of communicating.

H: I see.

E: Their withholding is essentially a mere matter of shuffling the order in which they present, and that's sufficient withholding.

H: It also forces them to think of what they would normally withhold, which they probably hadn't thought much of before.

E: There is the girl who had a series of affairs and is too distressed to tell you about it. You have given her permission to withhold. She knows you don't know about the affairs. She starts thinking over—well, number one is all right to tell about. Number five is all right to tell about. Not number two. And she tells about number four, number six, number three, number seven, number two. *She has withheld* number two. In fact, she has withheld all of them except number one. Because she didn't give—one, two, three, four, five, six, seven.

H: (Laughter) It's a play on the word "withheld".

E: The unconscious *does* that. You've got to be aware of it. Therefore, you suggest that they withhold, *and they do*. You also suggest that they tell, *and they do*. But they withhold and they tell responsively. As long as they are going to withhold *you ought* to *encourage them* to withhold. In discussing your body image – the way you view yourself, the way you appear in your mind's eye, the way you think about your body – certainly you don't want to tell me about certain parts of your body, and yet there are parts of your body you do want to discuss. For example, your chin and your mouth. You may even think about your ankles. You may think about your abdomen, the hair on your head. By saying "the hair on your head," how many girls are aware of the maidenhead? The part in your hair, and how do you feel about it?

H: That's the play on the word "part"?

E: No, it's a play on the fact that there is a genital grove. And there *is* a part in the hair.

H: Those are also called "parts." You do this, apparently, not just to get an idea of their body image, but to make them very conscious of their body.

E: Make them conscious of their body. And, "*As you sit there*, you can think about what you ought to discuss about yourself." "As you sit there," seems to be a transitional phrase, but what do you sit on? "And what kind of a body do you want? The kind of a body that would please a woman with another type of personality? Or the kind of a body that would please you with *your* personality? And how much do you know about it?"

H: You assume that a menstrual pain is related to this kind of difficulty?

E: Yes, I do.

H: Naturally, with my background, I get curious about the

history. You can't do brief therapy by dealing with the patient's past. This is something that keeps coming up again and again. As you say, it's really irrelevant since the problem must be solved in the present. But I keep dealing with a patient's past when talking to them. It interests me that this girl lost her menstrual functions for a year, from age 13 to 14.

E: Yes, and one of the first things I would want to know about would be what she thought about the impermanence of life, and the impermanence of the body, and how a body can come to a sudden and violent end. And the threat of death. This body of hers is doomed to go only to dust, and every menstrual period brings her closer to death, and it's a painful thing.

H: This is a different way to look at menstruation altogether.

E: But it does, you know.

H: Oh yes, it does, I know. But it also tells her she is a woman, that she is not pregnant. That's the sort of thing I think about.

E: But you think of menses in terms of male thinking, in terms of biological thinking.

H: How does a woman think about it differently? In terms of aging?

E: What does every woman think about—when she gets old enough she won't menstruate. When she gets old enough, she will cease to menstruate. Therefore it is a totally different thing to her as a person. Within the privacy, in the separateness of her own living, menstruation is a living thing.

H: This girl said that when she started to menstruate she was quite proud of it. It meant she had grown up, and there seemed to be no conflicts around it. She wasn't unhappy about it; she wasn't ashamed of it. She remembered walking down the street feeling quite grown-up.

E: Feeling grown-up, which was a nice statement. An

excellent statement. Then all of a sudden it became transformed into what? And what became of that grown-up, pleasurable feeling? It had been transformed *into* pain. Just consider how a woman thinks about her 25th birthday. It isn't a 25th birthday, it's a quarter of a century. How does she *feel* about her 30th birthday? She is forever leaving her 20s. Then the horrible dread of leaving . . . *leaving* the 30s. That 25th birthday is a quarter of a century. The tremendous emphasis that you find from Arizona to Massachusetts on the quarter of a century.

H: I haven't heard of that kind of emphasis on it. Once when I was inducing a trance, I had her do some automatic writing. I asked her hand what she lost during that bombing raid. She wrote a very interesting word that she read as "security." It also could have been read as "family." But she was quite impressed by the fact that it said "security." She was largely uprooted for so many years.

E: What did you read in the writing?

H: I read it as "family" when I looked at it, but she talked about it as "security" and let it go as that. I didn't think of it until after she left.

E: Even if it had been written as "security" with the plain letters, I would have asked her to spell the same word with another set of letters. So it would read like a different word. I think probably she would have written "family."

H: I see. I was trying to think of a way to go further with that, and I couldn't think of that way. I knew "security" was too general for what was really on her mind. She lost her father when she was three, and at the bombing she lost her stepfather in the sense that he went away to war. Then the mother divorced him shortly after that.

E: Now when did she stop menstruating?

H: She not only stopped menstruating; she developed a morning sickness. She got sick every morning, dizzy and nauseated. For a period of months. Almost as if she was trying to substitute a family of her own for the family she was losing. It was like a pregnancy situation.

E: She lost her father when she was three. And her stepfather after the bombing, by virture of his going into the service. If she were three years old then she could look forward to the return – *to having* a stepfather. How could she resume her three-year-old status?

H: I see, you look upon it as a regression.

E: Because at three, with her current memories and understanding, she could really look forward to having a stepfather come into the home.

H: She had a stepfather she didn't care much for, but I think from the way she talked about him he was of more use to her than she realized.

E: Your tendency was to apply general psychoanalytic concepts.

H: Yes.

E: Without recognizing that this is an individual patient who *may* fit into those psychoanalytic concepts. But let's find out what the individual concepts are.

H: She talked a great deal about how her girlfriend's fathers became like fathers to her as she grew up. They always treated her like a daughter, so that there was always some kind of father around, and she always enjoyed this.

E: How much blood did she see? How much did she hear about?

H: The only thing she reported was that she heard about the death of a little girl in the neighborhood. A neighbor girl who got hit by something that fell. But she didn't see the girl. All she saw really was the city way down in the distance, and she was up on the hill and could see the airplanes, and the fire. She was frightened, but her mother wasn't particularly frightened, she says.

E: The little girl who was killed, how was she killed?

H: She says, "I saw schrapnel come down and hit the little girl."

E: Obviously she could reason out that the little girl bled.

H: That could be.

E: Now you will agree that things equal to the same things are equal to one another, isn't that right?

H: O.K.

E: Death equals blood. Menstruation equals blood. And blood equals menstruation. Menstruation is hidden. It's concealed, it's not seen. The little girl's bleeding was hidden, unlooked, unseen. It's purely an individual equation. And when you think of all the individual equations.

H: How do you deal with that with a patient? Or do you?

E: You do, because you are thinking of all those possible variations that might possibly apply to the individual patient.

H: But what I mean by deal with it: Do you use this for your own estimate of the problem, or do you discuss this with the patient?

E: Something like that, yes.

H: So you would discuss the possibility of the little girl bleeding and what's being hidden about it.

E: No, I'd mention it casually. Not as an interpretation, but just as a casual mention. If it's true, she'll show it. Now with the bombing, the city didn't function, everything in the home was thrown out of function. *Her* function was thrown out too. She is part of a totality.

H: Yes, she describes it as if everything stopped functioning, if not quite in those terms, very close to it. She was taken out of school, she was taken away from her friends, she was taken away from her stepfather, and so on.

E: She wasn't big enough to go to school. She was taken out of school. Not big enough to go to school, not big enough to menstruate.

H: Why would it begin again painfully?

E: Why not assume a legitimate painfulness?

H: What do you mean by legitimate painfulness?

E: The first beginning of menstruation could occur easily, naturally, without any particular associations. So it could be painless. Then you interrupt a function for which you have learned all the sensations, and then it occurs suddenly and unexpectedly. The loss of it has been a painful thing. Here all of a sudden you are reminded, by the reappearance of all the painfulness, of her loss of affection, plus the normal congestion of the tissues. So it's a legitimate painfulness. You break your arm, it's put in a cast. Gradually you become accustomed to the cast, the cast is taken off, and you try to bend you arm—it's painful.

H: Yes.

E: It's a legitimate pain too. The pain of disuse. Yet you want it to be a moveable arm. But it's painful, not because of conflicts. Why shouldn't interrupted menstruation recur with pain? That in itself could frighten her and raise the question in her mind, "Is it always going to be painful?" Then she could look forward to painful menstruation. She will have a month's time in which to anticipate painful menstruation, and verify it.

H: I am sure that's exactly what she does in that way—spends a month expecting it.

E: Yes, she has had added proof. And I would raise with her the question, "What is your cycle?" "How many pads a day do you use?" "Does it always come regular-

ly?" "Is it in the morning?" "In the afternoon, or at
night?" "Or just at random?"

H: Apparently regular and in the morning.

E: I would throw in the question "How many pads a day?"
because that really makes it an embarrassing intimate
question. "Do you soak the pads through?" "Or do you
change them as *soon* as they begin to get moist?" She
has already told me that it's regular, it's in the morning. "And how would you feel if it happened a day before you expected it? And not in the morning, but at
night? How would you feel about that?" The first
thing I would want to do is displace the time of the
hurt.

H: You mean displace the time, then you can do something
about the pain?

E: If I can displace the time, then it's not the *expected period*, and the expected period is a painful period. The
unexpected period is not painful, because it happened
unexpectedly. Then you have that implanted in her
mind. She is too intent on questions about, "How
many pads?" "Do you let them soak through?" She
isn't paying too much attention consciously to the
suggestions for displacement.

H: They are more effective if she gives less conscious attention to them?

E: She is within hearing distance of you, she hears everything you said, she came in to talk to you, she is going to listen with both her conscious mind and her unconscious mind. You just remain aware of that fact.
"And how would you feel if it occurred unexpectedly —
during the night?" But you see I use the word "feel,"
but it has a different connotation than "pain."

H: Oh, I see.

E: So I have actually changed a feeling of menstruation
from pain into another kind of feeling. Now another
thing is to emphasize the handling of painful menstru-

ation. So many therapists, medical men, overlook the
patient's rights. They try to relieve a girl of painful
menstruation by a blanket removal. When any girl
comes to me to be relieved of painful menstruation I
make it very clear to her that she wants to be relieved
of the pain of menstruation, as far as she knows. But
there certainly is likely to occur, in her lifetime, an occasion in which she *might want* a painful period. She
might like to escape some social engagements, by virtue of complaining about her painful menstruation.
She might like to skip the university examination. She
might like to get an extra day off from the office. So
be realistic about it. She wants to be relieved of painful menstruation when it's convenient for her. The unconscious is a lot more intelligent than the conscious.
The girl comes to you for relief of painful menstruation, and you blandly, blithely, give her suggestions
to be free, and her unconscious knows that you don't
understand the problem. You are telling her now, as
a menstruating creature, to be free of pain, and she
knows very well that she's going to get married, and
she is going to have a baby, and she is going to have
interruption of menstruation, and that not one of the
suggestions you have given her is so worded that it
applies until after she begins a new history of menstruation. She rejects your offering of relief because
you haven't taken in consideration the natural course
of events. She is acutely aware of that in her unconscious and really scorns you because you just assume
that she's never really going to have an interruption.
But she is. She may get sick. Maybe in her past she
did get sick and had to interrupt menses. And her unconscious, seeking help from you, *wants* you to consider her as an individual who is going to encounter
such and such things. When you give her the privilege
of having painful menstruations as a way of talking

her husband into buying her a new fur coat, you have given her the privilege of keeping pain and not keeping it. Then it's her choice, you are not forcibly taking something away from her that she feels belongs to herself. You are just offering her the opportunity of dropping it when it's convenient, and keeping it when it's convenient. Just as you let them withhold.

H: Well, that's true of most symptoms, isn't it? It's the proper attitude.

E: It's the proper attitude. A woman in her 30s sucked her thumb, scratched her nipple until it was always scabbed, and scratched her bellybutton until it was scabbed. She had done it ever since childhood. She sought therapy for that, and I told her no, I wouldn't give her therapy for it, that I would just simply cure it—in less than 30 seconds' time. She knew that was impossible. She wanted to know how I could cure it in 30 seconds' time. I told her all she had to do was say "yes." She knew *that* did not alter anything. "To say yes and mean yes." "The next time you want to scratch your nipple, I want you to do it. You can come into this office, expose your breasts and your nipple and do it. Will you do it?" She said "Yes," and then said, "You know I'll never do it. I never will." And she meant, "*I never will do it.*" She was talking about not coming into the office.

H: Yes.

E: "That's right, you never will do it." (Laughter) Her unconscious knew and her unconscious took all of *her* intensity, and transferred it to her.

H: Complicated. What about all the other purposes that it served? Whatever they may be?

E: Your assumption is that it served other purposes. Have you ever thought about symptomatology wearing out in serving purposes and becoming an habitual pattern?

H: What about it?

E: What oral security does a 25-year-old gain by sucking his thumb? When he sucked his thumb as an infant, he was hungry. It serves no real purposes now. The extension of the symptom into habit.

H: Yes, that kind of a symptom. There is a nice phrase, "Often people need a graceful exit out of a symptom that no longer serves a purpose."

E: In brief psychotherapy you always give them the graceful exit. In prolonged therapy you also do the same thing. You have to prolong therapy often because they fight so desperately against accepting a graceful exit.

H: They sure do. To get back to the body image and thinking about this girl again: When you get an idea of the defects of the body image, what do you then do in the way of revising this? Or is merely the act of discovering that they have defective areas in their body image enough?

E: What do you do? A girl came in to see me because she was nervous. She was fearful, tremulous, uncertain. She didn't like people and they didn't like her. She was so shaky it was hard for her to walk. She was afraid of people and when she ate in a restaurant she brought a newspaper to hide behind it. She went home by ways of alleys to avoid being seen. She always went to the cheapest restaurants, so people could look at her and despise her. Besides, she wasn't fit to look at. I had her draw her portrait. She tested out her sketching ability, and there is her portrait. You see it? (Shows drawing.)

H: It's obscure. Merely unrelated parts.

E: Finally she drew this calendar picture of herself in the nude. First, a head with no body, and then her final picture of herself.

H: Now, what did you do with her from the first drawing

to the last drawing? In the way of overcoming this
defective body image?

E: First I asked if she really wanted therapy. Would she
really cooperate with therapy? She said she had no
choice, and I agreed with her. She really had no choice,
except in the matter of therapist. Since she had come
to me and had made that first difficult step, it would
even be worse to have to find another, because she'd
have to make the first step all over. That insured her
staying with me.

H: I see.

E: She didn't recognize that I was putting a barrier into
her seeking someone else.

H: That's slippery all right.

E: But it *was* there, and I told her that if she wanted therapy it would be in relationship to all of her functions
as a person, which included not only the way she
worked, and walked in the streets, but in the matter
of eating and sleeping, and recreation. Eating implies
what? Urination, defecation too. Try to eat without
including those—you have to. Every little child learns
that you eat, and sooner or later you move your bowels. That's one of the fundamental learnings, and you
always retain that.

H: That's true enough.

E: And I had mentioned it to her through eating. All of
her functions as a person—not as a personality, but
as a person. A person who ate, slept, worked, and engaged in recreation. So that was inclusive of everything. And I would have to know all the things that
she *could* tell me. And all the things that I could think
about.

H: That's a tricky phrase there. You would have to know
all the things that she *could* tell you. That's an endan-
gering statement with the danger suddenly taken
away.

E: And all the things that I could think about, and I dared
to think about a lot of things. (Laughter) Which actually signified to her nothing – absolutely nothing –
won't be included. Everything will be included. All
that she can tell about, all that I can think about. And
I am a doctor, and I can really think, and I really
know. Yet it is said so gently . . . but every bit of
knowledge that she could ascribe to her physician was
put out in front right there. And one of the first things
I wanted to know about her was, how did she think
about herself as a person. Or perhaps the best way to
tell me would be to tell me what she felt she looked
like. "Well" she said, "I am a blonde." "And you have
two eyes, and two ears, and one mouth, and one nose,
and two nostrils, and two lips and one chin. What do
you think about those? And you are blonde you stated. What kind of a blonde?" "A dirty dishwater blonde.
What more do you need? And my teeth are crooked,
my ears are too large, my nose is too small. All I can
say is that I am just a very ordinary girl." "Very ordinary" implies what? When she went from her face
to "very ordinary girl" she was describing herself. All
the rest of her body was implied by "very ordinary
girl." Then I wanted to know if she would tell me
whether she took a tub bath or a shower. I asked her
to describe to me in detail how she got into the shower, to describe in detail what she did, and what she
did after she turned off the shower. She stepped out
of the tub, took the towel, dried herself, took off her
shower cap, put on her pajamas, and went to bed. You
see, I had her in the nude, in all of her thinking, and
I allowed her to dress in pajamas and to go to bed.
It's so very much easier *then* to discuss the details of
the bath, when she is in the nude. I wanted to know
if she stood on the bathmat, where the towel was,
whether it was handy or on the other side of the bath-

room, and I wanted to know if she took a drink before she dried herself, after she dried herself, before she put on her pajamas. She would have to visualize herself. I am keeping her in the nude right in front of me, am I not?

H: (Laughs) You sure are, and without ever mentioning it.

E: Without asking her to really.

H: By very carefully not mentioning it.

E: But she was in the nude, and once having been in the nude for me, then, "Now if you were to see your body in the nude, without your head being visible, would you recognize your body? You know it is awfully hard to recognize your voice on a tape."

H: What answer do you get to that? Did she recognize it or what?

E: She started to think about recognizing her body in the nude, but there she was again nude.

H: Yes, I can see. I never heard that question before; it's interesting.

E: "Now I can tell you something about your body that you don't know, and I never have seen it. You undoubtedly are pretty sure that you know the color of your pubic hair. I've never seen it; I never expect to see it. I don't think that you know the color of it." Now that's one thing she's certain about.

H: That not only makes her think about it, but it makes her go home and check it.

E: Her first answer was, "Naturally the same color as the hair on my head, a dishwater blonde." With the natural normal pigmentation of the body, your pubic hair is going to be darker than the hair on the head, that I know. Therefore, I can tell her, "You say your pubic hair is the same color as the hair on your head, and I say it isn't." She checks it, and she finds out that *I am right.* I've *really* demonstrated my knowledge. I've given her a chance to take issue with me. Disputing *her knowledge* of her body. But what about my impolite mentioning of her pubic hair? That isn't the issue. The issue is that I've challenged her knowledge. She's going to prove to herself that I am ignorant, not that I am intrusive. So she's fighting a false battle.

H: (Laughs) You're right.

E: She can't tell me I am right or wrong without bringing up the subject of pubic hair. "And what color are your nipples? I wonder if you *really* know." They can't miss the issue of intellectual awareness, "I wonder if you really know." "Naturally, the color of my skin." "I don't think they are, that's something you'll find out, that they *aren't* the color of your skin." So she's got an issue there to fight on, a purely intellectual one. She's going to fight, but fighting on my territory.

H: Yes, she is. And the fact that you were right about the color of the pubic hair must make it all the more clear that she has been in the nude with you.

E: Oh, yes. And the fact that I am right about her nipples. When she tells me that her hips are *too large*, I can flippantly tell her, "The only use they have for you is to sit upon." How can you dispute that without getting into an awful mess of arguments? They are made up of muscles and fat, and that's an unmentionable topic. But they are useful in climbing stairs.

H: And useful in attracting men?

E: *That* I mention later. Then I can point out later that people view things differently. Who is it? Which woman is it in Africa that has the duck bill? I can't remember the name; you know, the duck bill women with their lips sticking way out with platters in their lips. "And do you know that the men in that tribe think those are beautiful, and they're astonished that the American men would consider the kind of lips that you have as beautiful." What have I said?

H: You slipped in a very nice compliment there.

E: I'm presenting the male point of view. It's nothing personal.

H: Yes, and you've made it so general that it can't be just you.

E: I'm talking about her lips, am I not?

H: Yes.

E: That is the sort of thing one does in brief psychotherapy.

H: Well, one of the problems in brief psychotherapy, it seems to me, is getting the patient to feel that this isn't just your personal opinion, but that everybody else would have the same opinion, or at least other men would.

E: Not that every man will have the same opinion, but that men have a masculine point of view. That women have a feminine point of view. Few men want to kiss a mustache, and very often women do. (Laughter)

H: But that's a nice twist there. If you pay her a compliment on how she has attractive lips, she can either deny it, thinking you were wrong, or accept it, thinking this was your opinion but not the opinion of men in general.

E: That's right.

H: The tricky thing is to use the male point of view on it.

E: "Now, you don't know whether I think you are pretty or not, but every man has his individual taste as well as his general masculine views." Some men like fat wives, and some like skinny wives, and they're really in love with their wives. For example, I know a man who thinks his wife is something sent from heaven. She's 5′8″ and she weighs 90 lbs. To me she's a collection of bones and the most unattractive thing, and he thinks she's beautiful. I am glad he does. I know a 6 footer, who thinks his 5′ wife, who weighs 170 lbs, is beautiful. I think she's a lard tub, but he thinks she's beautiful, and I am glad he does. Yet both men, the man who is in love with his lard tub and the man who's in love with his living skeleton, are tremendously attracted by the very feminine things that both women have in common. They are females in the first place. They both like to wear silky, satiny, pretty underthings. No man in his right mind wants to wear those things himself, but he likes to look at them. That's the masculine point of view. I'm not telling you anything you don't know already.

H: Not a thing? You're telling me an approach I don't know.

E: Yes, but just the things you already know.

H: I wish I was seeing this girl with the menstrual problem all over again. My difficulty is this: Since she was not capable of a deep enough trance, and she came specifically for that, I saw her a couple of times and I told her I didn't think I'd be able to help her. I felt very disappointed, and she felt very disappointed. I don't think I can help her with deep hypnosis, you know, but I think I can with some kind of an approach like this.

E: Now this girl whose portrait you saw, I asked her if she'd really like to find out how afraid she was of her body, just how afraid. She said she didn't think she was afraid of her body, but she'd do whatever I told her. "All right, Saturday at 1 o'clock sharp, be at the door of one of the downtown stores where they sell perfume. At 1 o'clock, turn and walk in and buy a bottle of perfume." She was there on the street, looking at her watch. At 1 o'clock she tried to go in the store. I told her also to have it purchased by 5 o'clock. But she couldn't walk in. She paced up and down the street trying to walk in the store. At ten minutes to 5 she dashed in, handed the girl at the perfume counter a $20.00 bill, and said, "Give me a bottle of perfume." The girl said, "What kind?" She said, "Any kind, any kind. Here I'll take this. Is that enough?" The girl said,

"But your change, Miss." But my patient was outside the store. She went home and squalled and squalled. Four long hours of anger. What do you do with perfume? You put it on the body, don't you?

H: Yes.

E: And the *mere* acquisition.

H: That's extreme.

E: Then I told her that she had to get herself a box of powder. She got that without much difficulty. Just walked in, hesitantly, asked for a box of powder, took it home, and put it beside the perfume. She dreaded to come to the next session. I told her I wanted her to take a shower, to dry herself carefully, and then to put powder under her arms and here, and here, across her abdomen and on her hips. "You put a dab of perfume here, here, here, here, here." She told me that was silly. I said, "All right, it's silly. Those are medical orders. You'll find out whether it's silly." She went home, took a shower, stepped out of the tub, dried herself very, very carefully, reached for the powder can, and collapsed on the floor, and squalled for hours, until exhausted. It wasn't so silly was it? When she finally cried herself out of every thought, she got up, put the powder and the perfume on the body, didn't even bother to put on her pajamas. She just collapsed shuddering, shivering.

Then she came in and said, "I know, there's lots wrong with me." I teach the functions of the body. "You eat. What kind of stomach trouble do you have? What kind of constipation do you have? How well do you eat? What respect have you got for your stomach? Do you eat good food or do you insult it with anything that's handy?" With that sort of a frontal attack, which cannot be objected to, it was possible to inquire what is the attitude she should have towards her breasts, her genitals, her hips, her thighs, her ankles, her knees, her abdomen. Were her teeth too crooked? Were they really? How *would* a man looking at her smile react to it? Would his eyesight be so deficient that he could see only those too crooked teeth, or would he see her lips? Would he see her chin? Would he like her smile? Did he have the *right* to see what *he* wanted to see? What he liked to see? Did she have the right to say, "I'm now smiling, and look at my crooked teeth?" He might prefer to notice the shape and the thickness of her lips.

H: You try to get her interested in the possibility of feeling attractive, is that it?

E: No. To recognize that any man who chooses can look upon her and behold something beautiful. And men vary in their taste. I don't know if I told you about Dottie. Back broken, age 21, her fiance asked to be released from the engagement. No sense of feeling from the waist down, complete paralysis, incontinent, urine and feces. Age 31, living in a wheelchair, taking her Ph.D. in psychology for lack of anything else to do. Sought psychotherapy for one of two things. A philosophy of life that would make her want to live or an acceptable reason to satisfy her for committing suicide. Since she was a psychologist and had studied clinical psychology, about the first thing I mentioned was the giraffe neck women of Siam. How when their rings are taken off their heads collapse over – they have lost their muscles for the support of the neck. And the duck bill women of Africa, the steatopygous Hottentot women.

H: Which kind?

E: Steatopygous. Those enormous fat buttock women. I stated that men have a variety of tastes. What made her think that, because she was incontinent with feces and urine, there wasn't some nice guy in the world who would find her attractive if she were she? That an attitude of expectation and willingness allows another to approach, and that romance was just around the corner for her. Then I took up this matter of displacement of symptoms. I don't need to explain to you displacement of symptoms.

H: You could explain to me how you took it up with her.

E: Well, she knew that symptoms could be displaced, and that worry over the mortgage could be transformed into a stomach ulcer. It was really a pocketbook ache. I told her that if people could spontaneously, unwittingly, displace one thing, they could displace another. She had the idea that because she was paralyzed from the waist down, she was sexless. Then I told her that the genitals were like the rest of the body. That the toe bone is connected with the foot bone. The foot bone with the ankle bone. Until finally the neck bone is connected with the head bone. That I thought that a woman's external genitalia were connected with the vagina, which is connected with the uterus, which is connected with the ovary, which was connected with the adrenal, which was connected with the hormone system, which is connected with the breast, which is connected with the thyroid, which is connected with the pituitary. In fact, everything we knew about physiology indicated that was the case. I was quite certain that the paralysis, the lack of sensation, hadn't interfered with the adrenals. They weren't paralyzed. The kidneys weren't paralyzed, even though they were connected with the adrenals. The adrenals and the kidneys were connected with the bladder. Her own wetting of herself proved that her kidneys weren't paralyzed. While she had lost the external genitalia, still the internal genitalia were connected.

That was in 1947. I did a lot of therapy on Dottie, laying that foundation, knowing that I could trust her to carry it out to its completion. She married a pathol-

ogist who was doing research in urine and feces. He
is a nice guy. Nothing wrong with the guy. I checked
him too. I didn't see Dottie again until last October
when I was in her city. I got the opinion of about 20
doctors on the subject of Dottie's husband. Exceedingly popular chap, everybody respects him, he's got
an utterly delightful wife. At their social meetings
back home they called him by his first name, which
is another good indication. They called her "Dottie,"
another good indication. Of course, she's got two children by Caesarian.

Dottie took me out to lunch. I asked her how she
felt toward me. She said, "Look, it's odd. I know that
I knew you in Michigan. I know that you tried to hypnotize me; it didn't work very well. I know I came to
you because I was depressed. I don't remember much
about that. I don't remember what we talked about.
I don't know what you said. All I know is that I am
profoundly grateful to you, and that you are a doctor of doctors to me. I don't know why, and I am
curious." I said, "Your amnesia is rather interesting,
Dottie. Suppose I ask you one simple little question."
She said, "You can ask me." I said, "Will you tell me
all the intimate details of your sexual life." Dottie's
reply was, "My first reaction to the question is a no,
but my second reaction is to you. That is, you are entitled to know. Sex relations? Three, four, five times
a week. I have excellent orgasms. I have plenty of orgasms in my breast, I have a separate one in each nipple. I get a very warm, rosy feeling of engorgement
in my thyroid, and my lips swell up quite a bit when
I have an orgasm, the lobes of my ears. I have the
most peculiar feeling between my shoulder blades. I
rock involuntarily, uncontrollably, I get so excited.
H: That's quite a case. I'm sure she must not have believed

you when you first said someone was around the corner.

E: But I emphasized the attitude of willingness and expectancy. The only way not to believe me is to have the attitude of willingness and expectancy – which was the essential thing.

H: You mean, *not* to believe you?

E: Because that would prove that willingness and expectancy in itself was useless, because there was no romance around the corner.

H: She could only disapprove by expecting it.

E: That's right, isn't that right?

H: It certainly is. This is related to another thing you often do, particularly in brief therapy, and that's tell patients what to do, like telling the girl to go get the perfume, or to go get the powder.

E: Yes.

H: I have often wondered how you set it up so that they do what you tell them to do. How you commit them to it.

E: "You want to know how afraid you are of your body, go and buy a bottle of perfume." She obviously knew I was stupid, so she proved it by going. Then she discovered differently.

H: She does it to prove that you are wrong.

E: Because it gives them contest, really. A contest between her neurosis and me as a therapist. I'll give you another patient – not getting along in her job, all the usual complaints. The first three times that she came in I noticed that her hair was very, very poorly combed. She noticed me looking at her hair and said, "Don't do what my boss does, he keeps telling me to comb my hair and I do my level best." I said, "You want to get along better in your job, and you do your level best with your hair, but I wonder how afraid you are of looking your best?" So I told her, "You can find that out by going home, and taking a shower and washing your hair. You are going to find out a number of things about yourself."

H: Leaving it that open?

E: That open.

H: What did she find out?

E: She says, "I came to comb my hair nicely." I said, "You can take a better attitude towards the rest of you too, can't you?" She told me later that she took a shower, dried herself very carefully, stood in front of a mirror, got her hand mirror out so she could get a backview, and she spent an awful lot of time examining her body. Examining it against the background of her boss finding fault with the way she combed her hair. She resented her boss criticizing her. The more she scrutinized herself, with that background of her resentment towards her boss, she kept on approving of her body.

H: It's extraordinary the way you manage to turn opposition in a contest to something productive for the person rather than something destructive to the person.

E: But all you are doing is using the narcissism with which you are born.

H: You could have a contest with a patient, in which the patient proves you are wrong by staying sick. But you ask them to turn it around so they prove you are wrong by doing something beneficial to them.

E: I am losing a battle with one of my patients who insists on remaining fat. So far I haven't devised any way. But you take a patient's own narcissism and you maneuver it around until it is useful to him.

H: (Laughter) It sounds easy.

E: I spent less than five hours with a 35-year-old transvestite male. A traveling salesman. He came for brief psychotherapy. "I am not expecting you to do a great

deal, but I do want some help with the transvestism."
Exceedingly compulsive about it. "I am married, got
a couple of kids, a nice wife. I have suitcases that lock.
In addition to that I put straps around them, and I
have little locks on the straps. I drag those around.
I get to a hotel, I lock the door very carefully, take
off my clothes, and I put on a bra and I put on panties and stay in front of the mirror. I put on dresses
and stay in front of the mirror, and I really enjoy it.
I keep standing in front of the mirror looking at myself." He was 35 years old. I don't even know how long
he had done this, since . . . all his life? I never inquired
when it started, nor how it started, nor what caused
it. My statement was very simple, "You stay in front
of the mirror, looking at yourself, wearing feminine
clothes, and you're looking at yourself and you are seeing neither yourself nor the clothes. You're seeing a
combination of them. But you *can't* see yourself because you are partly covered, and you *can't* see the
clothes because you are looking at the total. When you
leave this office, go to some restaurant, and see if you
can discover how a woman wears her clothes. Try to
find a waitress with stockings on, and see how she
wears her clothes." "Are her clothes the only thing?"
"You've got to examine the clothes and you have got
to examine every feminine gesture in order to appreciate the clothes." You should have heard the rapture
he gave me about the beautifully dressed women. He
sat that night and watched them, and watched and
watched them.

H: Did he give up putting on women's clothes?

E: Then I told him after watching them that one of the
things he could really do is take his collection of feminine apparel and really look at it, examine it. Look at
it, examine it, and feel it. Then wonder how a woman
would really wear those panties; look at her shoulder

movements, arm movements, hand movements, head
movements, leg movements, she would make wearing
those clothes. The same with the bra. To feel the cloth
of her dresses, and her slips. *To wonder how it would
feel to a woman's skin.* The first session was three
hours, the second session two hours. He came in later,
said that he had been absurd, that he had been trans-
vesticising himself for so many years and that it
didn't make sense. I said it didn't make sense. Unfortunately that set of apparel he had wouldn't fit his
wife; he didn't know what to do with it. He gave it to
the Good Will. Said his wife had become tremendously more attractive to him sexually.

H: And that was using his narcissism?

E: No.

H: Isn't that an example of what you were trying to say
about the girl?

E: *There* he was using his narcissism in a distorted way,
by using feminine clothes on a male body. I was using his narcissism in a different way. He could really
feel the clothes, he could *really see* the clothes, and
that should be his narcissistic experience. Instead of
the distorted thing of wearing them. His capacity to
appreciate feminine clothes was when it started to be
narcissism. Let me show you how to *really* handle a
rifle said a friend of mine. He showed me the feel of it.

H: You were doing a little more than that with this guy.
You were getting the guy to deny.

E: Deny what?

H: To deny what tendencies he has by having him think
how a woman would feel these clothes.

E: All he does is look in the mirror at that body of his.
There was no sense in trying to insist on femininity.
He has got all the evidence to the contrary.

H: Why do you ask him then to think about how a woman
would feel with these clothes?

E: No, *how these clothes would feel on a woman's body.*

H: If he was feeling a woman's body under these clothes, is that what you mean?

E: No, How a woman would feel wearing those pretty things. How they would feel to her skin.

H: Isn't that a way of getting him to deny that he has any feminine feelings like that?

E: But he *hasn't* got any.

H: I know. He just thought he had feminine feelings.

E: He just *thought* he had. I introduced him to the real ones.

H: That's a tricky one that.

E: He only *thought* he *had*; he couldn't have — he has the wrong shape of body.

H: The question is how you get them to think differently. That's what I am getting at. One of the ways you got him to think differently was to imagine how a woman would feel in these, thus making it impossible to a man.

E: I gave him the permission to *feel* the cloth of the dress. Isn't that a nice thing to do? (Laughter) Being a man they really ought to feel it this way. Not feel the texture of the cloth here on this thigh but with his fingers, and to look at the panties that he is *holding with his hand*, not that he is wearing *but that he is handling*.

H: You make it sound simple, but a lot of complicated things happen there again in that little sequence. What's most interesting to me about it is how you dismiss the whole etiology of it. This is what I have difficulty doing. In brief therapy, my first impulse is, when did it start, what purpose did it serve, and so on.

E: If you want to work out with a man his difficulty in working a correlation in statistics, would you start with his difficulty in school in adding one and one, and two and two, and would you laboriously go through the addition of one place numbers, the addition of two place numbers? The addition and subtraction.

H: My idea was the fact that his older brother was a mathematician.

E: Yes, but you wouldn't go through addition and subtraction of one digit numbers, two digit numbers, three digit numbers, four digit numbers. You wouldn't take up the multiplication of one digit number, and two digit numbers, and you wouldn't take up short division, and then long division, and fractions – all ⌣ ᶠ this difficulty. You'd really tend to stick to this matter of the correlation. Isn't that right?

H: That's right.

E: But what is the etiology anyway? Mathematics begins with how do you make the figure one. How do you make the figure of two? How does the three differ from the four? And how come you say that two plus two equals four, and then you change your mind and say, five minus one is four. Just don't go into that. But psychotherapy, so often, goes way back to outgrown, outmoded, literally forgotten non-surfaceable experiences.

H: I agree with that.

E: Virtually searching the history. This man was 35, and he was wearing panties and a bra, and slips and dresses, looking at himself in the mirror. But he was 35 years old; he was married and a father of kids. Looking at himself wearing feminine apparel. Age 35. He couldn't possibly see himself as a little kid playing with his mother's panties. I could spend months and perhaps years building up that scene. (Laughter) But as long as he wanted to look at the wearing of feminine apparel, put him where he can see it worn.

H: I am not disagreeing with what you are doing. I am trying to get it clear in my own mind how much of the past is necessary in order to do brief therapy.

E: You know, I had one patient this last July who had four or five years of psychoanalysis and got nowhere. Someone who knows her said, "How much attention did you give to the past?" I said, "You know, I completely forgot about that." That patient is, I think, a reasonably cured person. You can imagine what it was — a washing compulsion, as much as 20 hours a day. Tremendous mother hostility. Utterly tremendous mother hostilities, brother hostilities, father hostilities. I said, "Do you know your mother is psychotic? You are not going to believe me about your mother. Your father? I think he is a weakling, for the simple reason that he hasn't divorced your mother, and he won't admit that she is psychotic. He isn't man enough to divorce her, and he isn't man enough to tell her that he is living apart, living with a mistress. So let's drop him. Your brother, he is a pain in the neck so far as I am concerned. I don't know him. Very glad I don't." I haven't gone into the cause or the etiology, the only searching question I asked was this, "When you get in the shower to scrub your self for hours, tell me, do you start at the top of your head, or the soles of your feet, or in the middle? Do you wash from the neck down or do you start with your feet and wash up? Or do you start with your head and wash down?"

H: Why did you ask that?

E: So that she knew I was really interested . . .

H: So that you could join her in this?

E: No, so that she knew I was *really interested.*

CHAPTER 2

Voice Problems, Enuresis, Insomnia

1957. Present were Milton H. Erickson and Jay Haley.

H: I'd like to find out what information you want to get from a patient. For example, a 55-year-old woman came to me because three years ago she lost her voice and can't speak above a whisper now. If she does try to speak above a whisper, she goes into very heavy breathing. Now what do you want to know about her to deal with this problem?

E: What do I want to know about that woman? I want to pose her, first of all, some very simple questions. 'Do you want to talk? Do you want to talk aloud? When? What do you want to say?" I absolutely mean these questions because the answer to them puts her in a spot where she is committing herself.

H: I see.

E: It puts all the burden of responsibility on her shoulders. This idea of coming to me and saying, "I wish I had my voice." Does she really want to talk? How well? When does she want to talk? Today, tomorrow, next year? What does she want to say? When you have that problem, define her thinking clearly by asking,

"Do you want to say something agreeable? Do you want to say something unpleasant? Do you want to say 'yes,' or do you want to say 'no'? Do you want to speak aloud expectedly, or do you want to speak unexpectedly?" I would treat this situation as I would with a patient with a psychiatric pain and they want an operation; the best orientation of the patient is, "Where is your pain, and what do you think you want to be operated on for?" Might as well clear that up. Then I could do a physical if need be.

H: This woman had worked for the government for 30 years, and then she got a son of a bitch of a boss over her who made her life very miserable, and she lost her voice. In discussing him, she says, "Nothing I said had an effect on him." She also had a public speaking course the year before she lost her voice. When she got up in front of the class to speak, the teacher criticized her breathing and she quit the class. This same difficulty in breathing came up when she lost her voice. In the last three years she has had speech therapy. She has had breathing exercises where the teacher tried to teach her to sing and to hum. She has spent some time with a psychiatrist who antagonized her by telling her that her father made a coward of her, and then he tried to hypnotize her and failed.

E: What did she seek therapy for? Humming, singing, breathing, standing in front of people? Was she seeking therapy for speaking?

H: Yes, for speaking.

E: Then why all these other approaches?

H: They were handed to her, I think. She went to the clinic and stated her difficulty and they sent her to the speech clinic – the woman can speak. In fact, some days she'll be almost perfectly all right. Then at work she'll have some annoyance and she'll lose her voice

again. But she has eight months to go before she re-
tires on a pension. Even though she's very hostile to
work she wants to finish there. The boss who treated
her badly is gone, but a new administrator is in, so
she doesn't deal directly with the new boss anymore.
They also put in a secretary who is a very ambitious
girl, and she has to talk to the secretary rather than
the administrator. She is a supervisor and has worked
her way up from the bottom. But she feels now that
she doesn't get any rewards for anything she does. For
example, she wrote a complicated manual on procedures, put it on the administrator's desk, and he didn't
look at it for two months. This sort of thing is going on in her office all the time. She's lost interest
in her job, and all she wants to do is ride out her eight
months. She thinks she'd like to talk while riding out
her eight months. But she isn't very anxious to talk
really. She has the feeling that nothing she says is
very important anymore.

E: Do you know arithmetical progression? One, two, four,
eight, 16, 32, 64, and then 128 and so on?

H: Yes.

E: I think I would give this woman the concept of arithmetical progression. When she understood the progression, then I would point out to her that there are
some words you just wouldn't say. I'd have her think
about all the words that she just wouldn't say – and
let her make a deliberate choice, of one word, two
words, four words, eight words, 16, and so on.

H: Her own choice of words she wouldn't say – or would
say?

E: Words she *wouldn't say* of her own free choice. And the
words she *would say*. I would emphasize her voluntary refusal to say an obscene word, and her recognition that she could and would say the polite term.

H: How do you tie them together in the arithmetical progression?

E: That if she *would not* say one four-letter word – voluntarily would not – there are also *two* four-letter words she would not say. In fact, there are four. In fact there are eight. Actually there are 16 four-letter words she *would not* say – voluntarily. But she would and could say one polite word, in fact two, in fact four, in fact eight, in fact 16. In fact, if we could pick up 16 more obscene words, that would be 32 that she wouldn't voluntarily say. If there were 32 other terms she *could* say, she would be very happy to say them instead of the 32 obscene terms. In fact there probably are 64. So you are taking the attitude of *voluntarily wouldn't say*, voluntarily *could* say, and you are building it up.

H: I gather you are dealing with two different meanings of the word *could say*. "Could say" because it's proper, and "could say" because she is able to speak.

E: I wouldn't define that for her.

H: Yes, I see.

E: I just wouldn't be bothered with that. I would have her attention *on the progression*. I would choose obscene words because they have such a tremendous emotional endowment. They are very strong. They are distractive.

H: Would you have her merely think of the obscene words? Or say them? Or discuss them? Or what?

E: I would tell her those are the words she voluntarily would not say.

H: And you wouldn't name which words they were.

E: Oh no.

H: I want to make sure of that. (Laughing)

E: This is simply a maneuver from "could" into "would."

H: I see.

E: With arithmetical progression added, it really goes along.

H: That is an interesting approach. You aren't concerned with the function of this in her life?

E: How can you best find out the function in her life if she can't function at *that* level first? When she maps out in her own mind all those words that she *wouldn't* say, and the words that she *could say*, then of course she comes up with what words would actually be appropriate even though she wouldn't say them. One can think freely about the descriptive terms for that boss. One can think about the inflection. Take inflection – is inflection speech to her? It isn't.

H: I see.

E: The pause in utterances, those aren't speech. Just like the magician – he'll say, "You can see me put my hand here, and you can see me put my hand there. The rabbits are going to show up there." The pause, then a word here, a word there, and the pause. She is really going to look for that pause. The pause is not speech, and she *can* pause. But to pause she has to say a word, and then pause, and then say another word to define the pause. But the pause is emphasized as the important thing.

H: You'd teach her the importance of pauses?

E: That inflection which is not speech to her conscious thinking; inflection, tone qualities, pauses, are not speech.

H: I am rather obligated to use hypnosis with her since she came for that, and I find she goes into a pretty good trance, once she got over the resistance she developed after seeing that psychiatrist. She can at least levitate her hand. How would you use hypnosis with her?

E: How well can she levitate her hands?

H: It goes up slowly – about six inches.

E: And she can *think* while you are levitating her hand. When you tell her "lifting higher and higher," she can think, "It's not going up higher, it's moving to the left." Everytime you say the word "higher," she can think "left." What have you done with the levitation?

You're still levitating her hand, but you're making her think and giving her your use of the words "higher and higher." And *she* has to think "left."

H: What does that do?

E: It relates speech and the movement of the hand. The same thing can happen to the left hand. Only that time when you say higher it's *"right."* Then I would shift her chair around and put her in a different position. In a different geographical relationship. She can say "left" and she can say "right" in a variety of circumstances.

H: You mean have her say left or think left?

E: Think left, think right. But think it with intensity. You're going to have subliminal speech.

H: I begin to see what you're after. (Laugh) Producing subliminal speech will produce speech?

E: Yes. You can say "yes." You can say "yes" (louder), you can say "yes" (louder), and you can say "yes" (louder), and get more and more insistent. I told a patient that she could think just as strongly, just as forcibly, as she can speak the word "yes," but the only answer to me was "no," *"no," "NO."* I kept insisting, "you can say yes," and finally her subliminal speech exploded into *"NO."* She was convinced that she was absolutely aphonic. So aphonic that she could not even whisper. But she prided herself on her intelligence and her ability *to think.* So I built up her pride in her thinking, and the more insistent I became, the more I kept on saying "yes," the more she was thinking "no." And subliminal speech became speech.

H: You don't seem at all concerned about, for example, what function this has in relationship to her husband. In other words, in your thinking, what's the purpose behind losing the speech?

E: The purpose behind her losing her speech is very narrowed and constricted to you, and the purpose of speech is very wide and comprehensive. Now, why give all your attention to that very, very narrow sequence of it? Because she is entitled not to say something to her husband, she is entitled to defeat her husband. But she is not entitled to defeat herself in all the rest of the areas of her life. Therefore, you try to limit her aphonia to the things where the aphonia belongs. Just because strawberries give you hives, that's no reason why you shouldn't eat potatoes and broccoli, and meat—right? If there's going to be any dietary restriction, let's make it strawberries. The general reaction of these patients is to react to strawberry hives by cutting out all the diet.

H: Well, if she does this for a reason—let us say hypothetically because she wanted to defeat her husband— then she couldn't have aphonia for that purpose without making it quite explicit in their relationship unless she lost her voice completely. As an excuse for losing it with her husband, she'd have to lose it also at work.

E: I'd be perfectly willing to teach her that she could blank out thoughts, that she could say the inappropriate thing. I could teach her the art of misunderstanding. To give you an illustration, I was rushing to class in college on a windy day, and I was really hurrying. I rushed around the corridor and crashed into somebody. That person said, "You goddamned clumsy fool," and I hauled my watch out and said, "Quarter past two," and went on. He stood there looking, wondering (laugh), "Quarter past two," and he'd called me "goddamn clumsy fool." "Quarter past two." What could he do? It's quarter past two.

H: That's the art of misunderstanding? (Laugh)

E: What could the guy do? It would take a long involved explanation to tell me that he hadn't asked me what time it was. He couldn't cuss me out any longer. He was completely helpless.

H: What do you mean by blanking out thoughts?

E: How often in normal, everyday life, do we have the experience of being introduced to somebody and we repeat the name, "Pleased to meet you, Mrs. Jones." Ten seconds later, what was that name? We blanked it out. And she can blank out the various things in relationship to her husband, if her aphonia is in relationship to her husband.

H: Here's what happens with her husband. When she begins an argument with him, he gets up and leaves the room, comes back in a little while, and talks as if they hadn't an argument. So she has the feeling that nothing she says makes any difference.

E: So he wins?

H: Yes.

E: Why can't she take that over?

H: How would she take it over?

E: During the next argument with her husband, get her to notice and appreciate all those minimal movements he is making in preparation to leaving the room. Have her really note them, memorize them, because there are going to be certain minimal movements that tell her when her husband is going to get up and leave the room. She waits for a certain number of them, and then she says, "*I'm* leaving the room," and exits. What happens? Now and then some obstreperous intern or resident nurse or attendant lost their temper with me. They'd come into the office and cuss me out. Some would resort to profanity. "I think you're a goddamn dirty stinkin' son of a bitch." He'd wait for my blast to reply, but I would say, "But you omitted a couple of words there. What you meant to say was, "You're a goddamn stinkin' bloody dirty son of a bitch of a bastard." Where was he?

H: He was in the one-down position.

E: Very thoroughly, very helplessly so. He couldn't say

"no," and he couldn't say "yes." If he said "yes," he had
to admit he was incomplete. (Laughing) If he said "no,"
he had to dispute himself.

H: That's a double bind.

E: Why shouldn't a woman tell her husband, "Now it's *my*
turn to leave the room," and she herself interrupt the
argument. She herself put an end to it. I can assure
you that they can get great glee out of it. (Laughter)
"Every time I get in an argument with my husband,
he listens just so long, then he goes out and smokes
a pipe, and he comes back after he smokes his pipe.
He acts as we didn't have an argument." I'd point out
to that particular woman, "Yes, you have flowers in
your front yard. Watch him carefully. When he starts
fumbling for his pipe, you know he's going to walk out
in the yard. Say something scorching to him, and add
to it, 'Now, it's my turn to go out in the yard.' Then
go out and get some flowers. You'll like your flowers;
you'll enjoy your flowers."

H: I see, you train people how to deal with a relationship.

E: Yes, because out of that relatonship will come the adjustment they want. When you instruct a woman how
to handle her husband, you are showing her how to
change a relationship which is unsatisfactory to her,
in the sense that she is left feeling one-down, into a
more symmetrical relationship in which she can handle her husband. But I add to it, "Pick some flowers."
She likes her flowers.

H: What does that add?

E: Her total integrity. Those flowers are *hers*. She is the
one who is taking care of the flowers and she is the
one who plants them and is interested in them. And
so her superiority over her husband is but a mere incidental thing in that total life situation. The important thing is that she has put her husband down as
a part of going out and really enjoying her flowers and
picking some.

H: You make the issue not the contest between them but the satisfaction of something else.

E: The contest should be an incidental part of a greater whole.

H: Well, it seems most psychopathology comes when the relationship is the contest and there is nothing else.

E: I know, and it is overemphasized in psychopathology. "Yesterday my husband put me down, today I put him down – so we are equal." But they *aren't* equal. He put her down in relationship to the argument by walking out on her and then returning to the room in relationship to the closed argument. That's as far as he went. She put her husband down by walking out of the room. She came back in relationship to the flowers that she arranges in a vase, which is a totally different type of return.

H: Yes, it certainly is.

E: And those flowers are her complete satisfaction. She's put her husband down again. She's beautified the room. Her husband *only* returns to the room – with a silenced argument.

H: Yes. You teach a patient how to take charge in a positive way. What I admire about your work is how successfully you do that yourself with patients. It seems to me taking charge is an essential aspect of therapy.

E: But you must be willing to put the patient one-up.

H: When *you* put the patient one-up, the patient isn't one-up.

E: The patient believes that, he feels it. But to maintain that feeling, that belief, the patient has to put *me* one-up.

H: I see. I notice you sometimes tell a patient that you can solve his problems and that it is simple. Do you consistently present that?

E: Oh no.

H: I just wondered.

E: With some patients I point out that this is an exceedingly difficult complicated thing and it isn't going to be easy.

H: Here is another thing I want to ask you about relationships. I find that symptoms seem to arise when a relationship shifts. For example, an insomnia patient of mine seemed to develop insomnia at a time when his wife got sick. I think before that he had a relationship where she tended to take care of him. She developed a variety of afflictions: bursitis, and some stomach trouble and a couple of operations for this and that, and some lumps that might have been cancer, all in a period of a year, and he began to have insomnia. It seems to me that he began to compete for the one-down position with her as if he would feel better if she was taking care of him because he developed some infirmity like being unable to sleep. I find consistently that when a relationship is established a certain way, when something affects it so that it's changed, then the person tries to reestablish it back the way it was with a symptom of some kind. That is one of the reasons I am interested in the kind of instruction you would give to a wife to get one-up on her husband, or to win an argument, or to change the relationship. That is, this woman handles her husband by not being able to talk. If she could handle him better in other ways, she wouldn't need this symptom.

E: Yes, she needs to handle him comfortably, rather than handle him in a helpless way.

H: Yes.

E: Therefore, you can teach her how to handle him comfortably and there is no reason why she should be helpless. Not only helpless in relationship to him, but helpless in relationship to all the other areas of her life.

H: You have to know quite a bit about relationships in order to help people handle relationships in more competent ways.

E: *You* don't have to know. *They know* the relationships.

You merely get across to them the idea of handling it in a more competent way. And the willingness to do so. I remember a woman who couldn't stand her in-laws visiting her three or four times a week and she developed a stomach ulcer. She had a stomach pain which incapacitated her at work, in her own family relationships, and in her social relationships. My statement was, "You really can't stand your in-laws, but you *can* stand church."

H: You can stand what?

E: Church.

H: Oh.

E: "You can stand the card games with the neighbors. You like your work, but you *really* don't like your relatives. They're a pain in the belly. Why not have the pain in your belly everytime they come? It ought to be usefully developed; they certainly can't expect *you* to mop up the floor if you vomit." (Laughter) She hears that statement, "They can't expect *you* to mop up the floor if you vomit when they come." What did she do? She vomited when they came, and she weakly and piteously had them mop up the floor.

H: (Laughter) Did they come back again?

E: She would hear them drive in the yard, she'd rush to the refrigerator, and drink a glass of milk. They'd come in and she'd greet them, start talking, get sick to her stomach, and vomit. She had her wherewithal, she just wasn't sure if she had the wherewithal to vomit.

H: And she did this every time they came?

E: They quit coming. They started calling up to find out if she were well enough. "Not today, not today, not today." Then she might say, "I think I'm all right today," but unfortunately she made an error.

H: Now that's teaching her to handle them in a weak way and helpless way, isn't it?

E: As long as she wanted to be helpless and have a stomach ulcer, fine – go along with her. The relatives got sick and tired of mopping up that floor. (Laughter) She had her way, and she saved all her pain in the belly for their visits and had her own satisfaction. It is an awfully good stomach she had; it could throw the relatives out. (Laughter) That reversed pride.

H: Pride on the usefulness of the stomach you mean?

E: The goodness of it, and the usefulness and the effectiveness.

H: She gave up the stomach ulcer?

E: Oh certainly. She didn't need to keep it. So much simpler to vomit and make them clean up the mess. After they stopped coming for a couple of months she invited them to come over *for the afternoon*. They came warily. She could control them. After they'd been there the afternoon and she wanted them to leave, she merely had a distressed look on her face and her rubbing on her abdomen. They were very ready to leave. She hadn't asked them. Why should they mop up the floor again? (Laughter) Was it a weak way, or was it a strong way? Anyway, the relatives were whipped by it.

H: It was weak in the sense that it inflicted the punishment without taking responsibility for the punishment, and her husband couldn't get mad at her for inflicting punishment on his relatives because this was a helpless thing she was doing.

E: But it was a strong thing when she kept that glass of milk handy in the refrigerator. That was deliberate, intentional. The old joke about the person who always dropped in for Sunday dinner and was always served sponge cake – until he finally caught on. (Laughter) And the enjoyment of asking that courteous question, until finally he understood.

H: Let's talk about another case that I am faced with. It's kind of a complicated one. It is a boy who is 17 who is an identical twin. He developed a speech block in which he tries to say a word, and the harder he tries to say it the more he can't say it. He has to make a substitute word and he can say that. He's had this for years. It developed when he and his twin were young and had a private language. It was more of an accent than an actual language and they still have it some. No one could understand them but their sister. They went to school and no one could understand them at school, including the teacher. They were given speech therapy to teach them to speak more clearly. When they were kids the teacher couldn't understand them, and this boy started to block. They stopped the speech therapy and he stopped blocking. Then when he was about 12 or 13 they gave them speech therapy. Once again he started to block and they stopped the speech therapy, but he continued blocking. Now it seems to me, looking at the problem, that blocking serves some function with him in the sense of separating him from his twin. It's the only thing that really identifies him. His difficulty is that anything he does, any talent he develops or any skill he develops, he immediately teaches his twin, so that he never has anything that is his own that he can do and that his twin can't do. Except block. That appears to me to be the problem.

E: That he won't develop a personal identity?

H: Yes. He's doing better with it. He has his girl friend he goes steady with and so he doesn't double date with his twin, and he has somewhat a life apart from him, but not really. I think they were very close as little kids and they sort of hung on to each other as the mother went through a divorce and was separated from the father for some years, and so on. When I try to think of some substitute, or something I can develop in him, it's very difficult because he feels guilty if he doesn't teach his twin how to do it. I had an idea you would know mechanically how to handle this, as well as finding a substitute. He blocks badly when he reads because he can't substitute any words then. One day in a trance I had him develop the feeling he was his brother and had him read something and he read it perfectly without any blocking at all. Of course, his brother doesn't block. But he is capable of doing just about anything in a trance I think.

E: This is something that happened yesterday with a patient who blocks. A musician blocks on reading bass in music. She just can't possibly read bass because the blocking developed in the late teens. Yet she can read all music except the bass. She says that it's ridiculous, but she has to read what's in between and all around and she just blocks out. Listen to this. (Reads a paragraph backwards)

H: Reading backwards?

E: Reading a sentence backwards. It makes no sense at all does it? It was read to you and it *was not read* to you. *Right?*

H: Yes.

E: You'll have to admit it was reading, you'll have to admit it was not reading. I think my patient is going to read the bass backwards. With these reading problems that now and then come in, I show them they can read and not read. It's marvelous sport. It's as ridiculous as can be. It's funny. You read a story backwards. A nice little joke. You memorize it, then you tell it to someone backwards. (Laughter) They look at you. (Laughter) What are you talking about?

H: What does this achieve?

E: What does it achieve? A child just simply can't read. He doesn't read by virtue of his blocking. He's perfectly willing to do anything else. So you teach him the trick of reading *backwards*. That's really not reading you know, because there's no meaning. What was the meaning of the sentence I read to you? It's a mish-mash, isn't that right? (Laughter)

H: That's right.

E: It is as meaningless *as if* I remain silent, unable to read the sentence, isn't that right? Yet it was more entertaining. But the important thing is *the acknowledgment* I can read this way – I can *read* backwards.

H: This boy can read. I had him cover up the words following. He can read one word at a time.

E: That's right.

H: The anticipation is where he blocks. He sees a "p" coming and he knows he's going to have difficulty saying "p." When he doesn't see it coming he doesn't block when he gets to it.

E: He can read the individual words. What does he block on? The succession of words. You read a sentence backwards and the succession of words is already defeated by virtue of reading backwards. He doesn't have to block; it's already been done for him – and he can read a succession of words. (Laughs) "Table the on." An intelligent man could reverse that, "on the table." He doesn't have to, but he can't avoid it. And the fun of reading a story backwards and then telling it. Now, not having it typed out I can't do it. But I ran across a story that I would use for grade school kids and high school kids that can read, and that would be redoing the story of the painting of "Custer's Last Thoughts." The artist was instructed to make a picture portraying Custer's last thoughts. In great secrecy the artist painted it but did not tell anybody what the painting was until the day of unveiling. When the picture was unveiled the audience stood horrified in bewilderment. Because it was a painting of a fish wearing a halo, and Indians with flowers growing out of their heads. He was asked to explain and he said, "Custer's last thoughts were, 'Holy mackerel, the blooming Indians are coming'." (Laughter) You teach that to a kid reading it to him backwards — and what a practical joke, what a charming joke it would be to tell that backwards to somebody. At grade school level, freshman and sophomore in high school, that story is irresistible. It would be a practical joke. It would be as charming as can be, as wonderful as all of this bee-bop language and all the other languages they invent. But you know you have to read that story to enjoy it — he wouldn't know that. Because he'd have to read the story in order to memorize it backwards.

H: He can read it to himself without blocking.

E: Yes.

H: It's the reading aloud that is his difficulty.

E: Yes, but in reciting that backwards he would be vocalizing *aloud* with a full knowledge of a complete story forwards. *Aloud*, and he wouldn't know that.

H: I see.

H: How do you give a twin a personal identity?

E: I certainly would go into the physiological growth, the sexual growth, physical experiences, physiological experiences. Then I would acquaint him very thoroughly with point of view. For example, if I asked you to describe me as I sit here, you could. If I asked for a detailed description, you would describe everything. I can ask you to remember. Having done that, I ask you to pick up your chair, put it over in the alcove there, and then proceed to describe me. See how many different ways, how many differences there would be in the description. In this position you see the left side of my face much better than the right side. You see all the digits of my left hand, only part of the digits of my right hand. You can see my left shoulder; you can't see my right one anywhere near as well. Over on the other side of the room you get a different view.

The twin would not recognize what I was doing. But he and his twin can sit side by side; his twin would see me from one angle, and he would see me from another angle. Right?

H: Yes.

E: And the first dawning of realization that his point of view is different. He could really wonder what the difference was, and then I could point out, "You sit *there*, you see me, and while you're describing me a chain of stray thoughts go through your mind because of this position. Leftness would be more predominant. When you sit over there rightness would be more predominant. Even within yourself, when your twin is sitting over there and you're sitting here, over there you'll have a different point of view and your twin will have a different point of view sitting there." That's something that he can understand and it is a separateness and a difference, and the nucleus of individual orientation. "You can put your twin in your seat, but I've shifted my hand and your twin has to see something totally different. And he never will see this because I haven't got my hand back in the same position. I don't remember how I had it. The next appointment I want you to come after eating a good meal and see how differently you feel. Then come to see me with an empty belly. Because you're a constantly changing person. You change in relationship to a full belly or to an empty belly. When you come out before your evening meal you'll still be thinking about eating and what you would like to eat. When you come after a meal you'll think how good what you had eaten was or how disappointed you were that it didn't taste as good as you hoped. A totally different person before eating, after eating." And the build-up in here of a sense of personal identity. "I light this cigarette—and will your twin certainly think the same thoughts as you think when I light a cigarette? You're sitting over there, he is sitting there. He's going to see from a different angle." Until at that very simple level I demonstrate that he had a personal orientation that was individual with him.

H: Here's one of the difficulties. I find now there are examples of those who can't do things, but also people who can do them at times. Now this twin who blocks can, at times, not block, and at other times he blocks. So it isn't that he doesn't know that he can do something without blocking. He does know this.

E: This arithmetical progression is so easily comprehended by patients. Sometimes with the insomnias I ask if there is anything wrong in believing that they slept one second longer than they actually did. One second longer tonight, two seconds longer tomorrow night.

H: Believing that they slept that much longer than they actually did?

E: Yes.

H: What does that do?

E: Two seconds longer tomorrow night, four seconds longer than the next night and they have comprehended the arithmetical progression because they have worked out the old arithmetical problem: A blacksmith has horseshoe nails, 32 nails for a set of shoes for a horse. One cent for the first set of horseshoe nails, two cents for the second four — the farmer discovers that he owes 28 million dollars. (Laughter) Patients can understand that. And to think that they slept one second longer tonight and two seconds longer tomorrow night, and four seconds longer the next night. I am not asking very much of them. But there's arithmetical progression. And they can go to bed, toying with that idea of arithmetical progression. It's very sedative.

H: What happens when they think they have slept longer

than they have. Does that mean they *do* then sleep longer than they have?

E: Isn't that what you want them to believe? Because they'll make good on that sleep. They are always making good on the belief that they *don't* sleep. "I only sleep one hour, that's all the sleep I get at night!" "I only sleep two hours." "I only sleep an hour and a half." "I only sleep three hours. I'd give anything if I could sleep eight hours." I am not asking them very much when I ask them to sleep one hour plus one second tonight. One hour plus two seconds tomorrow night.

H: You are not asking them to sleep that long; you are asking them to believe they have slept that long. You assume that's the same thing?

E: They're going to put their belief into action, you know that.

H: Then in a week do they report to you that they've slept one hour plus whatever the increment?

E: Yes. One second, two seconds, four seconds, eight seconds, 16 seconds, 32 seconds, 64 seconds. It's a whole week of accumulated belief, accumulated performance, and tremendous alteration in their thinking about their sleep. "Of course, I don't really know if I slept, I don't really know." But whether they express it or not, there's an equal probability that they did sleep as well as a probability that they were awake. Previously there had been no probability of their being asleep, and they do want to sleep, and you've given them a probability. A completely acceptable probability. They've had a whole week in which to emphasize one minute and four seconds. It's such an insidious thing that they can't fight against it. You have arithmetical progression by constantly doubling it, and at one minute and four seconds you can halve the doubling, so it's only one minute and 30 seconds and just add another 30 seconds every night. Just add 30 seconds. Anybody can do that. It really is just a game, you know, but it's a cumulative thing. Then they discover that they are adding hours.

H: Is that the way you usually treat insomnia?

E: Oh, no. I had a 65-year-old man come to me who had suffered a little insomnia 15 years previously and the physician gave him sodium amytal. As the years went by he became habituated to sodium amytal. Three months previously his wife had died, and left him alone living with his unmarried son. The man had been regularly taking 15 capsules, three grains each. A dosage of 45 grains of sodium amytal. He went to bed at 8 o'clock, rolled and tossed until midnight, then he'd take his 15 capsules, 45 grains, a couple of glasses of water, lie down and get about an hour and a half to two hours' sleep. Then he'd rouse up and roll and toss until getting up time. The 15 capsules no longer worked since his wife died. He'd gone to the family physician and asked for a prescription for 18 capsules. The family physician got frightened and apologized for ever allowing him to become a barbiturate addict. He sent him to me. I asked the old man if he really wanted to get over his insomnia, if he really wanted to get over his drug addicton. He said he did and he was very honest and very sincere. I told him he could do it easily.

In taking his history I learned he lived in a large house, with hardwood floors, and that he did most of the cooking and the dishwashing, while the son did the housework, especially the waxing of the floors which the old man hated. He hated the smell of Johnson's floor wax and his son didn't mind. So I explained to the old man that I could cure him, that it would cost him at the most eight hours' sleep, and that's all, which would be a small price to pay. *Would he willingly* give up eight hours' sleep to recover from his insomnia? The old man promised me that he would.

I told him that it meant work and he agreed that he could do the work. So I explained to him that instead of going to bed tonight at 8 o'clock, he was to get out the can of Johnson floor wax and some rags. "It will only cost you one hour and a half of sleep, or two hours at the most. And you start polishing those floors. You'll hate it, you'll hate me and you won't think well of me as the hours drag along. But you polish those hardwood floors all night long and go to the real estate office the next morning at 8 o'clock. Stop polishing on the floor at 7 o'clock, which will give you a whole hour for rising. Then the next night at 8 o'clock get up and wax the floor. You'll really polish those floors all over again, and you won't like it. But you'll lose at most two hours of sleep. The third night, do the same, and the fourth night do the same."

He polished those floors the first night, the second night, the third night. The fourth night he said, "I'm so weary following that crazy psychiatrist's orders, but I suppose I might as well." He lost six hours of sleep, he had two more to lose before I cured him really. He said to himself, "I think I'll lie down in bed and rest my eyes for half an hour." (Laughter) He woke up at 7 the next morning. That night he was confronted with a dilemma. Should he go to bed when he still owed me two hours of sleep? He reached a compromise. He'd get ready for bed and get out the Johnson floor wax and the polishing rags at 8 o'clock. If he could read 8:15 on the clock, he'd get up and polish the floors all night. A year later he told me he had been sleeping every night. In fact, he says, "You know I don't dare suffer from insomnia. I look at that clock and I say if I'm awake in 16 minutes I've got to polish the floors all over, and I mean it too!" You know, the old man would do anything to get out of polishing the floors—even sleep. He didn't dare to stay awake.

I had a 29-year-old man who wet the bed every

night, for 29 years. He came to me for therapy one winter and said he wanted quick therapy, brief therapy, nothing more. Would I take him on. I asked him what his symptom was. His routine was to go to bed, and by midnight or half past 12 he would have the bed wet. He would get up, change the linen completely, go back to bed and sleep the rest of the night. Next night he would come home, wash out the linen, hang it up to dry, go to bed, at 12:30 get up and change the linen, stack it up, go back to bed and sleep. The next day he'd wash out that linen and fold the other pair of sheets.

I said to him, "Since you get up at 12:00, 12:30 or 1:00 o'clock, whatever it is when you wet the bed, all you have to do is change the linen, prepare your bed, dress completely, walk 20 blocks down the street, and turn around and walk back." He would be glad that he had that much of the night left to sleep since he'd be tired walking that 40 blocks. He refused to accept this suggestion, saying he preferred to wet the bed to walking the 40 blocks. Three months later he came back and said, "How does that go?" I told him again and he said, "You know it's worth a trial." I said, "All right, you rejected it once. So you can give it a trial and reject it again. I'll add something to it. Regardless of whether you wet the bed or not, you set your alarm clock every night to arouse you at 12:30. Whether the bed is wet or not you walk 20 blocks. After you have done that every night for two weeks, you'll do anything to have a dry bed. Promise yourself absolutely that if at any time you ever wet the bed for which you cannot get a medical excuse from me – such as unconsciousness, cold, or pneumonia, or something like that – then you'll walk every night 40 blocks for one whole week."

He said, "I'm fed up with it. I'm going to do that

for two weeks. Then I'll go to sleep, and if I wet the bed that will mean one whole week of walking 40 blocks whether I've a wet or dry bed." He came back to report to me that he had a dry bed. He still has his week's walking in reserve. He came back to report to me again, "I haven't had to put in that other week's walking. I'll tell you something else you might be interested in. I've worked at a job I've hated for nine years. Since I quit wetting the bed, I developed an impulse to ask my boss for a raise. He gave it to me, and was very generous. He told me I should have asked for it before. I took the raise and was grateful about it for a couple of weeks, and then I got mad as hell. I still didn't like my job. So I went to my boss and said I want a transfer. He said, 'Well, I think it's about time you ask for a transfer.' So now I've got a job at even higher pay from the raise I got. What happened to me?" "Since you have a dry bed, you respect yourself." As he worded it, "You mean as a bed pisser I didn't dare ask for a raise?" I said, "That's right. A normal man, sleeping normally, is man enough to ask for what he wants. When he was nothing more than a piss-the-bed, he wasn't entitled to anything."

H: Why did you choose that suggestion in this case?

E: Wouldn't you do anything to have your bed dry to avoid walking 40 blocks, at midnight in the wintertime?

H: What you're dealing with in both insomnia and bedwetting is an involuntary thing, and you get them to overcome an involuntary thing by voluntary behavior.

E: That's right, voluntary behavior. They'll resort to anything to escape that voluntary behavior, even control involuntary behavior.

H: You first get them thoroughly commited to how much they want to get rid of the problem.

E: That's right. Do they really want to? How much sleep would the old man give up? Eight hours wasn't asking very much, only one hour and a half, two hours at the most. He gave up plenty of sleep every night anyhow. I wasn't asking him for much. But boy, it was effective.

H: Well, this brings up a case I had of insomnia which I cured, and I didn't know why it was cured. That's one of the reasons I decided to come and see you. He is a successful attorney. Last May he went on a trip and had difficulty sleeping. For seven months he got about two hours of sleep per night. A couple of nights he'd stay awake all night. When I saw him he had been on about six grains of amytal a night, as well as on a tranquilizer, and still he wasn't sleeping. He was one of these guys who insisted he had nothing wrong with him – perfectly happy with his work, perfectly happy with his wife and children – the only thing wrong was he couldn't sleep. I helped him in a few sessions, and I have no idea why he really was better. We did a lot of talking about his life. I didn't really know what to do to get him over this, except to reassure him about some of the things that were on his mind. But I did some things related to what you're talking about. He was saying that every time he was going to sleep, something would pull him awake. I thought that it was some kind of a thought that he had on his mind, but he couldn't get anywhere near it because everything was perfectly all right with him. So I suggested that he think about all the most horrible things that he could do, or could see himself doing. He couldn't think of any, so I had him think of all the horrible things Mr. Smith, some hypothetical person, might have on his mind. He then thought of murder, homosexuality, putting his wife in a whorehouse, and various things like that. I told him to go home that night, and before he went to sleep he must deliberately try to think of all the horrible things he could bring to his

mind. He did that and had a good night's sleep. The
following week he came in cured and he still is six
months later. I don't know whether it was my assigning him this or not.

E: It was your assigning him that.

H: I could have done that three weeks earlier.

E: One of my professional cases had insomnia, never got
to sleep before two, always awakened at four. He was
a hurried man, and had erratic working hours. He
hadn't been reading for years. This insomnia had been
going on for some 12 years, and I led him out on all
the books he had promised himself to read since college. He named this book and that book. He did want
to go through Dickens, and he did want to go through
Scott. In college he had promised himself to read some
other set of books. I asked him what he thought about
all these book reading promises that he had renewed
and broken throughout the years. I made him feel as
guilty as I could, and I told him there was a cure for
his insomnia. He was to go to bed at 11:00 o'clock and,
if he was not asleep at 11:30, he was to get up and
keep his promises one by one. But he could not sit in
a chair and read because he'd fall asleep. He was to
fix up the lamp on the mantel and lean on the mantel
and read for the rest of the night. (Laughter) He went
to sleep at 11:30 very shortly, because he knew if he'd
waken at 2, or 3, or 4, he'd be up for the rest of the
night standing against the mantel reading and have
the guilt feeling for not keeping his promises. That
was an evasion for him. He was in to see me a year
later, laughing at the "swindle" I had worked on him.
But he said, "It's a good swindle. My practice is much
better, my income is much better. I am healthy, I am
happier, I sleep nights. I am reading some of those
books, but I've got a whole set of Dickens waiting in
case my insomnia comes back." (Laughter)

H: Is that what you typically do – assign them something that they don't want to do, that's very difficult for them to do?

E: Yet in some way they want to do it.

H: When would you use arithmetic progression with a patient rather than the scrub the floor approach?

E: Some people haven't got enough strength of character to scrub the floor, so you present them with this arithmetical progression. Also, a patient can come in and tell you, "I sleep a great deal, eight hours at night; I wouldn't have believed it was possible." Then you can ask him, "Well, since that's solved, are there some other problems of personality that really need solving?" A negative approach, yes. "Well, I suppose you can work on my sex adjustments with my wife. I suppose you can work on my relationships with my inlaws."

H: Why would you say that's a negative approach?

E: What did I say?

H: "Are there some other problems of personality that could be worked on?"

E: "That could be worked on." It's a negative approach. You're just raising this as an unimportant question. "Do you suppose there are problems that could be worked on?"

H: It doesn't sound very negative to me. (Laughter)

E: "That's a beautiful job that you have done on the lawn. Do you suppose you *could* clip the hedge?" I'm raising the doubt.

H: I see.

E: But the goodness of the job on the lawn is going to overweight the negativeness of the quesiton, "Do you suppose you could clip the hedge?" "The devil, I did a good job on the lawn; of course, I could clip the hedge and do just as good a job." You're reinforcing the goodness of the lawn job. And your patient is always entitled to a respect of his doubts. You let the correction of his doubts come from within him. I don't think you should say, "Now that I have taught you to sleep eight hours a night, I can straighten out the rest of your problems." No, you say, "Do you suppose you have any other problem that might be worked on?" "I suppose you could straighten out some of my marital problems."

H: When they say that, they're committing themselves to the sleep problem being solved?

E: Why yes.

H: I see.

E: That's no longer an issue. How many patients have I done brief therapy on for some definite problem, presenting problem, and have them come back, "You handled that so well, I think I better have you discuss *this* with me." I knew that she'd discuss it with me anyway.

CHAPTER 3

Headaches,
Unconscious Conversation,
Assertiveness

1957. Present were Milton H. Erickson and Jay Haley.

H: Once again I would like to present to you a type of case and ask you what information you would want from the patient. What would you want to know about a patient who is referred to you because she had severe headaches once every two weeks, often once a week. These headaches last about three days and she has to be knocked out with drugs to get some sleep.

E: The first thing I would make clear to the patient is this: She undoubtedly has those headaches for a reason. The first important consideration is how many of these headaches she needs for that unknown reason. Does she really need them every week, or every two weeks? Does she really need to have them last three days? Would it be sufficient for whatever the reason is to have the headache last only two and a half days instead of three? Or, since she has some unknown reason for the headaches, is it necessary for her to have the headaches at an inconvenient time? Could

62

that reason be satisfied by having the headaches at a time most convenient for her and for the shortest length of time that satisfies the reason? Need the headache be continuously sharp and painful or could it be a slow dull headache culminating in a brief period of pain and then trailing off in a slow dull headache? Thereby I emphasize that she has the headaches, that she can keep the headache, the duration, the severity. I would put it to her in such a way that she is not going to confront me with the idea, "But I can't get rid of the headache." I am just suggesting a modification, and she is going to accept that. She can't help herself. She knows I am not overpromising her, that I am taking a completely reasonable attitude. She knows that I am being definitively too conservative. She wants me to be less conservative – but it's her want, not my insistence. When she has these headaches, is it really necessary for her to have other somatic manifestations with them or are the headaches in themselves enough? Does she need any special emotional components or are the headaches in themselves enough?

H: That's an interesting way to handle a headache.

E: It's often a very, very effective way. I had a patient with a headache for three days every week. The first interview I introduced that systematic presentation of those ideas. She skipped the next three weeks, and then came in and told me that this fourth week she was going to have a headache. I asked her to outline her program for the week. When would be the most convenient time to have the headache? Would it be possible for her to precipitate the headache a few hours in advance, or even a day in advance? Or could she delay it a few hours or even a day? For how long a time did she want it, and did she really feel, since she skipped three weeks, that she ought to make this headache

more severe than usual, or did she want to make it
less severe as a *possible* result of her learning during
the past three weeks? All I was asking her to do really
was to take some kind of control over the headache,
which she didn't really consciously recognize as voli-
tional control. No matter what she did she could make
it more severe, or less severe. She could speed it up,
or she could delay it. Whatever she did to the
headache was an expression of her control. Her reaction was, "It might as well be just the usual headache,"
which *was* deliberate control.

H: I see.

E: "And it might just as well last the usual three days. It
might just as well occur unexpectedly, the way it
usually did." I said, "That would be a sensible thing,
because a month from now you might want to alter
it. You'd really like to study this headache thoroughly,
so a month from now you can put into force any special alterations you want to make." What was I telling
her? – Skip another three weeks.

H: You were?

E: She didn't know I was saying that, just as you didn't
realize it.

H: No. (Laughter) Now you presented it as an unknown
reason for the headaches. Do you try to find out the
reason?

E: No. You tell me, because if you can, you will be the only
one who can tell me: How did I fall in love with Betty?
It seems to have lasted a good number of years, now
why? Do I need to know the reason?

H: I don't think you need to know the reason for that, no.

E: Yet it has altered and changed and influenced and directed my life so very, very extensively. How important
is it for one to know? Will it add anything?

H: Well, to my mind it would, but it doesn't if it doesn't
to you.

E: In what way would it add anything?

H: Well, for example, this particular woman I am talking about with headaches, they follow certain sequences . . .

E: (Interrupting) No, what I mean is, would it add anything to my happiness?

H: Oh, you're talking about you and Betty.

E: Yes. Would it add anything to know the real reason why I fell in love with her?

H: No, I don't think it would.

E: When I first saw Betty walking across the campus at the University of Michigan, she was about 60 feet away from me and I looked at her and I thought, I'll sit beside her at the luncheon meeting of the Academy of Michigan Arts and Sciences, because that's the girl that I'm going to marry. I managed to get a place beside her, and I was determined that I was going to marry her. I didn't see her again from March until June. Then I really knew I was going to marry her. Now, what did I see in that girl some 60 feet away from me walking down the sidewalk?

H: I don't quite understand why you equate an incapacitating physical symptom with love.

E: Because they both influence your life so tremendously.

H: All right.

E: Whatever the reasons were, they certainly have governed and controlled me in so many ways. How many incapacitating symptoms and problems do you get for utterly irrelevant reasons?

H: I wouldn't agree that they were ever for irrelevant reasons.

E: Just because you saw your father beat your mother over her head and knock her around, and you were a little child, and then years later you happen to have a bitter quarrel with your husband, and thereafter you have periodic headaches. It develops on Friday, it last three days; finally the psychiatrist digs out that the mother got her head beaten on Friday. It scared the daylights out of you; your mother didn't seem to get over it until late Sunday evening. Then you knew you could still have your mother. You dig that out and your patient stops having a headache.

H: Well, I don't think that's a fair presentation of insight therapy. Usually you find that if somebody has a headache it is a way of handling a situation they're in, and usually they have done this all their life in some form or another with some kind of infirmity. Perhaps a headache, perhaps not, but something that makes them withdraw. It may be because their mother got beat over the head, or it may be that they learned from their mother this was a good way to get away from the husband for a period of time.

E: Yes, and they keep on having the headache.

H: When they get in a similar situation, yes. Now you can teach them to control the headache, or you can change the situation that provokes it.

E: Yes.

H: To me the latter would tend to be a more productive way than just getting and keeping control of the headache. I don't know whether you assume that when they get control of the headache they also get control of the situation or not.

E: And, "What are you going to do in place of your headache, because it serves some purpose? Can that purpose be served adequately, pleasantly, competently by something else that's not so painful, that's not so distressing, that's not so destructive as the headache?"

H: The patient will say, "I don't know. I don't know what purpose it serves."

E: "You don't even know what purpose the headache serves, but it serves some purpose. And it's a physical thing.

Why couldn't an enjoyment of classical music be a substitute? You'll use your head, you'll listen to it, you like classical music, you would like to include it in a rather systematic fashion in your day-by-day life, and why not that way? It's pleasurable, it's going to alter all of your thinking and all of your feeling, all of your attitudes toward yourself to sit and listen to the classical music that you like. You're inspired, it changes your mood, even as your headache does. You've always wanted to make provision for a fairly good program of listening to classical music, but you've never really organized your daily routine to fit it in. You've just organized your daily routine to have a weekly three-day headache. Your unconscious can use a headache, use a bellyache, use constipation, use classical music, it can use a bestseller, it can use a trip out to the park. Your unconscious is capable of using so many things, either for your profit or for a loss. The headache is a loss."

H: Now when you put it that way, are you suggesting a substitute or are you suggesting a *kind* of substitute?

E: A *kind* of substitute—because how long is it going to take to find out the cause of the headache and the special purposes it serves? If you can get that same amount of energy devoted to something useful, constructive, pleasant. Against *that* background they can handle these situations much more adequately.

H: One of the reasons I bring up this headache case is because it's another one of those where I cured without knowing why or what happened. This woman had these headaches three days at a time, and I saw her for about six weeks, and she didn't have any headaches from the day I saw her. That was three months ago. She has had these headaches since she was 14 years old and she has a number of other problems. She had previously seen a psychiatrist for three years without relief. She's been married to a man now for some years and she has a lot of boy friends, but she doesn't have any affairs. The boy friends just hang around her. She's really setting up a situation that could involve murder, because she attracts the kind of men who want an affair but not an affair, you know, and she drives her husband to distraction with this. She was handling this kind of a situation by having these headaches about three days a week. She'd have an argument with her husband and two days later she'd come up with the headache. Before she developed it she'd become very perfectionistic around the house. She would scrub the walls and clean the house beautifully.

E: You say she does how around the house? Perfectionist?

H: Perfectionist. Everything had to be just right.

E: Yes.

H: Then she developed this headache. The first day would be perfectionism, the second day would be a headache and she'd go to bed with it and couldn't move. Then about the third or fourth day the headache would let up and she would become very sloppy, just sit around and do nothing. Then for a few days she would be all right and back she'd go into the routine. It was just like this week after week after week.

E: I would want to see her husband.

H: Which I did.

E: And I would want to see her. Those boy friends of hers, that she sets up so carefully to tantalize. She thinks she's tantalizing them, but she's only tantalizing herself. Isn't that right?

H: Yes.

E: That's where I would start. In tantalizing herself, what is she doing? Consciously she lets her thinking go just so far – and her unconscious thinking goes a bit further. Then she really cleans house, externally, but symbolically she is cleaning her own head out.

H: Interestingly enough, when she has the headache, she objects to the drugs they give her because they take away the pain but they don't put her to sleep. She's still awake and she can still feel the headache somewhere in her head, but she can't control her thoughts with the drugs, and she experiences something like an hallucination. She sees her mother standing over her saying, "You're doing wrong, you're doing wrong."

E: Yes.

H: She's a very interesting woman in many ways. She wears too much makeup, and she combines this with sort of a helpless, withdrawing way. If she attends a party, men swarm to her even though she is merely sitting.

E: That aggressive promise and that weak yieldingness.

H: One of her unfortunate difficulties is she doesn't feel she is a woman. She avoided ever being in the nude. I suggested that she go in the bathroom, get in the nude, examine herself, and see if she could accept herself. What she most objected to was hair down there, pubic hair. She didn't like that at all. Until she was about 12 or 13, she took showers with her father, and it was about the only time he paid any attention to her, and they had a fine time in the showers. She grew pubic hair and the showers stopped. So she cut off the pubic hair, hoping the showers would continue, but they didn't continue anyhow. Her body image of herself is a very unfortunate one, and I was led to that almost immediately by the way she talked.

E: How do you introduce a person to the idea, when they don't dare to get into the nude and look at themselves?

H: How do you?

E: The patient tells you, "I can't possibly get in the nude and look at myself in the mirror." Then there may be many efforts and they can't possibly do it as a deliberate, motivated thing. "I can't stand in front of the mirror and look at myself. I can't possibly do it." So they won't undress, and they can't. How would you get them to do it?

H: I don't know.

E: You get them to do it on their own terms. They tell you, "I can't possibly get in the nude, stand in front of the mirror, and look at myself, I can't possibly do it." You say, "That's right, I am going to make you prove it. I think you'll laugh at me when I tell you what to do. On a very dark night, with the curtains drawn and the lights out, undress and stand in front of the mirror and look at yourself, and you can't possibly see yourself in the nude. You can do that because you can't possibly see yourself in the nude." Once they've done it — "See what you've done?" You've got them to do it and they can't possibly do it, and they've done the thing they can't possibly do. (Laughter) So you've put a completely different construction on it.

H: Yes.

E: Once they go through that, they agree it is a silly thing to do; they might as well do it with the lights on the next time.

H: Well, I saw her husband. She described him as a very rugged, strong guy, quite a rigid guy who wouldn't give in on anything. I spent an hour with him and he seemed to me frightened and unable to handle his wife.

E: The husband really needs the therapy?

H: He does, and he won't accept it. He keeps insisting she's the one who needs a psychiatrist.

E: Then I would tell him, "Your wife needs a great deal of management, much more than I can give her, the kind of management that I would have to rely on *you* to give her." How often do they have sexual relations, and *when*?

H: Very rarely now. Apparently when they were first married it wasn't so.

E: He's the one that needs therapy.

H: I think she has quite a good potential for therapy.

E: I think she's going to wait until he gets it before she takes it.

H: Possibly.

E: I'm treating a husband and wife. The husband knows darn well his wife needs the therapy. I know he needs the therapy, so I am talking to him about the management of his wife. His wife really wants to be managed. She's trying to force him in every conceivable way to manage her. The ways she has hit upon are to be nervous, to be underweight, to spend recklessly, to have to rest instead of washing the dishes. And he is a guy with great potentialities.

H: I'm still interested in the way you approach symptoms. You seem concerned solely with the symptom and how to handle the symptom rather than what's behind it.

E: Remember the symptom is the handle to the patient. What are you going to do with the pot? You take hold of the handle.

H: (Laughter) OK.

E: You keep your hand on the handle, and whatever you do with the pot you still have your hand on the handle.

H: If someone comes in with a constant nervous stomach or stomach upset, do you handle that the same way you would a headache? Do you deal with it in terms of whether the stomach needs to be upset every day, or every other day, and so on?

E: Well, that's my first approach. You sooner or later discover either that they have an upset stomach or that's the way they like to think about themselves, and that's the way they want you to talk to them. When you talk about an upset stomach your patient knows very, very well, just as you do, that you are not talking about an upset stomach. Even though those are the exact words that you say, you're really talking about an upset sexual life. Let's call sex the stomach, and you politely stick to stomach as another way of saying sex.

H: How do they really know you are talking about their sexual life? You mean, because that's what is on their mind?

E: That's what is on their mind.

H: So instead of talking directly about their sexual life, you deal with it in terms of their stomach. Is this easier, or what?

E: A woman came to me because of the tastelessness of food. She couldn't get any satisfaction out of her food, couldn't taste it, didn't feel it. She wasn't the least bit regular about her food. I talked about the size of the bolus of food, and the movement of food in the oral cavity. What was I talking about and what did she know I was talking about? We both kept up that polite pretense, and she knew darn well that I understood. But if she wanted that kind of language, why not discuss a bolus of food instead of a stool?

H: You deal in whatever language the patient brings to you, and if they shift to another language you deal with that then?

E: But it is awfully easy to shift from bolus of food and tastelessness of food, and no satisfaction with food, to the question of constipation, about the size of the stool, the odor of the stool, the color of the stool, but what is the patient really doing? They are testing. And I measure up to that test. But I make it so awfully easy for them to shift to the real language.

H: I see.

E: Why should I tell them, "Stop this nonsense, talking about the tastelessness of food. You are really concerned about your spastic constipation."

H: One of the differences between you and the analytic

school would be the fact that they use silence to get the patient to shift languages.

E: They use silence, they use passive resistance to the patient, and they wait the patient out. The patient who had the phobia for going into drugstores. Not always present, not always the same drugstore, but a very definite phobia. She goes into the drugstore and the bright lights, the big windows, all that stuff affects her. Yet sometimes she can go in easily, comfortably. What are the things you can buy in a drugstore? I could run over in my mind all the things that you can buy in a drugstore, and I know what a woman could buy in a drugstore. I wonder if she is raising the question of menstruation. "In six months' time how many drugstores do you suppose you could have a phobia for?" She thinks I'm talking about half a year; I am actually talking about six monthly periods. I said six months. She says, "Five or six." "About how long do you think it will be before that horrible feeling will come over you again?" What am I talking about?

H: Yes.

E: The unconscious picks it up. I also know what I am talking about. When she says, "In about a month's time," I say, "Have you ever noted the very special purchase that you may have made?" Now that's getting down to definitive language: "the very special purchase you may have made." That choice of words: "very special." And she is a woman, it is a drugstore, and a very special purchase that she made last month and a month ago and was making this month. What does her unconscious think and feel about that? The topic is being discussed, safely so, and I am giving her every opportunity of saying the things clearly but unrecognizably, to herself.

H: If the patient never deals explicitly with the problem, do you work entirely in terms of the drugstore?

E: I am thinking of a patient where we never did call spades spades. At the termination it was so charming – the patient's statement was, "We never did really talk about the thing that troubled me. We just had an understanding with each other, and we still don't need to talk about that openly." The understanding is sufficient. I have had patients describe in detail to me how they felt they ought to cook dinner for their husband, and they go into a tremendous wealth of detail about preparing the meat for the evening meal. "What kind of spices should I use? How do you really season it? What about the natural juices or should you put in flour and cornstarch and make a jelly-like gravy?" You talk about the preparation of the evening meal. And she can state, "I like steak – rare – or rarely." What does she mean by "rare"? Just plain steak. No comment. What does she mean: "natural juices" or "jelly-like gravy"?

H: You don't ever make a shift to let her know that what she's really talking about is a parallel with sex?

E: I make it very easy for her.

H: In analytic therapy an interpretation would be made that would, later perhaps, put these two together.

E: Yes. And what would I say after I have answered all of her questions, resolved her problem for her, and we are still talking about the evening meal? When I have made it very, very easy for her to say something about sex, and she still hasn't, and I don't think it safe, my interpretation is, "Now we really understand each other. You yourself understand – and I hope you'll come back sometime to tell me how things are going along." I have had patients come back to tell me boldly, frankly, "My sex life has been completely readjusted, thanks to you. I don't know why I was so silly that I wouldn't come out and tell you *what* I was talking about. Now I can, and is there anything more you think I ought to know about *sex*?" And I tell them that the French language, the Italian, the Chinese, the English – all serve to communicate meanings, and as long as the meanings are communicated that's sufficient. As long as she understood, that was the important thing. "Sometimes it's interesting to shift into another language; there might be some nuances of meaning, some special connotations, that are better expressed in another language, and if you have any other questions about sex you can discuss those." That makes it very very easy. "Nuances and meanings and other connotations" – best expressed in English.

H: Would you feel that merely the understanding of what's on their mind is therapeutic?

E: Yes. I think that too many therapists think that *their* understanding is the important thing. *They* want to understand, and then they want to present *their* understanding to the patient. The patient is another breed of cats.

H: You're talking about therapeutic change now. If a woman discusses dinner in a way that is obviously discussing sex, if you accept this discussion of dinner and say, "We understand each other," has some therapeutic change been produced?

E: I can discuss the preparation of a meal, a roast of meat, a steak, the feel of the steak, the texture of the steak, the appearance of the steak.

H: The therapy comes in making the steak attractive then?

E: Yes. They know what I'm talking about.

H: What I am trying to get at is this: It's more than merely a common understanding; it's a shift in the attitude towards the steak.

E: Yes. I approve of it. I like steak. I like roast beef. I like to handle it, I like to enjoy it. And you can really see your roast beef if you like it. But you always make your own choice. Theoretically it might not be any better than the others, but it's *your* choice, and it really is because *it is* your choice, not because it's steak, U.S. choice beef. You can always use words that symbolize a tremendous amount, if you are willing. A patient who came to me and launched into a diatribe, vituperative as could be, about her father, and her mother, and her brother. The longer she discussed it the more I realized that she couldn't *possibly* be talking about her father, her mother, and her brother. Then what was it she was talking about?

H: You're asking me?

E: Yes. What was she talking about: father, mother, and brother. Her father's god-like dictatorial ways. Her mother's assumption she was the mother of all mankind. Her brother seemed to be a little Jesus. I finally told her, "I don't quite understand your criticism of your father, mother, and brother. You seem to be trying to talk about a trilogy but that's the wrong word. I can't think of the right word." Trilogy? That's a three: father, mother, and brother. Father and his god-like ways, mother the mother of all mankind, brother the little Jesus. Her boy friend wanted her to become a Catholic, and there was her religious conflicts about the Trinity. She was Protestant, and a very doubtful Protestant. Protestant doubtful, Catholic doubtful. She really wanted that religious question straightened out. She did not want to think that Catholicism had something to do with her doubts about her boy friend. She just was going to exclude religion from all discussion of her boy friend. Trilogy? Trinity? And I admitted that trilogy was the wrong word. I couldn't think of the right one.

H: Sounds like your statement about hypnosis. Sometimes you hesitate, seeking for a word so the subject will supply it.

E: That's right. But we got that entire situation straightened out. She just was *not* going to solve her problem on a religious basis.

H: One of the things that I am curious about is how you handle the patient who tends to belittle himself. He takes back everything that he says, derogates everything that he says. This is so common among some of these patients. The patient sits down and says, "Oh, I've been thinking, if you can call what I do thinking."

E: "What would happen, if you *did* call it thinking? Would the walls crash in? You are here to get an understanding of problems. I think you recognize that your thinking isn't good. At least that's the interpretation that I placed on your statement, 'I've been thinking, if you call what I do thinking.' From my point of view I am going to call it at least an honest striving towards it, an earnest striving toward thinking." That permits him the failure of thinking, but credits him his trying.

H: (Laughter) That's nice all right.

E: So he gets credit, and he can't possibly reject that credit. Because he's always doing thinking, *if* you can call it thinking. He is always striving, striving in real earnest.

H: What you do is take a positive point of view about what he *is* doing.

E: Yes, and place a validity on it, a wealth of significance. Sooner or later he's going to tell you, "I've been doing some thinking. This time, I think it's thinking." So this time *I* think it's thinking. "And what was it *this* time?" And by saying that I shift it.

H: You do?

E: "What was it *this* time?" What does "this time" mean? "This time" is really selected out of a number of times, isn't it?

H: Yes.

E: So I've conveyed another idea to him.

H: Well that's an interesting one. You emphasize this special time and so indicate this is happening continuously, is that it?

E: That's right.

H: I'll be damned!

E: Well, it's correct, isn't it?

H: That's one of those tricky ones where the patient can accept it as, "This is a special time," and not realize that he is accepting it, because this is happening consistently.

E: And you are awfully undecided, and not very much interested in, taking a cigarette when I offer you one. You can say, "No, thank you." I can say to you, "There are three cigarettes here – this one, this one, and this one. This one sticks out partly, this one less far, and this the least. Now do you want this one, this one, or this one?" It's no longer a question of rejecting.

H: It's a question of choosing.

E: It's a question of accepting, but only *which* one. The patient must accept an idea, and this one seems to be appropriate this way, this other idea seems to be appropriate another way, the third one seems to be appropriate still a third way. Now, which one will you take?

H: I see.

E: You volunteer for a hypnotic trance. You are a bit reluctant, and it's your first experience, you really ought to be a bit reluctant. You can use the coin technique, you can use the house-tree technique, or the hand levitation technique. Which technique would you like me to use to put you in a trance?

H: What's so important in that is the early statement about accepting their reluctance.

E: That's right, you accept their reluctance. This reluctance becomes attached to the coin technique, and the house-tree technique, which he rejects. (Laughter) Isn't that right?

H: I guess it is.

E: He presumably has made a free choice. You don't want to discuss your problem as you sit there in that chair. You certainly don't want to discuss it standing up. You agree, don't you? But if you move your chair to the other side of the room it would give a different view of the whole situation, wouldn't it?

H: (Laughter) Did you ever have them actually move the chair over?

E: Oh yes. "I just can't tell you about my homosexual activities last night. I just can't do it. I'm too ashamed, too humiliated, I can't tell you." "I don't blame you. You are sitting there in the chair. You know you ought to tell me, but as you sit there you know you can't tell me, and you really know that as you sit there. Why don't you sit in that chair over *there*? I can bring one in or you can move that chair over there, that will give you a different view of the whole thing." (Laughter) Then you get that nice account of last night's experiences on the desert with a Mexican punk, with all the details.

H: That ties in the resistance with the sitting *there*.

E: Yes, I better tie it to that, because that's something I can handle.

H: I see.

E: It's something he can handle, and all of your resistances are really false, and they are tied to things, so why not tie 'em up.

H: What other things do you do when a patient takes things back? I mean, so often you find the patient will begin to move a bit and they'll take it back, or the patient will tend to assert himself and then have to apologize for it.

E: Give me an example.

H: I'm trying to think of one at the moment. All I can think of is extreme ones because I have a couple of extreme patients, but it often happens with little things with patients.

E: "I took care of my house, I cleaned the house, I did the laundry, did the dishes, cooked the meals, all week. I am too incompetent to do that again. I just can't do it again."

H: That's a good example.

E: Is that it?

H: Yes.

E: "But you have learned a lot of things, haven't you? You have learned that somehow or other you did it last week. You didn't expect to, did you? Isn't that a surprise, and you really didn't expect it, did you? In fact, Monday you didn't think you would do it on Tuesday. On Tuesday you *really* didn't expect to do it on Wednesday. On Wednesday you *really* didn't expect to do it on Thursday. On Thursday you really, really, *really* didn't expect to do it on Friday, but you did it. Then, on Friday you didn't know you were wearing out, and you didn't expect to do it on Saturday, but you did. You did despite the fact that it was wearing you out. You didn't expect to do it on Sunday, *you really didn't*, absolutely didn't, expect to do it on Sunday because it was wearing you out, but you did do it on Sunday. Then, on Monday you couldn't do it, and you know that now." I'll have gone all the way out.

H: Yes.

E: But let's go back. "You didn't know last Monday, you *really* didn't know but you did it on Monday. You had doubts about Tuesday, and more about Wednesday, and still more and more and more—that's something that you had to find out that it would wear out. It wore you out last week, but it was something that happened last week. Seven days in a week—Sunday, Monday, Tuesday, Wednesday, Thursday, Friday, and Saturday. Or did that week begin with Monday,

Tuesday, Wednesday, Thursday, Friday, Saturday, Sunday? The week can begin with any day – and the most unexpected things can happen; they've happened to you many times in the past. You surprised yourself more than once in the past and the past is an extension of a remoter past into the future." (Laughter) What have I done? "Many unexpected things have happened in the past, things that you really didn't believe, couldn't believe would happen, but they did happen, and the future is going to become the past. In eight days' time, only eight days' time, next week will be the past, and many things have happened unexpectedly in the past."

H: That was an awfully good example. I had a woman sent to me who is in psychiatric treatment with someone else. She is overcome with apathy and expects to die. She called me on the phone the other day and said she thought she'd live, and then immediately said, "Of course nothing's changed." This is typical of her, but actually to say she thought she'd live was a tremendous statement.

E: On January 1st one year I got a patient who told me that he was going to die that night from heart failure and he'd be dead in the morning. I said, "All right, call me up tomorrow morning and tell me you are dead." (Laughter) He called me up at 11 o'clock in the evening and told me he was dying. I said, "Well, you don't know at what time, but I want to be notified tomorrow morning." I got my call in the morning, "I didn't die last night, but I'll die tonight." Every night he called me at 11 o'clock to tell me he'd die that night. In February he called in the morning, and I said, "Yes, you tell me that you will die tonight. If I remember correctly you told me January 1st that you would die that night, but you didn't. You told me January 2nd that you would die that night but you didn't. This is

February 1st and you tell me you'll die tonight." February 2nd he called me up and said, "I'm dying tonight." I said, "Yes, you're telling me you'll die tonight. You told me on January 1st that you'd die that night. You told me January 2nd you'd die that night. You told me January 3rd that you'd die that night. You told me January 4th that you'd die that night. But you didn't. You tell me you'll die tonight. You told me you'd die January 1st, but you didn't. You told me January 2nd, but you didn't. You told me you'd die January 3rd, but you didn't. You told me you'd die January 4th, but you didn't. You told me on January 5th, 6th, 7th, and 8th that you'd die, but you didn't." (Laughter)

By March he said, "Goddamn it, I don't care about what I said last January about dying." I said, "I do. I had to take those calls every night, and I didn't believe a one of them." In April he said, "I was mistaken in January, in February. I was mistaken in March, but I am going to die tonight." "Call me tomorrow morning." In May, "I think I'm going to die tonight." "I know, you thought that you'd die in January, you were sure you'd die in February. You were positive you'd die in March, you had some doubts about it as April started going by. This is May. Call me up, will you?"

H: This happened entirely on the phone?

E: It was fun. By June he called up, "I'm going to change that record. I don't think I'm going to die tonight, but I don't know about tomorrow night." (Laughter) I said, "Call me up next week." He called me up next week, "That really settled it, didn't it?"

H: Why did you handle him in that way instead of in some other way?

E: He didn't have cardiac disease. I handled him that way because he couldn't afford to see me regularly. He was honest, he wanted to pay his bill, he couldn't afford to see me. Besides, all of his thinking was that obsessive-compulsive thinking. Then I took that one item and I ran it into the ground, thoroughly. It always left him so enraged — January 1st, January 2nd, January 3rd, and 4th.

H: Is that what you tend to do with obsessive statements? Run them into the ground?

E: Sometimes. But if you try to have an interview with that man he just talks on that one item. You couldn't budge him. As long as he insisted on that one item, let's have it. (Laughter) He can talk with me now and laugh now about all the futile helpless anger he developed. He said, "At first I thought I was mad at you, and I was really mad at myself for saying a silly thing like that." He's finishing his college work.

H: One thing I'd like to learn more about is this: A patient has a symptom all the time, and he gets better and has it only part of the time. How do you get rid of it completely? You suggested arithmetical progression as one way of solving this. Do you have any other ways?

E: I was thinking about you this morning when I was seeing a patient of mine. He has his mother. He also has bronchial asthma. You only need to see him to recognize from the shape of his chest that he is asthmatic and that his asthma will increase and decrease according to the seasons. There's nothing you can do about it; there is nothing you can do about his mother. Now, I persuaded him to take a job in a bank. He's completely, totally uninterested in banking. (Laughter) Then I see him once a week, once in two weeks, once in three weeks. Every time I have seen him I have asked for some little detail in banking that he could answer. He got great pleasure in telling me about them. Today I thought it was about time to give him a review of himself, so I let him out on banking. He really knows a lot about it. He was most enthusiastic. He looks upon it as a delightful temporary job. He earns money with which to go to college. When I saw him, he was mama's pitiful little asthmatic boy, with nothing except asthma. She was a *very* sweet mother who would bring him a glass of water, bring him a sandwich, bring him a napkin. She told him when to go to bed and when to get up, and she sympathized with him. Now he is an enthusiastic young man. I took up this matter of time perspective with him. To view himself as he was a few months ago, and to see himself now. To view the attacks he has had of asthma in the past few months, what to expect about the attacks in the future. He said, "They're damned nuisances." That's all. And his enthusiastic view of what he's going to do at college.

H: This was done partly by an occasional question, building up cumulatively, about banking?

E: Yes. Every time he made a mistake in his work, what interested me *always* was the procedure by which it was corrected — never the details of how he made the mistake. How was it corrected, and what the attitude was of so and so who helped correct the error.

H: How to emphasize the positive.

E: Yes.

H: You really feel, then, that anything that tends to be cumulative is effective?

E: Yes.

H: That it builds on itself, so to speak.

E: It builds on itself.

H: The biggest problem is to give that feeling of accomplishment to the patient. There's another thing I want to ask because I am still trying to get straight your attitude about symptoms. Now, I know you assume that a symptom has a function, a purpose of some

kind, which is why you don't just take one away. But
I haven't got it very clear what kind of a function or
a purpose you look for in a symptom. Take this as a
hypothetical example—this is the way I tend to think
about it and I don't think you do. A woman has a back
pain with nothing organically wrong. You ask her
what it keeps her from doing and she might even
manage to bring up that it keeps her from having sexual relations. She loves to have sexual relations but
she can't because of the back pain. Her husband thinks
it's unfortunate because he'd love to have sexual relations, but he can't because of her back pain. This marriage may go on like this with both of them using the
back pain as an excuse for not facing the fact that
they both have problems about sexual relations.

E: Yes.

H: Now I tend to think about a symptom in terms of that
sort of function. When you just approach the symptom directly, as you tend to do in your discussions
here, but not so much in your papers, it's a little different. I mean, you wouldn't deal directly with that back
pain; you would try to find out what was behind it.

E: In a woman with a low back pain you always suspect
sexual difficulties.

H: You don't have to inquire into this. You just tend to
take it for granted?

E: Yes.

H: Then you treat the sexual difficulty, is that right?

E: Yes.

H: That's just something that I want to be sure of, because
when I posed to you the problem of a headache or a
voice difficulty, you would deal very specifically with
the headache or with the voice without getting the
history, trying to get the function of it. A lot of it
then, is less inquiry on your part and more assump-
tions from previous experiences, isn't it?

E: On that particular symptom. I might approach it by dealing with the back pain and give her a dissertation on stance, high heels, foot movements, body balance. I would do this so the woman would *know* that I considered her back pain something that would progressively leave, as these other matters would alter. Then I could inquire about what all the backache interfered with. Does it cause her to be constipated? Does it cause her to have diarrhea? Does it cause her to have urinary frequency? Does it interfere with sex? What particular position in bed can she assume that relieves her back pain and permits sex so that she can *have* all the sexual pleasure that she wants?

H: Would you slip that in, or bring it in that way before she had said that it interfered with her sex relations?

E: I'd ask these questions, and of course the constipation question, the urinary frequency question, permits me to blanket the question about sexual difficulties. It implies that it could cause constipation, urinary frequency, and might even interfere with sex.

H: I see.

E: Might *even* interfere with sex, which is the contradiction of her attitude, and her husband's attitude.

H: The *even* is?

E: That's right, but it's accepted and she has accepted the contradiction — then it's much easier. What position could she assume in bed that would permit sexual relations so that she could have *all* the sexual pleasure that she wanted? Then we'd discuss positions.

H: You are laying premises for what is permissible to discuss? If she accepts these as you go along, she . . .

E: And in discussing positions she is committing herself to the idea that she *wants all* sexual satisfaction. She does not recognize how she is committing herself. She is accepting the premise without knowing it, which makes it very difficult to deny it, right?

H: Yes. I can find out some idea of what's behind a symptom by asking a person what it interferes with, and usually that's the sort of thing they're avoiding.

E: Yes. But if you blanket it in safely.

H: You don't isolate it out. You blanket it in?

E: Very often I blanket it in. Constipation, urinary frequency — what's in between? (Laughter)

H: OK. There is another thing I wanted to get to. I know you will behave in a certain way with a patient sometimes, and I wonder how you manage to maintain the consistency of that behavior with that patient if you see him over a period of time.

E: Could you clarify that question?

H: I think sometimes you deliberately assume a role with a patient. Perhaps a role of being angry with them, or a role of being very omnipotent. I wonder if, or how, you manage to maintain that consistently over a course of treatment.

E: A role of omnipotence is a very helpful role. To maintain it you had better show your weakness pretty thoroughly. You are omnipotent with the patient, and yet you let the patient deceive you on some minor little point, so that they can accept your omnipotence in every other regard.

H: Then you use the inconsistency to maintain the consistency?

E: Yes.

H: One of the things that's argued by particular schools is that you need to be as much yourself as possible with a patient and be consistent. Now this is a different sort of thing than behaving in a certain way to produce an effect with the patient.

E: But naturally you are inconsistent in your behavior. So you get a reputation with the patient of being omnipotent. Under normal expectations, sooner or later you've got to be inconsistent. They are watching for it, waiting for your fallibility. So you satisfy their need. I can think of one patient with whom I *had* to take an omnipotent role. She was insisting on taking up with me all the details of her rows with her mother and father, particularly her rows with her mother and the untidy housekeeping. She'd sit like this (with legs apart), and I'd say, "Is there any other topic?" "No, there isn't." (Legs pulled together) (Laughter) I'd say, "Well, are you ready to discuss that matter about your father and mother?" She started discussing that. "Are you sure there isn't any other topic?" "No, there really isn't." (Legs pulled together again) (Laughter) All I had to do was to watch that. Then I made another play. She discussed her mother's attitude about hanging clothes up. I noticed that she said, well, she always threw her slip, her girdle down, her stockings down, her bra down. After a few such recitations, I noticed the absence of panties. She came in one day and I commented on how windy it was outside. She said that it *certainly was* windy and pulled her legs together. So the next time I asked her how long had she gone without wearing panties. I had my absolute omnipotence. She came in to the next interview very smug. I promptly confessed that I didn't know whether she had panties on or not, and I knew darn well that she did. She was going to test me out. Yet I was so omnipotent that I knew that she didn't wear panties, and she had to test me out.

H: Do you tend, in general, if you take a particular posture with a patient – and I don't know really what you do on this – but if you are consistently angry with a patient in order to have some effect, do you also give a contrast to that?

E: Oh yes, somewhere in the situation there is laughter. I'd be very angry, and then sometimes come up with this ringing laughter.

H: One of the things that you've never commented on and that we haven't discussed much is the problem of countertransference when you *do* get angry with patients. Do you think much about that?

E: I had an experience of countertransference the other night. This woman irritates the life out of me. Horribly so. The previous patient had come in a bathing suit and got the seat of the chair all wet. So I got a towel and draped it over the seat of the chair. Then the patient that irritates me so much came in, sat down on the towel, and irritated me very much. I suddenly realized, with a great deal of amusement, that after she left I had taken hold of the corner of that towel and very carefully, gingerly, picked it up and put it in the laundry. (Laughter) That really amused me. My own more or less phobic response to the towel — which took up all of my anger. I think I must have looked funny taking that towel out to the laundry. (Laughter)

CHAPTER 4

The Unconscious,
Insight, and
the Use of Analogies

1957. Present were Milton H. Erickson and Jay Haley.

H: You don't make transference interpretations apparently. That is, you don't interpret, "You must feel a certain way about me." Or do you?

E: Hell's bells, no. I don't think there is any need for it.

H: You feel it's just implicit?

E: It's implicit. It serves a purpose, but why manufacture
a great big production out of it and take up valuable
time? Sure the patients develop a tremendous transference, but that isn't what's wrong with them. That's
their method of getting rid of what's wrong with them.
I feel that it's a bridge. You're traveling over a road,
and just because you come to a bridge is no reason
why you should take it apart and examine each part
of it before you cross over. Speaking as an engineer,
it is nice to know how a bridge is built.

H: Well, when you had that boy, the Italian boy you mentioned, swear at you for a period of time, and then say,
"But you're not my father," wasn't your purpose to get
him to say that? Or feel that?

90

E: Yes. And suppose I had tried to tell that to him. He would have wasted a lot of valuable time explaining to me that I was not his father. I already knew that. What he needed to do was to go down the cursed highway. But think of how much delay any effort on my part to explain that I wasn't his father would have occasioned.

H: Well, I don't know if it would have occasioned delay. I don't think it would have done the same thing at all. That's something he has to discover for himself, that he was treating you like his father.

E: He was treating me the way he wished he could treat his father. The way he had treated his father unconsciously. But he was discovering all the things that he had done unconsciously to his father without daring to manifest it.

Editor's Note: The "Italian boy" referred to was described by Erickson in 1955. His conversation describing that case is inserted here. Present with Erickson were Jay Haley and John Weakland.

*   *   *

E: Pietro came to me as a patient. His lower lip was about two inches thick. Italian, his father trained him to be a flutist, and he developed this thick lip. Italian family, patriarchal family setup, very, very rigid. Father ate first, and all the choice morsels went to father. Father worked hard. Each day every member of the family, including mother, gave a report on the day's activities, for approval or disapproval. But father always gave a report on himself and mentioned his mistakes too. Father dictated how many hours each day Pietro should practice, and he specified what exercise, and so on, that Pietro should do, and exactly how long.

So Pietro developed that thick lip and couldn't play the flute. It had been treated for at least a couple of years, x-rays and everything, and it remained that way. So Pietro became my patient. Pietro was desperate for help, and usually twice a week for nine months Pietro would come in regularly for his appointments, and he would tell me what a son of a bitch I was. He never minced any words. He would shake his fist under my nose and threaten me. He raged up and down the floor, cursing at me continuously for nine months. And all that resistance. Pietro was infuriated because I always made little casual remarks, especially when he was on the other side of the room. I would throw in some casual remarks which he could not recognize. I hypnotized him the first time and told him that he had to unburden himself and free associate. Those casual remarks didn't seem to make much sense, at least Pietro told me they didn't make any sense. At the end of the hour he'd say, "What is my next appointment?" I'd take my calendar and say, "I'm recording the hour and day, be here on time." (Demonstrating closing his calendar)

He would go back to Detroit raging all the way, and he always guessed what time it was. When he arrived, he would come in and go look at my desk calendar, and sure enough, when he walked into the office and over to my desk calendar, it said 2 o'clock Saturday, 6 o'clock Wednesday. Yet he knew that I had not given him the appointment. He never did solve that matter. I always knew ahead; I never told him the hour or the day. I'd switch from Wednesday to Thursday, to Sunday morning, to Monday afternoon. How would I do it? "This isn't 2 o'clock Wednesday, it's 20 minutes after 9 on Tuesday." Or I would just say, "This isn't 2 o'clock," and sometime later mention, "My birthday occurs on Wednesday." Sometimes he'd spend the entire hour cursing me out because of my omniscience as to the hour when he would show up next. But I'd give him his appointment.

H: Why did you do it that way?

E: Any patient who has to pace the floor and shake his fist and explore my ancestry and describe me way back to the days of the Vikings, and all the looting, the raping, that my ancestors did, describe in detail the murders they committed. All the way down the line thoroughly. That guy wanted me to give him every opportunity, until one day he declared, "But you're not my father."

H: Wait a minute. Would you say that again?

E: But one day he suddenly declared that I was not his father. Then he sat down, and three months later his lip was in normal condition. He got a job with the Detroit symphony orchestra as first flutist, then went to New York and got a job as flutist in the New York Symphony with the privilege of private teaching.

H: Was that an answer to my question, "Why did you do it that way?"

E: Yes. That is, with that patriarchal family, the father dictating literally everything, the enforced routine. Father picked out the instrument, father set so many hours of playing the piano, so many hours of just wiggling the fingers, and father really had a tremendous sense of music. He had Pietro pick up the flute and handle it with the right kind of touch and go through that movement without blowing it, then put it down in the case and take it out of the case and handle it. "The musical instrument, it is something that has feeling. And you gotta learn the feel of the instrument, the feel of the music." He would make him practice by the hour picking up and putting down the flute to get the "feeluh the flute." Yes, he was an excellent flutist. And his father's favorite American expression was, "Don't give me any lip."

W: And he was giving his father a great deal of lip.

E: Yes.

H: When you didn't directly tell him the hour to come, this made you not his father.

E: Oh, I didn't give him the hour because father always knew everything. Remember the daily reports; father knew everything.

H: And you made yourself even more omniscient than that.

E: I made myself more omniscient than the father. I really outfathered father.

H: Well, isn't there something else you're doing there. Aren't you making him come voluntarily? Or damn near voluntarily?

E: No, I wrote down the appointment. When father said something was to be done, that's all there was to it. No response was ever given by father. "I have spoken. I have written. It's recorded!"

H: It's recorded but you don't know what it is.

E: You've got to do it though. Because I have recorded that you are coming in. When father left word that there must be so many hours practicing the piano to keep the fingers nimble, father could phone to mother. Well, Pietro knew he had to do it. And things were done that way.

H: When you say you put him in a trance the first session, was he more cooperative the first session?

E: He was very resentful about the failure of all the other doctors. When Dr. Wilson sent him to me, he gave me a buildup as a *good* psychiatrist, and someone who could hypnotize him and cure his lip.

H: Was the lip swollen or just thick?

E: It was swollen. About two inches thick.

H: So you put him in a trance and suggested that he free associate and get off his mind what was on it?

E: Yes. Get every unpleasant thing out of his system.

H: For any definite period of time?

E: No, I was curious to find out how he'd work it out.

W: You were more omniscient than father, but presumably he did not curse father up and down at home.

E: Oh no.

W: There are two things going on very much at once.

E: I was even more powerful than father.

W: And he could curse you out for nine months.

E: And never get a batting of the eyes from me. I'd sit and smoke my cigarette and just stare blankly at the floor while his fist was under my nose being waved around. That really was greater than father. Because he knew darn well what his father would not do to a thing like that.

H: Well, in the three months after he said, "You're not my father," was it just regular psychotherapy then?

E: Yes. Discussion of what he should do. "None of your lip" and its variations had become a standard of daily cliché; nobody ever gave him any lip had been his father's constant boast.

H: Well, he gave you one kind of lip and he gave Pa another kind of lip.

E: Yes. The father discussed music with him so that Pietro could "learna the soula of music." He must fall in love, marry, and father children, so that he could "learna the feela the sweetness to loveuh the woman, her beauty."

W: He must do all these things that cannot be done voluntarily.

E: (Reading from case notes) "He appeared exactly at the time for the next appointment and launched into another diatribe, even as he closed the door behind him. The interview was terminated in the same manner. I merely said, 'Your hour is up, goodbye.'"

H: This is something you mention often, this causal mention of "May," and then they happen to drop in in May. Does that consistently work?

E: That they may drop in?

H: There's two "mays" in that.

E: Yes.

H: But you mentioned, I think it was with the urinating couple, you just mentioned "next month is May" in conversation and they came in May.

E: Yes. Well, it was the next month.

H: Does that consistently work? If you want somebody to drop in the next month, do you just mention in passing the month?

E: Yes. "I'm not going to be particularly busy next week. Probably I'll have a chance to write some papers." What have I told you? The door is open. Yet at the same time it just seems that I'm offering a casual observation.

H: You haven't quite closed the door by saying, "Maybe I'll get a chance to do some papers," but almost . . .

E: Yes, so it doesn't look like an urgent invitation, nothing compelling about it. So they can *feel* they've come spontaneously. "We just happened to be driving by so we dropped in to see you." Boy, did they go out of their way to happen to be driving by!

*   *   *

End 1955 excerpt. 1957 conversation continues.

H: Could you elaborate on just what you did with this Italian guy to give him that next appointment?

E: Yes. Here's this chap ranting and raving about me and my neglect of him and my incompetence, and so on. "I was born in December." Well, now just who is interested in that? Nobody at all, especially not the patient, and he would rant and rave some more about me. But here is my important statement — it's important because it has no meaning. It's an unwarranted intrusion — "December."

H: You just say "December" in the middle of all this.

E: "I was born in December."

H: Oh, you told him that. I see. Which isn't true, I suppose.

E: Well, it just happens that it's handy, and let us say this is the last of November. "I was born in December." So he rants and raves some more at me, and I can say, "Well, I have five fingers." Well, now every damn fool knows that.

H: So it *must* mean something else.

E: That's right.

H: And he comes back the fifth of December. Now, is it possible to set this up experimentally?

E: Oh yes. I've done it.

H: How?

E: Well, "You know, next month – I'm awful glad you gave me that amazing account, and I'm awfully pleased, and would you continue – I would like to continue to be pleased. What more could be asked?" All of the other nice appropriate things, "and you know, next month is May," and a . . .

H: You really just slip it in that irrelevantly?

E: Yes.

H: Now, if it were woven into a context which had meaning in itself, it wouldn't work?

E: No. You slip it in as a completely irrelevant, meaningless thing.

H: Then is when it works. It sticks out like a sore thumb.

E: Yes. Now, "I was born in December." Next month is December. "I have *five* fingers on this hand." It's very disgusting to have somebody do that, and you wish you could forget that they said anything as assinine as that.

H: Oh, that's where it comes from. That the irrelevancies you try to forget.

E: You wish you could. Then you look at your watch and it's 4 o'clock and you say, "Well, it isn't 1 o'clock." On December 5th at 1 o'clock he shows up wondering, "How come?"

H: Well, this is the thing that's always puzzled me, why they wonder, "How come?" Why don't they remember at least the December, you know? I'm interested in the amnesia end of it.

E: Because, you see, it's so irrelevant.

H: You don't have to use a trance for this?

E: No, well, they're watching you and they're all absorbed. You give them three completely irrelevant statements that they wish you hadn't made, that they wish they could forget about, but they can't forget about because there's no meaning to them.

*   *   *

H: Well, this again might be related. You often speak of a patient discovering something when it seems to be a kind of unconscious discovery.

E: Yes.

H: Your structure of the mind sometimes confuses me a bit. The conscious and the unconscious are complicated enough, but when you have the unconscious discovering something, then it gets a little too complicated for me.

E: I expect you know this. What do you see there?

H: It's a square.

E: Now this is what I mean about the unconscious discovering something. You know everything that's there, and you look upon it as a square with diagonals, verticals and horizontals. Yet you know everything that's there. There's a lot more there than what you see.

H: You mean more in terms of planes and things?

E: More in terms of what you see. Because you see this, don't you? And what is that? That's "B." They're all there. There's an "X" there too. There's even a cube. A square cube. Now you saw every one of those parts but you didn't identify them. There's been nothing

added to the picture, and you can recognize every individual part. You have now suddenly discovered the
alphabet. And you know all the alphabet. You see
what I mean? You've often looked at a thing and
taken it that way and then all of a sudden you happen to get a different view of it, and why didn't you
know it in the first place? You're amazed.

H: Well, that's a conscious discovery though.

E: Can't the unconscious do exactly the same thing, because it just hasn't gotten around to shifting the parts
about? In the reasoning process, the two strings. Students would labor for hours on them. Now they know
what a pendulum is. All of a sudden they put it together. Their unconscious has known what a pendulum is. They haven't acquired any *new* information;
they've just discovered what they have there. And it
comes as a flash of unconscious insight.

H: Well, it may be an unconscious insight, but it comes
as a flash of conscious insight.

E: Then it comes as a flash of conscious insight, but it first
came as a flash of unconscious insight.

H: In your therapy do you often leave a problem at the
level of unconscious insight?

E: Yes. Often. "You probably won't be ready to know this
consciously for some time, so keep it out of your
conscious mind. Filter it through gradually. Don't
blow off, with a sudden discovery that you hate your
mother."

H: Do you ever use this with them in a waking state? Such
a statement as, "Don't discover this consciously"?

E: Yes. But literally I'm speaking on two levels. "Don't discover this consciously," really means, "Unconscious,
keep it to yourself for a while."

H: Well, that's something relatively new — unconscious
insight — or new to me. Do you find this common in
the literature?

E: But in everyday life you show unconscious insight. You step into a social group fully prepared to discuss something, and all of a sudden you discover, "Well, I'm not going to discuss that. I wonder why." And you really don't know why. I can think of one of the doctors who's Catholic, and he disagreed with me on the Catholic church in some matters. He presented a case before the staff, and he forgot to mention his recommendation for sterilization. Then after the staff meeting was over, I said, "You know, Henry, how come you didn't mention sterilization?" Henry said, "God, that was the entire point of this staff meeting. That's why I presented the patient, to get the staff approval of sterilization. That means I'll have to present it at another staff meeting." I said, "Well, why did you forget it?" He said, "I don't know." I said, "Didn't we have visitors?" He said, "Yes, but what of it?" I said, "What insignia did those visitors wear?" He said he didn't know. I said, "You stop and think for a while." Then he said, "Oh yes, I just got some kind of a flash that they were wearing something. They were in civilian clothes but they had certain Catholic badges." Visiting Catholics in a tax-supported hospital? No, you don't mention it. That's unconscious insight. And you see that all the time.

H: That's a little different though; I mean, that's pretty typically Freudian. But it's a little different, unconscious insight into one of your own emotional problems, which is, I thought, what you were on the edge of. A guy has to touch a doorknob three times before he opens it.

E: Yes.

H: Now can he have an unconscious where he naturally — this problem of unconscious and conscious is tricky — naturally his unconscious knows why he has to touch the doorknob three times.

E: Does it? It only knows this part.

H: And you can get the unconscious to know the full part?

E: So then you cover up that part and then you can see this part. Then you cover it all up, and you slowly show it that way.

H: I gather you feel this can be done without his conscious ever knowing?

E: Yes.

H: There are objections to a therapy done without insight. For example, if a man has to pee through a ring, or a tube, and you manage it so he doesn't need one, the analytic feeling would be that he never discovered why he had to do it to start with. Would you feel that was irrelevant?

E: I feel that's irrelevant. Is it the knowing why he used to do it that way, or is it the pleasure of doing it this way, forevermore, which is the vital thing?

H: I'm surprised you're not a Zen Buddhist, really.

E: The analyst has the feeling that you must know the "why." For a knowledge of human behavior, for an academic knowledge, the "why" is important. But for the functioning of the individual, it's his adjustment to the present and the future that's important.

H: Do you feel you have to have a pretty good idea "why" before you try to change it?

E: I haven't the slightest idea, and only an academic interest, in "why" that couple were lifelong enuretics.* I hadn't even bothered to speculate on "why." Nor am I even interested, psychiatrically, though I am slightly academically, in how they managed to find each other. (Laughter) I'm much more interested in the fact

---

*"Indirect Hypnotic Therapy of an Enuretic Couple," in Haley, Jay, *Advanced Techniques of Hypnosis and Therapy: Selected Papers of Milton H. Erickson, M.D.* New York: Grune & Stratton, 1967.

that they're happily married, and sleeping in a dry bed. (Laughter) That seems to me *the* important thing. The "why" of their enuresis, and the "how" of their meeting, and the "why" of their concealment of it – well, that's past history, water under the bridge. (Laughter) Or water into the bed. (Laughter)

H: Well, if you take a symptom like that, it's going to be a symptom of a hell of a lot of other things in a relationship. Now, solving that symptom doesn't solve the other things in a relationship necessarily.

E: That little hole in the dike won't flood the land, except that it will, because once you break through an altered pattern of behavior in some way, the cracks keep traveling.

H: Yes. I got that feeling from most of your patients that if they once overcome one symptom, they'll overcome the others. Do you do much in the . . . I don't know whether you'd call it long-term therapy or a reconstruction of the personality?

E: Yes.

H: Now do you do that on the "why" basis?

E: Sometimes. Often you get one little "why" here, and then they assume that there is a reason for it, and it's just not nonsensical manifestations on their part. That there is a "why" for the other neurotic manifestations. That they can accept those neurotic manifestations as not purely a defect in themselves but a response in themselves. Therefore, if they can make a wrong response, they can learn a good response.

Something happened the other day. I sent one of my patients to date a certain girl. He enjoyed luncheon with her. Yesterday he took her out to lunch again. A two-hour luncheon. During the course of it, the girl happened to mention that she was of Russian Ukranian origin. The previous luncheon he remarked about how intelligent she was, how pretty she was, how very capable she was. Yesterday when she mentioned her Russian Ukranian origin, her face suddenly became hideously homely. He felt nauseated at the thought of being in her company. Then he heard his mother's voice, literally telling him about the neighbors next door, and he really got a view of his mother's snobbishness and how much a part of him it was. He was literally sick all afternoon yesterday. But he's going to have a luncheon date with her again, because she is a bright, intelligent, competent young woman, and he's not going to let his mother interfere. What that will do to the entire construct that his mother forced upon him isn't . . . you can hardly speculate on it. He's really going to destroy his snobbishness in so many, many ways now.

H: You say you suggested he have a date?

E: The date was the luncheon engagement.

H: Well, the more typical analytic situation is that you give no advice, no suggestions, no recommendations. You deal with what they bring you.

E: A colleague said he had a minister come to him for psychoanalytic therapy and the minister announced and discussed his plans of visiting a series of bawdy houses. As my colleague thought it over, here's this man with his background and his current occupation. If he goes to bawdy houses, accepts clandestine prostitutes, he may get venereal disease. If I don't run counter to psychoanalytic theory and practice and advise the man that there's no hurry about it, no rush about doing it, that he ought not to do it, and really discourage him, I may wreck that man's life. Right then and there my friend decided that he would step in.

Why should I let a girl discuss with me her intention of having an affair without stopping her from it? When I see a man withdrawn from all of his social contacts, even leaving his home town, coming to a strange town to live, withdrawn completely, why should I not select some girl that I know is good company, and safe company, and suggest a luncheon engagement? Why shouldn't I suggest that he join the church choir, instead of letting him fret around in his room wishing hopelessly? Letting the days and the months and the weeks and the years pass by, while I wait for him? I certainly wouldn't advise a patient to do anything contrary to society. I wouldn't even suggest to a man who's promiscuous that he engage in sexual activity. I would raise the question whether or not he were really interested, and let him examine his urges, see if he's genuinely interested. Phrase the question that he might be more interested in good feminine companionship.

H: Well, what comes to mind is your suggestion that the man go home and masturbate three times. Now that's the most remarkable suggestion I ever heard given by a psychiatrist. So the man wouldn't have an erection when he went to bed with his wife.

E: Yes, why shouldn't he?

H: True.

E: He had a history of masturbation. There's nothing criminal about masturbation.

H: I just never heard it suggested before by a psychiatrist. Yes, excuse me I have. Wilhelm Reich comes to mind. In a paper he says it took him nine years before the man could masturbate with pleasure.

E: What does the analyst do when he lets a man free associate on masturbation, week after week after week, but keep that topic of masturbation in front of the man's mind? So he masturbates and free associates and masturbates and free associates and masturbates and free associates. Why not let him do it and get it over with?

H: OK. I gather you mean by that they often suggest it without meaning to suggest it, or without being aware.

E: Without being aware of it they are suggesting it. I can think of a resident at the hospital being analyzed. And that voyeurism. After several weeks he just simply couldn't avoid it; he had to go out and do some voyeurism. After he got out of jail he came to me, and he said, "I think the analyst is wrong. I'm quitting him. What is your advice about voyeurism?" I asked him to describe what he would like to see.

H: What did he describe?

E: He certainly described his idea of a female body. His idea of the kind of clothes that she would wear, and how she would take them off. I had him go through that a few dozen times, and then I said, "Where will you find this girl?" He said, "She's nonexistent. It's just my idea." I said, "Well, do you think you'll go out and try to find her?" "Hell no." But he wanted to know something about voyeurism. Well, let him find out. Therefore, have him visualize it, speculate, and really tell all the things, and then add them up. I held him to the problem of describing the girl, describing the clothes, type of lighting in the room.

H: Have you had many cases that analysts had given up?

E: I've had a considerable number of analysts as patients. Even training analysts. There was one well-known training analyst in New York who said the 15 hours spent with me had taught her more than her seven years of analysis. Another one was my patient for a considerable period of time, while still engaged in active psychoanalysis. I've had a very considerable number of patients who had completed their analysis and came to me for therapy thereof. (Laughter)

*   *   *

H: Sometimes a person or a couple has difficulty conceding there is a problem.

E: It's up to you to appraise a person, and to require them to participate. You see, I like to use analogies.

H: I know you do, and I can see how useful they can be.

E: Because they can't reject the analogy; they can recognize the parallel. If you just talk about the problem, they can refuse to recognize that. The analogy they have to recognize; they have to recognize the parallel. In doing so, they partially recognize the problem.

H: I see.

E: And they don't know that you forced it.

H: Talking about metaphors or analogies or stories, you have said you reach the unconscious with them.

E: Yes.

H: Now you chose the word "unconscious" as a description of this process. I wonder if it is really essential, or if you could deal with it in terms of how to get someone to follow a suggestion which they cannot resist beause they are not aware of it. They are not aware they are receiving the suggestion. An awareness difference, rather than an unconscious-conscious difference.

E: I'm trying to think of a patient. She told me about her horrible self-consciousness in a bathing suit because it seemed to her that whenever she wore a bathing suit her genitals were too prominent and everybody looked at that area of her body. She didn't like to go swimming for that reason. Another thing she mentioned was the question that had come to her, whether or not at the age of 35 she should relinquish her virginity. She wasn't willing to talk about that, and she only talked about the temptations she had had. But she was utterly, utterly indefinite, and so I steered her away from the subject. I knew that she was self-conscious in a bathing suit, everybody looked at her genitals, and that she had, at the age of 35, wondered about the desirability of keeping her virginity. She was a decidedly attractive woman. Of course, if she

wanted to wonder about the desirability of keeping
her virginity, and she mentioned the age of 35 – well,
I drew my own conclusion. So one day I told her, "You
know, Eisenhower, and Patton and – who was the
other general? Suppose you tell me about the Battle
of the Bulge?" And I got the whole story about the
time she went to bed with a man and then wondered
and wondered and fought the man off on the battle
of the bulge.

H: Milton, that's a remarkable metaphor. But suppose the
idea of conscious and unconscious had never been proposed. Now, how else would you explain what you did
in that example? If there was no such concept as the
unconscious.

E: Are you going to get rid of the back of the mind?

H: Well, how else would you explain the way you slipped
the suggestion in? I mean, suppose we were born in
1840 and observing the same phenomenon, but prior
to the idea of the unconscious.

E: Well, now let's go back to that "Battle of the Bulge."
Here is a patient who had told me in the therapeutic
situation about her self-consciousness about her genital area in a bathing suit. How does a woman's genital area look in a bathing suit? It has that very definite curve and a very definite bulge. I didn't ask her
to define it in that way because that would be offen-
sive to her. Then her question about her virginity at
age 35. What pinpointed the age of 35? The calendar?
No. She'd had plenty of experience with calendars, and
calendars could pinpoint it at 34, at 33. But she tells
me 35. She didn't come to me to be educated in the
matter of history, World War II history. "Eisenhower
and Patton, and what was that other general's name?"
Well, obviously I don't know much about history either.
Do you see that? I know Patton, I know Eisenhower,
but I don't know the other general's name. So I dem-

onstrated my lack of knowledge of history. Well, when you demonstrate your lack of knowledge of history, you're pointing out very directly, by implication, that you are not talking about history. Do you see that?

H: Now, how do you know that the patient is going to recognize an implication unconsciously and is going to behave in accordance with this implication?

E: When the patient discovers you're not talking about history.

H: How do you know he's going to make this discovery?

E: But I don't know who the other general is.

H: It's so obvious to you, Milton. (Laughter)

E: You see, I make apparent my ignorance. Why is that patient there? For purely personal reasons. The patient then has to think, "Well, he can't be talking about history. And I'm here. He must be talking about me."

CHAPTER   5

Alcoholism and
Giving Directives

1957. Present were Milton H. Erickson and Jay Haley.

E: You should have been present when I made a house call yesterday. He said to me, "You certainly put me in a mess. I think it's unfair of you. I've had to sit down all day there, and I've had nothing to do. I don't think you were fair. I don't think you were honest. I think it was underhanded. You're really keeping me in. I woke up last night going to bed, and I looked around for my bedroom slippers. I decided to sit on the patio. My wife was sitting there. I decided that maybe I needed a drink. I knew she'd put up a row. So I decided to get dressed. I couldn't find my clothes. I looked in the closet. Every damn bit of clothing I had was gone. I asked my wife where the closetful of suits had gone. Your instructions. That's what I call kicking a man in the ass when he's down." He proceeded to rub his rear.

   I said, "Really, was it a kick in the ass? Was it underhanded? Didn't you and your wife and I stand on my front porch while I explained to your wife that if you had another drink, that was to constitute your agreement that your wife should dispose of your

109

clothes?" He said, "Well, I didn't quite understand it. Yes, I did agree to it, but I really didn't believe you'd do it. I didn't believe you'd call up and tell her to do it." I said, "I didn't call her up. We reached the agreement in your presence, and I didn't call her up. You agreed, and you told her that was what she was to do, in my presence. You went and took your drink Thursday, you took your drink – three of them – on Friday. Friday night, last night, she took your clothes." He said, "Now that you've explained it, it doesn't seem so unfair." He immediately sat down and continued with the discussion. He'd been pacing the floor, holding his rear, pacing the floor. He felt kicked.

*   *   *

E: Another alcoholic came to me. He was 42. He was a nationally known man. Set up many of the early aviation records. He'd been drinking since the age of 12, and he was a confirmed alcoholic. He'd been locked up, I don't know how many times, with the d.t.'s. He'd been in jail I don't know how many times. In spite of that he hung up some aviation records. When he walked into my apartment, he must have been sobering up from a drunk lying in the gutter. Dirty, filthy, unshaven, and he stated, "You're a Norsky, I'm a Norsky, and I think I'm worth salvaging. I tried AA. I always fall of the wagon. I'm just getting over a three-month binge. I'll stay sober about a week and then I'll go on another. I've lost literally everything, and that's happened to me before. I'd sober up for a year. I'm a good businessman. I'd always get back into good financial shape, and then I'd shoot the wad. I brought along my scrapbook to prove to you that there is something good in me, though it's pretty well washed out with alcohol. Now will you take me as a patient?"

I said, "Yes, if you let me handle it my way." He

said, "I'll do anything. I'll cooperate with you. Drunks can talk straight from the shoulder to one another. I think Norskys can, so I'm putting my faith in that. Let me show you my scrapbook." He showed it. He went through it. Newspaper headlines, this aviation record, and that one, winner of this race, and so on. When he finished, he said, "Now you can start, if you think I'm worth it."

I said, "All right, I'll start my way. Why do you come under false pretenses? That's not your scrapbook. That is the scrapbook of a man who is doing things, and you are a dirty, filthy, foul-smelling, unshaven bum. You've got no right to carry that man's scrapbook with you. When you go home tonight, lock it up. Don't ever look at it again until you, too, are a respectable man. Now I'll tell you a few things about yourself." So I really delivered a diatribe for an hour and a half, all derogatory. I wound up by saying, "Now, as you mentioned before, you are on Nembutal plus the alcohol, and you always start your drunks by ordering two schooners of beer, one in each hand. You drink one, and then you drink the other, and you order a whiskey. When you leave here you go down Michigan Avenue to Middlefield. You'll find a beer garden there. Go in there and order your two schooners of beer and say to yourself, 'That psychiatrist is a son of a bitch.' Then next Saturday crawl in the doorway and tell me how right I was."

Well, he just simply leaped down the stairs in a furious rage. He had taken my diatribe, my vituperation of him, delivered calmly, dispassionately, with every nasty word I could think of. He went down Michigan Avenue, walked into that beer garden, ordered two schooners of beer, and said, "Well, that son of a bitch said you would do this, the hell with him." (Laughter) That was September 26, 1941. A couple months ago I got another report on him.

H: He's still off it?

E: When he came back, I said, "Well, do you really want to enter therapy?" He said, "Yes." I said, "Good, that dressing down I gave you last time was just a mild introduction. Now I'm really going to tell you what you are." For three hours I denounced him. Sent him home. It was a week after September 26th. You know, that man hasn't had a drink yet. That is, up to last April.

H: Just two sessions did it?

E: Oh no.

H: He went into therapy?

E: He came back the next week, a couple of weeks later. In the meantime he'd gone down to Detroit, entered a gymnasium, and he really got himself in good physical shape. The latter part of November he joined the Air Corps. He was given the rank of Captain, and soon Major. He called once in January and said, "I'm going haywire, I've got a bottle of rum on my desk." I said, "Bring it over. I have the glasses and the ice and the chaser." He brought it over. I had the ice, soda water, glasses. I said, "Do you want a drink?" He said, "I do." I said, "Well, if you drink, I'll match you drink for drink. This won't be enough for the two of us. We'll rest around here for awhile, and then we'll go to Detroit. We'll travel in taxicabs. You'll pay the bill. Either you drink me under the table, or I drink you under the table. Pour the drinks." He poured them. I said, "Here's how." He looked at it, and he said, "You really mean it that you'll get drunk with me?" I said, "I do." He said, "You'll have to get drunk alone." He was promoted to Lieutenant Colonel and sent to the Pentagon.

H: Well, now when you say you asked him if he wanted therapy, and then you saw him for one more three-hour session, did you then take him on in therapy or was that the last time you had a session except for the drinking bout?

E: No. He'd come in and report he was doing all right. I never really did discuss his problems.

H: He'd just drop in and talk to you for a while?

E: Just for a visit. A social visit. In the Pentagon, he'd call me up at night, or from his residence, and inquire all about me. He frequently flew up to Detroit. When he did he always took Betty and me out to dinner, and he ordered fancy drinks for us. He took coca cola, or orange juice, or lemon juice. Therapy? An hour and a half of diatribe, and that three hours of vituperation. Thereafter it was social visits, except that one time with the bottle. I had to drink both drinks.

H: You mean you thereupon drank the other drink, or did he make you the offer?

E: He offered it to me. "You can't pour it back in the bottle. It's good liquor." I said, "All right, as a favor to you, I'll drink it."

H: As a favor to you. (Laughter)

E: The "why" I don't know. After the war he went into civilian life, decided that he didn't like civilian life, and went back into the Air Force. He's a Colonel now. That was 13 years ago.

*   *   *

E: Another alcoholic who lived here worked one mile distant from the beer gardens. I impressed upon him, "It's your own idea. You want to quit drinking. You can't walk down the street on the way to work because you go into the first beer garden you come to. You can't ride the bus down the street because you always get off and go get a drink. You feel so perfectly free, and so full of good intentions when you step out of your house. All right, I know that street, and I know this street, and I know this street. There are no beer gardens. You are free, and you are full of good resolve. It's a distance of six miles. It's a good, healthy walk for a broken-down alcoholic who is full of good resolves.

H: It worked I gather?

E: He did it. The question was, there are some beer gardens in here. How close can you get to those? He could get within a block of them. Then he found out that he could walk on the opposite side of the street. So he began walking this way on the opposite side of the street. Cross over on the opposite side from this beer garden, zigzagging down the street, until finally, he said, "I can walk down this street." But why shouldn't he? He was a free citizen when he stepped outside the house. That was many years ago.

H: He's still not drinking?

E: He's still not drinking. Now, of course, the statement can be made that it is just fortuitous.

*   *   *

E: When patients come into my office, I greet them with a blank mind and I look them over to see who and what and why they are without taking anything for granted. For example, I look a woman patient over and I notice that she has two eyes and one of them is not glass and she obviously is using both eyes. I also look at her hands, because, you know, I have met a girl who wore gloves and she had one artificial arm. I look at her feet and she has two feet and rather broad heels. I look to see how many breasts she has, and I look to see what her elbow movements are, what her arm movements are. Then I listen to her voice to see what kind of intonation she has — all to verify the fact that this *is* a female. Why should I assume that because she has a woman's name she's a female? It isn't necessarily so. You just look at the person and you appraise all of those things. All you know is that a human being has approached you. So you look them over and decide, on the basis of the evidence available, what that human being is. The general tendency is to look at a skirt and say, "Well, that's a girl." It isn't so.

A woman came into my office very beautifully dressed, beautiful coiffure, her makeup was excellent, and she had a very nice voice. Her introductory statement was essentially this, "I wonder if you are the psychiatrist that I want to see?" I said, "I am the psychiatrist you want to see. I have looked at you." She stalled around asking a few more questions and I gave her the same cryptic answer. She wanted to know what I meant when I said, "I am the psychiatrist you want to see. I have looked at you." Well, she didn't have any feminine, real feminine things inside of her. "She" was a transvestite, had been a transvestite for years.

H: How did you pick this up? I mean, could you state what you observed that was non-feminine?

E: Well, that total picture was non-feminine.

H: With this transvestite, did you do that thinking on the basis of being posed that question, that you were being posed a test?

E: Well, I was looking at the patient as she sat down.

H: Did you feel the patient was testing you and therefore you had to see what you were being tested on?

E: Oh, the patient was testing me.

H: I mean, is that why you started looking more carefully? Was it because you felt you were being tested? That this was a testing question, "I wonder if you are the psychiatrist I want to see?"

E: I had my answer then. I had already looked at her but I wasn't going to tell her that. I was going to see what

she could understand – or he. Of course, I found out
that she'd been in to see I don't know how many other
psychiatrists. And had always rejected them.
H: They couldn't tell.
E: If they couldn't tell.

*   *   *

*1958. Present were Milton H. Erickson, Gregory Bateson, Jay Haley,
and John Weakland.*

H: Let's deal a bit with the question we have brought
to you before: how you get patients to do what you
tell them to do. Now there are three ways you've discussed. One, you've said they want to get over their
difficulties so they go ahead and do it. Another way
is they want to prove you wrong, and they go ahead
and do it to prove you're worng. A third way is it's
something they're going to do anyhow, or is a character trait of theirs, and therefore you just tell them
to do what they would do anyhow.
E: Well, suppose I give an illustration of where I ask a patient to do an apparently ridiculous thing. It's out of
keeping, out of character. The patient is decidedly
seclusive, retiring, and afraid of the dark. A man. And
afraid of lonesomeness. I asked him, "On Sunday afternoon, at about 1 o'clock, I want you to get in your
car and drive down – and I named an avenue – South
Nineteenth Avenue. You'll find a jog in it, but nevertheless you continue on to the end of that avenue just
as far as you can. It's a rather lonesome place. It's up
on the mountain side. There's no good reason that you
have for going there. You stop the car and you get out
and you walk around until you find a reason for being glad you went down there." He said, "That's an
awfully silly thing." Nevertheless he made the trip.

He went down and parked his car and looked around, and looked around, and looked around. It's a nice mountainside, a lot of broken rock, palo verde trees, saguaro cacti. He came back and told me that he'd seen a most unusual thing. There was a saguaro cactus with a stalk, a central stalk, about that high, with four mesops going up from it. Practically equal in size, so many feet away from this palo verde tree which was in full bloom. He said it was a most remarkably beautiful scene. A perfect picture. An unusual saguaro, an unusual relationship to that palo verde tree in full bloom. He was glad I sent him down. I didn't know what he would find there.

Bateson: You hadn't planted the cactus five years ago? (Laughter)

E: It had been planted at least 60 years previously. But I knew, in that utterly impossible situation, he would have to justify his trip there. I do know that if you've got any intelligence, any imagination, any artistic appreciation, that it's impossible to go over a mountainside without seeing something worthwhile. It's a safe thing. Because he's got to find something to justify that trip.

B: If we gave such an instruction the guy wouldn't even get in his car.

Weakland: Yes, that's the thing.

E: Yes, but you see you wouldn't say it with that absolute certainty that I had when I told him I knew he had to find something. I was dead certain of it. Nobody's going to go down there without finding a good reason for being glad he went.

W: You have sufficient emphasis on finding the reason to be glad that he will get started on the trip, but then you tie it into the goal down at the end.

E: I can call up that same patient anytime and tell him to do any other absurd thing. His attitude now toward

me is such that, "Well, if Erickson says so, it's worthwhile." (Laughter) He doesn't recognize that it is *he*
who makes my suggestions worthwhile. But I tell my
patients that, and I mean it. It's the fact that I mean
it. If they don't do it, I am genuinely disappointed,
and they know I am. I haven't lost face; I'm just horribly disappointed. Then I can tell them. "Well, you
missed that, and there's nothing can be done about
that now. Because you missed it. But this time I hope
you will go out, up Black Canyon Highway, and just
before you get to New River, I hope you will drive
about 1500 feet down that dirt road on the righthand
side." Well, my disappointment about the first assignment — it's too late now, they've missed it — but
they've got another chance of a different character,
and I'm awfully glad they have got another chance.
But you see, I know they have another chance. Because if they drive down the Black Canyon Highway
and turn right on that New River Road, I don't know
what in the hell they'll see, but they *will* see something
that interests them. They've got to. They've got eyes.
How many neurotics conjure up innumerable things
out of nothing. That's their pattern. Well, I'd like to
have them conjure up something beautiful. Something pleasing. Something rewarding. They've got the
skill at conjuring up things. I'm perfectly willing to
use it.

H: Well, if a woman comes to you and says, "I'm afraid to
drive out of town," you never tell her to drive out of
town.

E: A woman who can't drive out of town?

H: That's right.

E: Well, let's not take a woman, let's take Bob. Bob could
drive on East Van Buren, and West Van Buren, he
could drive on North Central, he could drive on Cy-
prus Street. There were two or three streets in Tempe

that he could drive on, and he could drive on Buckeye Road. He could drive out Black Canyon Highway to the city limits. That was all the driving he could do. He said, what on earth would he ever do if East Van Buren ever got blockaded and he had to get back to Tempe? Because that was the only street he could drive on to get to Tempe.

Now what I did with Bob was this. "What happens when you try to drive on the street?" He said, "I faint at the wheel." I asked him if he was sure. He said, "Yes. My heart starts pounding, and I faint." I said, "How do you know?" He said, "I *know.* I've had friends with me in the car, and I've tried, and I pass out at the wheel, and they've had to take charge."

So my approach to him was, "I'd like to have you go up to Black Canyon Highway and note the telephone poles. Drive up to the last telephone pole that you dare drive up to and stop at the side of it. Then look at the next telephone pole. Drive up there about three in the morning. After you've looked at the next telephone pole, start your car up in forward gear and get it going just fast enough so that when you reach the telephone pole safely, you switch off the ignition. Then you faint as you go past the telephone pole. When you recover, because your car will slow up and you're on the shoulder there," I knew the highway, "when you recover from the faint, wonder if you can get to the next telephone pole. So put your car into first gear, start it up, release the clutch, and as soon as the engine is really turning, turn off the switch, and see if you get to that third telephone pole before you faint." You know Bob had just a lot of fun, he got some 20 miles.

B: He got what?

E: He got some 20 miles.

H: How many times did he faint?

E: Oh, a few dozen times, but it got so, towards the last, he was figuring on – can he get another half a mile before he faints? I just had a letter from Bob recently: "I really enjoyed my vacation trip. I've traveled all through Florida, Alabama, Mississippi, and I'm thinking of staying awhile in Arkansas." He drove all the way. But you see the willingness to faint was the essential consideration.

H: The willingness to faint.

E: He looked upon the fainting as the absolute barrier to driving. It's not a barrier to driving. You start your car to rolling, you've got the Black Canyon Highway with plenty of room on that shoulder. It's a nice wide highway, you can drive along there on the side of the blacktop. From one telephone pole to the next. Perfectly good. You can start your car rolling, turn off the ignition, and shift into neutral and proceed to faint. Your car is going to come to a stop.

H: You progress by fainting.

E: That's right, and he used each faint as the starting point for the next trip down the highway. You see it was the *starting point*, not the stopping point. Do you see that? And he traveled down the highway and passed out.

H: How does he get a way to do this?

E: Three in the morning, deserted highway. He knew it was deserted. I did too.

H: He's willing to go out there and faint on the highway just because you recommended it.

E: Yes. I pointed out to him, he's a nice young guy, college student, unable to drive his car on certain streets in Tempe, and he had to walk. No sense in owning a car if you can't drive it. Was it worthwhile to learn to drive his car at the expense of fainting? A lot of people are willing to work hard to drive a car. Was he willing to work hard? Was he willing to faint? Which

didn't take much effort. He thought fainting was an
obstacle – I thought it was a starting point.
H: This is where it gets tricky all right.
E: I can approach that problem in another way. What was
her name? She lives out beyond Scottsdale, and she
couldn't possibly drive on Camelback, which is a few
miles north of Cypress Street. She had to go out there
by way of McDowell Road. She couldn't go Camelback. She thought possibly she could go East Thomas.
She knew that Indian School was too close to Camelback. These roads are a mile apart. She could go Van
Buren. But she couldn't possibly go Camelback, or Indian School, she might possibly go Thomas. She could
go McDowell, she could go Van Buren. So, of course,
I took in Baseline Road, which would be about five
miles out of her way and was south of Van Buren. It
would be a ridiculous way of getting to her home.
Then I asked her what about this matter of getting
absent-minded? "You know, you drive down Central,
and you're headed for McDowell. Why not absent-
mindedly turn off of Palm Lane. You can do that.
Palm Lane runs parallel with McDowell. Why not
cross McDowell in an absent-minded way and go out
East Roosevelt, which parallels McDowell? Just do it
absent-mindedly. Just be interested in your thoughts."
H: Hypnosis was involved in this?
E: Usually when I talk to people some hypnosis is involved.
(Laughter) "Why not just absent-mindedly drive out
East Roosevelt?" That's all I needed. "Why not plan
the next time to go out East Van Buren, and absent-
mindedly go out East Roosevelt, which is *north* of
Van Buren? Why not plan to go out Van Buren the
next time, and absent-mindedly go out McDowell instead, which is a mile north from Van Buren? Why
not absent-mindedly turn left instead of right and go
out East Thomas?" I got her to do all those. But re-

member, I've got her absent-mindedly getting further north and further north, and Indian School is further north. I had her go out East Roosevelt and absent-mindedly turn left, and absent-mindedly cross McDowell. Absent-mindedly cross Thomas, and absent-mindedly turn right on Indian School Road, and she arrived home before she noticed what she was doing.

Well, that settled that. When she told me about that, I pointed out to her very, very emphatically that she had told me that she could not go home by way of Camelback. There was no reason why she should go home, but she was absolutely positive that she couldn't go home by way of Camelback. We repeated that and repeated that and repeated that. She couldn't go home by Camelback. All I did was drop in one little suggestion; "Of course you can *come in* by Camelback." (Laughter) "But you can't *go home* by way of Camelback." You see, you hammer home, "You can't *go home* by way of Camelback. You can't, you can't, you can't, you can't. Of course you can *come in* by Camelback but you can't *go home.*" You never forget what you are aiming at. You are aiming at familiarity with Camelback. You emphasize all the *can'ts*, and you do a thoroughly competent job. Since you agree so wholeheartedly with the patient, they are in a position of yielding that one little inch. They can *come in* by way of Camelback. That's all you want. One little yielding.

CHAPTER 6

The Case of
Inhibited Ann

1959. Present were Milton H. Erickson, Jay Haley, and John Weakland.

H: Now that we are a little more familiar with the way you approach patients, what we would like to do is to start over again, and in a more systematic way deal with the way you do psychotherapy, from the way you classify patients to start with, to the way you terminate them at the end. Now obviously you don't classify patients the way other people do. A patient comes in the door, and you take a look at the patient and listen to the patient and you don't classify him as an hysteric or as a compulsive . . .

W: Well, you might, but in your operative classification, somehow that isn't the important point, it seems to us.

H: You have some way of classifying people in terms of what they need or what you're going to do, I gather.

E: That is, you recognize the patient as they come in, they may be an hysteric, or a compulsive, or a schizoid or a manic, something of that sort. The problem isn't trying to adapt therapy to that particular classification, but: What potentialities does the patient disclose to

123

you of their capacity to do this or to do that? You organize your therapy around whether they can think on this one topic – and do they think better on this one topic by the process of avoiding thinking on another topic? If you discover that they can think well on the topic of father by avoiding any mention of mother, fine. So then you ask them to do their best thinking on the subject of father. Sooner or later, after they've done their best thinking on the subject of father, it becomes possible for them then to think about mother.

In their functioning at home you discover that while they cannot function in the bedroom, they can take a tremendous pride in functioning in the den and functioning in the yard looking after the flowers and the grass. So you've built up a tremendous pride in what they can do *there*. The first thing they know they're working in the front yard, the side yard, the back yard, and working through the front of the house to the den, and working through the back of the house to the den. They start enlarging the number of particular things they can do in relationship to the bedroom. You do not ask them to function libidinally in the bedroom, but you ask them to take a particular pride, which they can do, in something in the bedroom. If it's no more than the painted wall, the placement of the furniture, and the pictures on the wall, the drapes, and as soon as they start taking some pride in some reality in the bedroom, then you've opened the door to bedroom functioning at the libidinal level.

H: So when they come in and they describe a problem to you, you're both listening for what they think is their problem and also for what is potentially possible in what they can do.

E: All right, I can give you an example. Let's call her Ann.

Ann came in because of choking spells, gasping spells, all-gone feelings in her chest. The fear that she could not survive another half hour. When do these choking spells, gasping spells develop? She said anytime of day or night. But it wasn't long before I discovered they tended to develop shortly before bedtime. I also found out that they developed at noontime, luncheon time, when friends came in to visit, if risqué stories were told. So I let my patient think that she was separating her symptomatology from the bedroom by relating it also to casual visits from neighbors, casual social groups. But I always managed to get my patient to think of some risqué story a next-door neighbor told, some risqué story that was told at a social gathering. Usually I tended to object to the patient telling me the story. Let's put an inhibition on the narration of the story. The purpose would be to get the inhibitions out and working, but let's inhibit something else. Let's inhibit the story, the narration of the story, rather than to inhibit her breathing. You see? When she chokes and when she gasps, she's trying to inhibit a physical function.

H: Now when she chokes and gasps, she's trying to inhibit a physical function. You assume she needs to do this, but you want her to inhibit something else rather than that, for the moment.

E: Yes. There's no sense in trying to deprive her of her pattern of using inhibitions. Give her lots and lots of opportunity to use inhibitions. So I let her inhibit herself from telling me the stories, but *I* instructed her to inhibit herself. She wouldn't have told them to me anyway. (Laughter) But I merely took that over. Then I pointed out to her that this choking, gasping, just before she went to bed must have made preparation for bed difficult. Did the steam from the shower bath aggravate her choking and her gasping? She had to think about that. What she didn't know was that she was thinking about herself in the nude. I was enabled by that question to get her to think about herself while in the nude, without asking her to go through the process of undressing. So she was doing that, and she studied that. Then I asked her if stepping from the shower out onto the bathmat, that sudden change in temperature from the warm, moist air of the shower into the relatively cooler air of the bathroom, did that sudden change of temperature on her skin aggravate her breathing in any way, or increase the choking or the gasping? If it did, did drying herself with the towel and rubbing her body improve it, lessen it, or what did it do? The patient is thinking, of course, rather extensively about herself, in the nude out in the open in the room, not behind the shower curtain, and she's discussing that openly with me. Then the next thing that I did with the woman . . .

W: So that by discussing the situation in terms of what affects her difficulty you get her to think about being there in the nude.

E: Being there in the nude. She knows she's in the nude when she steps out of the shower; I never have to mention that. That is something that is understood. Too often therapists want to hammer home, "But you're in the nude when you get out of the shower." You never mention unnecessary and obvious facts. If the patient wants to avoid things, well certainly help them to avoid, and it's very, very nice to avoid the *obvious.* You've satisfied your avoidance needs, but there's no . . .

W: But yet nothing is hidden.

E: Nothing is hidden. (Laughter) The next thing I wanted to do with her was to raise the question of what in the bedroom could possibly cause that choking, gasping, painful feeling in her chest?

H: Is this a married woman?

E: Yes. Because she would develop that maybe an hour, an hour and a half, before bedtime. Therefore it was the psychological anticipation of something in the bedroom. Something *in* the bedroom, not something *going to be* in the bedroom, but something *in* the bedroom.

H: Why do you make that distinction?

E: Because I don't want her to think that maybe lovemaking is involved in the situation.

H: You assume it is, but you don't want her to think so?

E: I assume it is by virtue of that extreme, laborious way in which she smoothes down her dress, tucks her feet very carefully under the chair, holds herself rigidly and primly, the high-necked blouse that she is wearing, the hair pulled straight back in a completely prim fashion, the fact that I know that she's got *one* child. Her entire manner is one of extreme and rigid prudish modesty. All of her behavior suggests that; I don't know if it's so or not. But she's rigidly, primly modest, and she chokes and gasps every night. She lays that preparation for entering the bedroom.

H: Well, the crucial thing is: Why don't you want her to know this?

E: She wouldn't have her symptomatology if she could face the issues.

H: Most therapy is devoted to getting her to face that issue.

E: Oh, I'll get her to face the issues.

H: Ultimately. OK, go on.

E: But let's get all of the issues out, and let's teach her that she can face this one thing already in the discussion I've offered. She's faced the fact that she's nude out in the middle of the room and a strange man is discussing her bare skin. It's been done so quickly and so easily, but it's a fact. It's already been done. That's going to teach her that she can face a lot of issues. Now what are the things in the bedroom? Very, very promptly, somewhere in the interview, I have mentioned that undoubtedly she has this symptomatology when she is on vacation, when she's visiting her mother or father, when she's visiting friends, signifying right then and there that it isn't necessarily restricted solely to *her* bedroom, and concealing the fact that I am aware that it might possibly be related to her husband. I'm helping her to conceal any awareness of the possibility of it being related to her husband. But I am helping her to conceal it. What are the things in the bedroom? And what *are* the things *in* the bedroom? Well, you know there are windows with drapes.

H: (Laughing) All right.

E: There's the chairs, and there's the dresser. The question I asked her was, "Do you have your hope chest there?" A hope chest embodies, or symbolizes, all of the hesitancies and uncertainties that the nubile girl has about marriage and about sex, and every possible uncertainty, every possible inhibition. Fortunately, she did have a hope chest there. I didn't know it, but I wanted to know for certain.

W: It also symbolizes the expectations too, doesn't it?

E: The expectations too. That whole tremendous complex. When she mentioned the hope chest, I inquired: Was it made out of cedar completely, or was it one of these lovely cedar-lined chests, or was it a combination cedar-lined, cedar exterior, plywood? I've forgotten what it was. She told me what a lovely chest it was. Then I made the statement, "You know, all the time you've been married, about how long has it been? Twelve years? There's been a lot of changes in your hope chest, especially after your daughter was born." A lot of changes in your hope chest. No further specification, no further analysis, but a tremendously long pause, thoughtful, giving her every opportunity, at the conscious level as well as the unconscious level, to think of all the changes since that hope chest first became a reality in 12 years of married life. What else is in that bedroom? "Of course there's a carpet."

H: You haven't got to the bed yet.

E: "Of course there's a carpet." Do you recognize what that statement is? It's a most emphatic emphasis upon the obvious. "Of course there's a carpet." I don't say there *is* a bed. It's obvious that there is a carpet. It's obvious that there is a bed. (Laughter) But I've mentioned that bed so emphatically, "Of course there's a carpet." (Laughter)

H: Okay.

E: So that bed is as good as named and described. That "Of course," you see, emphasizes the obvious.

W: This is like the meaning that you get across when you say, "Of course there's a (pause) carpet." I mean it's not the same but it's the same point.

E: It's not the same. It's the same point, yes. But it's said so casually, with a pause, and of course there are all the other things. Remember, I mentioned the dresser and the drapes and the chairs. Now you see, in originally mentioning the drapes and the dressers and the chairs, my patient has an awareness of the other furniture and I've made an incomplete mention of things. It's an interrupted, incomplete task. My patient knows it. My patient is not really going to be interested in the mention of the bed. So I have met my patient's need not to mention the bed. But there's still a need to mention it. That's why she's coming to me. My patient's description of her choking and her gasping, and I forgot to include the mention of her paling and her flushing and the hotness of her face, and the uncomfortable feelings throughout her body, as if she were burning up. Now with that incompleted task of mentioning the bedroom furniture – I finally achieved it by saying, "Of course there's a carpet." That "of course" means, "Well, it's a bedroom, you don't have to mention everything in the bedroom." My next series of questions relates to this: The patient knows that I'm going to inquire into bedroom behavior. What do psychiatrists do? My patient was a college graduate. Sex has got to come out. I've got to ask about what you do in the bedroom. And I ask her, "You know, in hanging up your clothes for the night, do you put them on the back of the chair? On any particular side of the room?" I've put the inflection too obvious there. Any particular *side* of the room (with a rising inflection). But I ask her, does she hang her day clothes up? On any particular side of the room?

H: Now, hold it a minute. Maybe you made it obvious, but not to me.

E: Well, which side of the bed? Where does she undress, on the right side of the bed or the left side of the bed, or at the foot of the bed? I don't know. But I'm not really talking about that, I'm talking about where she hangs up her clothes. Which side of the room? For example, "Do you put your blouse on the *back of a chair or the arm* of a chair?" As if that were an important question, and it is an important question. The word "back" and the word "arm" have crept into the inquiry. Nobody has noticed it, except the unconscious because of that sensitivity, because here's a woman that I suspect of having sexual conflicts or fears or anxieties. So we go into this question of where she drapes her clothing, clothing that she has taken off.

Then my question relates back to the bathroom again. "I really don't know what your metabolism is. Some people want to sleep very warmly in bed at night; they want pajamas and they want blankets.

Other people like to sleep with a minimum of night clothes. Some women really like these abbreviated nighties, and they really do. Some women like these abbreviated pajamas, and some like long pajamas or long nighties. It's usually a function of how their skin reacts to the temperature change." I've mentioned that in the bathroom. I mentioned in the bathroom rubbing of skin. My patient is still talking about getting into bed in relationship to body temperature, skin feelings, degree of covering.

Then I can comment to the effect, "You know, one of the problems, often in a marriage, is the difference in the reaction, physiologically, a matter of body temperature in sleeping. Sometimes a husband wants lots of blankets and sometimes he doesn't want any. When a husband and wife agree physiologically, it isn't necessary to put one blanket on one side of the bed and two blankets on the other side." But I've mentioned disagreement between a husband and wife and difficulties in adjustment. Her statement was, "Joe likes to sleep in the nude." She liked to sleep in a very, very long nightie. I've got my information, so very, very painlessly, by the process of cultivating every one of her inhibitions.

H: Cultivating them?

E: Yes. Having her continue to use them. But I've always directed where she used them.

W: Have you also used them in the sense that she is so inhibited that even the tangential mention of these things is going to be quite powerful to her anyway?

E: It's going to be sufficiently powerful. Now, the next step with Ann (and if I happen to slip and give her name, for heaven's sake be very sure to edit that out) was this: "Now we have different patterns of sleep. Some people sleep very soundly, some very lightly, some very restfully. I don't know what the effect of this choking and gasping is upon your sleep pattern; but I would like you to think about the sleep pattern of your daughter, your husband, and then speculate upon your own pattern of sleep."

She told me how daughter could sleep and the house could burn down. Daughter really slept. And I pointed out, "You know, if you had a second or third child, you'd undoubtedly note they had different sleeping patterns. Incidentally, was your daughter a planned child, and is it your interest to have only one child, or would you really like to have a larger family?" When I asked, "Was your daughter a planned child? Are you interested in having an only child or do you really want additional children?" what am I actually asking about? Did they plan sexual relations? Are they still having planned systematic sex relations? Yet it's a casual inquiry that you could expect. It's asked in a properly informative fashion.

Her statement was, "The child was a planned child." They desperately wanted more children, but it didn't seem to work. *It* didn't seem to work. So we got her mention, quite directly, of sex relations. Then I switched immediately to this matter of, "You said a long nightie – do your feet get cold at night?" Now we all know what "cold feet" mean. "And does anything in particular seem to intensify your choking and your gasping? For example, when your husband kisses you goodnight. Does that increase your choking or your gasping?" She said, "We don't kiss goodnight because he always wants to hug me when he kisses me goodnight, and I can't stand that pressure around my chest." I offered my sympathy about that, and pointed out, "Of course, that would interfere with lovemaking, wouldn't it?" But you see, that's a tangential observation. What we're really talking about is kissing goodnight, and I make the tangential observation that the difficulties of hugging would interfere with intercourse.

W: If I understand you rightly, what you're saying is that even when you get more direct, you do it in an indirect way.

E: Yes. But it's an awfully direct way just the same. You see, bringing it up that way, she could tell me very quickly and very easily, and I've given her a face-saving explanation. I've told her how to defend herself in explaining sexual difficulties. I much prefer my method of defending herself in her sexual difficulties than anything that she can think up. Because that places the situation in my hands.

H: Well, wouldn't that be her explanation anyhow?

E: Even so, I've given it to her.

W: You've also made the connection.

E: I've made the connection.

W: She might have denied it if it had come out in a different way.

E: If it had come out in a different way, she might have said, "There are no difficulties in intercourse." Did you ever take a person out to dinner and you know their liking for barbecued spareribs. You say, "Well, why don't you order the barbecued spareribs?" They look at you with distaste, thinking, "Why didn't he let me make my own choice?" That's right. They're going to choose it anyway, but they still want to feel it entirely their own choice.

H: You use that on a defense then?

E: Yes.

H: They want to choose their own defense.

E: Yes, but you see, I choose it in such a way that they're awfully glad I chose it for them. (Laughter) Just as you take your guest out and you know that your guest would like the $5.75 dinner and is going to settle for the $2.75. You say, "That filet mignon looks wonderful." Then what does your guest do? Orders the filet mignon. Just the same procedure entirely.

Then I've got this matter of difficulty in sexual relations brought out. My statement then is essentially this, "You know, sooner or later I really ought to go into this matter of your sexual adjustments with your husband. I suppose we might as well do it now. I'm not certain how much detail we need. I would say that anything that's particularly unusual, in your mind, ought to be enough to discuss. Now I don't know whether you enjoy sex, or you have difficulties in having orgasms. With your chest complaint, I suppose it interferes with satisfaction. But I wonder if there's anything in particular that *you* might think that *I* would consider unusual or different?" She said, "Well, I suppose you will laugh at me when I tell you I always undress in the dark, and if possible in a different room."

H: Well, now, you switch that from what *she* would consider unusual to what she would think *you* would consider unusual.

E: That's right. In other words, first I asked her to think in terms of her own thinking. Then I asked her to think in terms of her purposes in coming to me. Asking her to think in terms of her own thinking, well, she's used to her own thinking. It's utterly and completely safe. So she starts thinking in those safe terms. Then I ask her to start thinking in terms of her purpose in coming to me. It was she who came to me, and that was a safe thing because *she* decided to come to me. So she tells me that, and then she asks me not to laugh at her. I asked her if she thought that anything that governed a person's behavior over 12 years of married life is anything to laugh at? She said, 'No." It isn't, you know. I had said the words, "Governed her behavior through 12 years of marriage." What is her behavior through 12 years of marriage? It's a beautiful summary of 12 years of sex relations. And it governed her behavior. So I asked, "Is your husband sympathetic to this extreme modesty of yours?" He wasn't. "Do you blame your husband for being impatient with your extreme modesty, or do you recognize that he *is* a man?"

H: That's a slippery one there.

E: "And that he's going to think and behave like a man." See, I've been thinking of writing up Ann's case, and I went over it this weekend.

H: Well, now you leave rather ambiguous what a man is under those circumstances.

E: That's right. My idea of a man, your idea of a man. They're both utterly worthless ideas. What's *her* idea of a man? That's what I've got to deal with. And here I've got a very crucial thing about her behavior, a woman who has to undress in the dark, preferably in another room, which tells me her husband would like to have the light on. He would like to watch his wife undress. Therefore, I added, "Of course, you do the same thing even when you're home alone, isn't that right?" Which is doing what? She can't really admit that she's so afraid of her husband. I don't want the woman to humiliate herself by confessing that she married a man and was so unwilling to enter into the marriage relationship. Because she's going to condemn herself, and she is already condemning herself, frightfully. So I mentioned that of course she does that even when she's home alone.

Then, I have discovered accidentally that the drapes on the bedroom windows, the drapes on the bathroom windows, or the shades there, are unbelievable drapes. Now, of course, I've mentioned the drapes earlier, and I know this much about her undressing behavior; therefore, I go back and inquire about the drapes. I find that they are very, very special drapes. She has window shades, and venetian blinds and drapes. All on the same windows. She's got very special water-proof drapes over the bathroom window, which is frosted glass. Therefore, I've got all this material out of her, and it's been largely voluntarily and so, safely.

Then I ask her, "Speculate on the most horrible thing that you can possibly do. Speculate on it. Don't tell me. Just speculate on it, because I think it's going to open a whole new view of what your problem is. But I'm not at all sure. But don't tell me. Because I want you free to speculate on the most horrible thing you could do in relationship to getting ready for bed." She sat there and thought, flushed and paled. While she was flushing I said, "You really wouldn't want to tell me, would you?"

W: When you say speculate but say, "don't tell me," you're really saying, "Go further but still be inhibited about it."

E: Yes. And when I tell her, "You really wouldn't want to tell me, would you?" then she's got to be sure that she really wouldn't want to tell me, which is literally nothing more than an instruction, "Elaborate that fantasy, whatever it is. Dress it up because you really wouldn't want to tell me." Finally she burst out laughing, and she said, "It's so horribly ridiculous that I almost would like to tell you." I said, "Well, be sure that you would really like to tell me, but if it's funny as that I'd like to know." She said, "Joe would drop dead if I came into the bedroom in the nude, dancing." (Laughter) I said, "We ought not to give him heart failure." *We ought not to give him heart failure.* Do you see what that does? We're going to give Joe something, but we aren't going to give him heart failure. (Laughter)

And there is my foundation laid very quickly, very

effectively. I've told her that she is going to do something. Then I tell her, "Of course, you know, Joe really wouldn't drop dead with heart failure if you came into the room in the nude dancing. You can think of a lot of other things he'd be doing." She said, "Yes." I said, of course she could fantasize entering the bedroom that way. "You know what you can really do? You can undress in the dark and get in the nude, and your husband has the lights off usually, isn't that right? In the bedroom for you? Because he is a considerate man, isn't he? You can enter the bedroom dancing in the nude and he won't even know about it." (Laughter) Do you see what that's going to do to her attitude towards sex? I don't know how much more detail you want from me.

H: What we're interested in, particularly, is the various ways you make this shift from cooperating and encouraging them in behaving in some symptomatic way, and then you shift. Now you have her overly modest about her body, you manage to get her to think of doing the opposite, and then you shift her back to doing the opposite but in a situation where she can be overly modest about her body.

E: Yes.

W: Well, in this case in some funny way — there are times when you seem to make an abrupt sort of a shift from apparently accepting what they do just 100 percent or maybe 200 percent, and I think there are the . . .

E: Well, just stop to consider it. The patient comes to you on a very — what shall we call it — tender, intense matter. They've got all their defenses and all of their fears and all of that maladjustment behind them, and they're desperate enough to seek help. Now suppose you take somebody out hunting, and it's their first experience in hunting and you caution them to be silent, and to be alert, and to be responsive. As you're walking along

briskly you suddenly turn right. You have emphasized, "Maybe game is in sight." You haven't said so.
You have emphasized there is a need to avoid walking
straight ahead. When you make a sudden shift in your
interview with a patient, and you veer off to the right,
you have emphasized, "That particular point where
I veered off, *that* was important."

W: Well, what strikes me is that with this girl, the main
impression I get is that more or less consistently
throughout you keep going a step further. You're always going ahead in a somewhat inhibited way. So
that these two apparently contradictory things are
proceeding sort of together all the time. In contrast,
I'm thinking of a couple that you told us about that
came to you who were so phyloprogenitive that they
never enjoyed sex and you listened to them for a half
an hour and all of a sudden said, "Why don't you fuck
for fun?" One seems to me to be a gradual shift, and
the other a very abrupt shift.

E: Yes. But, of course, with that couple I told them they
needed shock treatment. And then I proceeded to give
them the shock treatment. Now in raising this question of dancing in the nude into the bedroom in the
dark, I was literally telling her, "You can enter the
bedroom in the nude. You can carry out this ridiculous
fantasy. You can find it amusing. You can experience
a lot of feelings within yourself very, very safely." So
I've got her in the process of actually dealing with her
own reality, her own feelings. Then, of course, the
double bind. I didn't think she ought to do that too
soon.

H: Well, then you did another little thing in there too, and
that was to handle it in such a way that she was doing it to defy her husband or to express some resentment of her husband.

E: To deprive her husband.

H: Yes. You start with a situation where the husband feels
deprived, because she undresses in the dark, and you
arrange it so that (Laughing) she can come dancing
into the room in the dark and deprive him.

W: While she's moving towards him at the same time.
(Laughter)

E: But this time he won't know he's deprived. I didn't think
she should do it too soon. I cautioned her very, very
strongly not to do it tonight or tomorrow night, or
even next week. But the week following that – I didn't
know whether it was the first part or the latter part
of the week.

H: That's your shift of "when" instead of "whether," right?

E: Oh yes. She did it. She wondered if she could really
engage in such a childish thing. I told her there was
one way of finding out. While her daughter was at
nursery school, and she was alone in the house, why
not darken the house and actually discover for herself
the niceness of a sense of complete freedom. Then I
went on to discuss the pleasure of swimming in the
nude. People seldom realize what a drag a bathing suit
is until they can feel water slipping, not over a bathing suit, but over a nude body. Swimming is so much
more pleasurable. If she had any doubts about it she
really ought to take a bath wearing a bathing suit.
She'd discover what a handicap clothing was. And
why not? Then I asked her what type of dancing she
liked. She likes round dancing, she's done square dancing, she takes in the ballet. She enjoys it. Incidentally, she does a great deal of knitting, embroidering,
crocheting, dressmaking. She makes pot holders and
she makes scarves for Christmas presents. She likes
sewing. I asked her then, when I found that out: Did
she make her own nighties? I pointed out to her she
ought to make her own nighties, at least, "run up one."
I use that same phrase sometime later.

H: At least, "run up one"?

E: Yes. That's a dressmaker's term, to "run up" a dress. "Run up" a blouse. At a later interview I spoke of letting her nightie run up to her neck. And still later, run up to the head of the bed. She did do that nude dancing. She enjoyed it. She told me about it. She said it was the first time in her life that she had ever really enjoyed entering the bedroom. She said she went to sleep giggling, and her husband wanted to know what she was giggling about. How does a little child feel when they've done something they consider ludicrous and daring? They giggle to themselves. Especially when it's something ludicrous and daring that they can't tell people about. They giggle, and giggle, and giggle. She went to sleep giggling, and she didn't tell her husband, and she didn't go to sleep choking and gasping.

W: I forgot that.

E: Yes, you forgot it. So did she. She couldn't possibly anticipate going to bed choking and gasping with that tremendous sense of the ludicrous. The daring, the embarrassing thing accomplished. She had plenty of inhibitions about telling her husband. She had plenty of inhibitions about showing off to her husband. She had plenty of inhibitions and they were all laughable. Then I pointed out to her, "You know, really, when you were full of giggles like that your husband must have wondered . . . it's really unfortunate you didn't have some lovemaking, because you were certainly in the mood for it then with all those giggles." You should have seen that awfully thoughtful look in her eyes. It was just a casual psychiatric comment on my part. Then I asked her what else ought she to do? Did she really enjoy that sense of physical freedom? Where did she have her nightie when she danced into the room in the nude? She said, "I was using it as a scarf. Then, before I got into bed, I slipped it on." (Laughter)

W: What's the difference between choosing the shock treatment in one, and this one step after another with this girl?

E: Well, this girl was shy, timid, fearfully inhibited, and reacting with these choking, gasping attacks upon her own body. This other couple were reacting with more or less paranoid reactions toward each other. "Getting so I hate him." "Getting so I can't stand her." You see, it's a different type of personality. When somebody says, in the presence of his wife, "Everytime I make love to her now I more or less hate it." Well, there's a person that can take a hard blow. He's giving a hard blow. When the wife says, in her husband's presence, "We've tried so hard to get a baby, and it doesn't work, when there's nothing wrong with either of us. And he's just such a disappointment to me." She's hitting hard too. Now here are a couple of people that can hit hard, but not with malice, with utter earnestness in depicting their situation. If they can hit hard with objective evaluations, so can you hit hard. You're just following their lead.

Here's a woman that tucks her skirt in unnecessarily and checks up on it repeatedly, brushes it down. I think you ought to be wary of her sense of modesty. But I think you ought to get at what's being hidden behind that exaggerated modesty. Now I've asked her what was the most horrible thing that she could think of to do. I asked her subsequently what she thought was the most utterly horrifying, amazing, ludicrous thing she could possibly pull on her husband. What sort of fantasy? "Don't tell me, but just think freely in your own mind. I don't know whether it will embarrass you or whether it will amuse you. I hope it will amuse you tremendously." She thought of a lot of embarrassing things. She also met my hope that it would be an amusing thing. She did some more laughing, and again she told me what it was.

She said if she ever undressed in her husband's presence with the light on, he would be sitting there in the bed pop-eyed. He'd be waiting for her to take her bra off, and she'd be just imagining what would happen to his eyes if, when she took her bra off, he saw little red ribbon bows on her nipples. (Laughter) We already see what the therapy is doing to her.

I asked her, "What size ribbons?" (Laughter) That's right. What size ribbons? I don't want her to present that sort of absurd, ludicrous, ridiculous fantasy and then react against it. Let's get down to matter-of-fact, common-sense considerations. "What size ribbons? You know, there's baby ribbon, it's narrow, it's bright red. If it were too wide it wouldn't be desirable. You couldn't tie it too tight. You probably ought to put it on just before you go into the bedroom, and that way your nipples will stay erect because of the tension."

Now, of course, Ann did do that. Joe reacted very nicely. He did sit up in bed. There was an awful lot of hostility in Joe's response. Hostility that she accepted because his response was – "I think you're beginning to get some sense." She came and told me. "I think you're beginning to get some sense." Intercourse for them had been about once a month, under protest by her, and usually very brief. Never over five minutes. When Joe told her, "I think you're beginning to get some sense," she knew exactly what he meant, and he turned on his side and rolled over and went to sleep. "Beginning to get some sense." He also told her, "Keep right on getting sense," and that he was willing to wait. Which committed her all the more. His own unconscious response.

So from then on progress continued. She said Joe meant a lot of things. "How do you feel about sexual relations with him? You know we really ought to get down to the hard, cold facts of your maladjustments. Just as soon as you think you can discuss your sexual maladjustments, let me know. Let me know directly, or let me know indirectly. I don't care which it is, and if I'm too stupid to recognize an indirect mention of it, be sure you make me pay attention."

In the very next interview she said, "I'd like to have you tell me all about sex relations. How a man should behave, and how a woman should behave." Then she gave me a very adequate account of her own frigidity, her own fears, her own anxieties. That choking and that gasping, the way she gasped at the thought of penetration, at the thought of defloration. Her own choking, gasping behavior, and Joe's own awkwardness and clumsiness, and his own uncertainties and his own fears.

Later Ann told me about the rigid, stupid teachings her mother had given her and her own inhibited behavior throughout high school and college, avoidance of any incidental sexual learning. Never able really to think it through. Ann's desire to know what an orgasm was, and to have me describe it to her. What should a woman's orgasm feel like? My statement to her was, "Every woman has her own individual orgasm. I can only describe to you what various women have told me. That doesn't mean very much. It has to be experienced; it has to be felt. Now what are the things you want me to do to insure your sexual behavior with your husband? You've used this choking, this gasping, for a long time to insure against it. Suppose I insist that you use this choking, gasping behavior for something else entirely? Something different?"

How many patients resent your taking their difficulty away from them? How many bottled up appendixes are there in the family treasures? Have you ever listened to someone tell you, "This is the appendix the doctor took out, and do you know how many attacks I had of appendicitis?" They treasure their problems, but they want to treasure them safely. What I was asking her was, "Let's put your choking, gasping into a specimen bottle of some kind. And you can have it. It's yours."

She told me what she wanted her choking, gasping behavior for. She said, "There's a couple that have been friends of ours for a long time. I don't like them. They always come and they always want drinks and they always drink too much. They always find fault unless we have the very best of whiskey for them. Joe likes them. I don't like them. Joe always ignores one particular thing. He ignores the fact that the man, whenever he gets the chance when his wife isn't in the room, always mentions he saw a good-looking blond recently. I know that he's stepping out on his wife. I want to get rid of them. I don't want to be friends with them." Every time that couple came to call, she had a choking, gasping episode. Now she's rid of them.

H: Is it typical that in the beginning you're extraordinarily careful to avoid suggesting what the symptom seems to be achieving, and then later you discuss it quite directly?

E: Very, very often.

H: And you behave as if somewhere they know what it's achieving. Well, now, that's the example of how you classify someone as having a symptom related to avoiding something about sexual relations, or that whole problem.

E: Now Ann is very, very free in discussing sex. She goes to bed in the nude. After sex relations she puts on her nightie. She likes to sleep in her nightie; she likes to make love in the nude. Sex relations, three times a week, four times a week, sometimes Saturday night, on Sunday morning, on Sunday night. Sometimes when they're alone, when daughter goes to visit a certain friend Sunday afternoon. Perfect freedom.

She modeled some negligees, nighties, shorties, for her mother in her husband's presence. Mother sat there in frozen horror. Ann said, "You know, I felt sorry for mother because I knew exactly how she was feeling, and I wish she wouldn't feel that way." Again Ann's reexamination of her own feelings and again her rejection of those original feelings. Ann's utilization now of her choking and gasping behavior as useful.

I think she's such a very nice, delightful person. This question of more children, another examination of herself and her husband. No apparent reason why they shouldn't have children. Apparently she's a one-child woman. When she reaches the age of 35, which is another year, she is going to abandon forever the idea of becoming pregnant again. Because your hope to get pregnant puts a certain amount of tension into things. You keep a record of your fertile periods. During them you make love for the purpose of getting pregnant. In the nonfertile periods you make love for the sheer pleasure of making love. Ann doesn't want to miss the possibility of becoming pregnant; but if by the age of 35 she's not pregnant, she better accept that reality. That was Ann's own reasoning. I had nothing whatsoever to do about it.

This differentiation between intercourse during the fertile period and intercourse during the nonfertile period is, again, of course, Ann's own reasoning. But it does follow some of Ann's rigid patterns. It's intelligently followed and intelligently utilized.

I cite Ann because she is such a nice, remarkably nice case. That horrible modesty of hers, that horrible rigidity, that horrible punishment of herself, made her such an easy patient to manipulate in the matter of ideas. She turned her aggressions onto herself. That left her the easy prey of others. That couple that called on them, of course, preyed on her too. Made her furnish the best whiskey. She did all the shopping. They knew that they could make her buy the very best whiskey. In other words, she let others assault her. Therefore, I made use of the tendency. Why shouldn't I?

H: Now, would you assume that her husband would not necessarily welcome her becoming less modest? That this would also be an arrangement that would be satisfying *his* needs?

E: From everything about Ann's statements to me, I felt that her husband was one of these people who tend to hope for the better. Of course, in his reaction to Bill and Stella, letting Bill and Stella demand that he furnish them with the best whiskey. One wonders what would have happened to Ann had she had a forthright, aggressive husband. Their sexual pattern after treatment was at least three times a week; previously once a month. That's a horrible contrast. Again it suggests a certain passive character on the part of the husband.

H: We find that very typically if a wife or a husband has some difficulty such as that, and one of them changes, the other gets disturbed or changes or flips in some way. This idea that the husband would like the wife to be more receptive sexually, and then when she is this is fine, doesn't necessarily hold up in a lot of cases. When she gets more receptive sexually, he can get more upset.

W: I think what you were saying, if I understood you, is that in this case the idea was that he was a passive, enduring guy, that he would endure this until he got used to the fact that things could be different and better. Is that right?

E: Yes. As he illustrated in, "You're beginning to get some sense," in turning aside and laying down and going to sleep. Part of an enduring type.

H: Well, there are a couple of possible interpretations of that. I mean you can interpret it as passive and enduring, and you can also interpret it as a protest to her changing.

E: You could at that time, yes, interpret it in those ways. But I think against the background of putting up with that sort of behavior — I think dressing in the dark in another room is carrying it too far. Therefore, he must be pretty passive and enduring.

W: Milton's got a positive view of the spouse, as well as a positive, utilizing sort of view of the behavior of the patient.

E: You see, if he were going to be negative and hostile about it, he'd make her undress in the dark in the bedroom.

H: In the dark in the bedroom?

E: You see, that would be a negative, hostile attitude on his part. That would be putting his wife in the nude in his presence, but also helping her to be completely unavailable. I would probably have varied my approach very greatly if Joe had arbitrarily insisted that she undress in the dark in the bedroom. That's a different sort of a picture.

H: You mean if he's capable of insisting that she undress in the bedroom and also insists that she undress in the dark in the bedroom, then something of him is being . . .

E: Something's wrong then. It would be hostile. It would be a negative thing, it would be a self-defeating thing on his part. When Joe let her go into another room to undress in the dark when the bedroom was dark, and then to come into the bedroom in the dark in her nightie, he was just enduring it. Keeping away from her and out of it, having no share in it.

H: Now I gather that one thing that might be said is that

when you see a new patient and you observe them and
listen to what they say, that you classify them in
terms of some function in the present of their symptom or difficulty. You don't classify them in terms of
psychodynamics in the past; it's something in the
present.

E: Something in the present.

H: Now suppose someone comes in and his problem is that
he fails. Well, I have one. He's a photographer and he
keeps making stupid mistakes. He leaves the camera
open, or he doesn't push a switch. Now when you see
that, what do you assume about this sort of a symptom? Do you assume that he's failing in relation to
somebody else? Or do you assume that he's failing in
relation to himself?

E: There are three possibilities. He's failing in relationship
to himself, he's failing in relationship to other persons,
or he's failing in relationship to the objective world.

H: What's the objective world?

E: The destructiveness toward the objective world. Failing in relationship to it.

H: I don't conceive of the objective world except as other
people. What do you mean by the objective world?

E: You take the child who is very well adjusted, very happy, gets along with himself, gets along with his
parents, and you bring him a new toy. What does he
do with that toy? He takes it apart with the greatest
of care and he puts it together again. That has nothing
to do with his father and mother. They can't understand it. But here is the objective world with which you
can behave. You can do things with this objective
world. You do it so nicely, with utter disregard of how
the parents feel about you taking a toy all apart.

H: It's a little easier to see it with a child than it is with
an adult. The objective world has got tied up with an
awful lot of people by the time you're an adult.

E: Oh yes. But just the same, people can react unfavorably to adults and themselves and treat the objective world with the greatest of care. The farmer may be very harsh toward his family, and he may punish himself with a tremendous amount of work; but his horses are well curried and fed and brushed down, and so are his cattle. His stock are prizewinners in every regard. But so far as people are concerned, he quarrels with his neighbors, he quarrels with his family, and he beats himself over the back all the time.

H: You don't feel that the good care of his livestock is related to being a good farmer, which is related to what would his father or mother think of him if he wasn't a good farmer?

E: It's the same sort of thing that allows a child to take a toy apart and put it together with extreme care so that he knows and understands and enjoys the toy all the more.

CHAPTER 7

Classifying People
and
Starting Difficult Cases

1959. Present were Milton H. Erickson, Jay Haley, and John Weakland.

H: Well, now, getting back to how you classify people, I think it's somehow different from the way other people classify. But it's hard to get at just how you do it. Now a woman comes in and tells you that she is always gagging, having difficulty breathing, and she acts overly modest, in the way she arranges her skirt. Now you also begin to look for something positive that you can use.

E: Well, you see she's come in, and she doesn't know how to act in that strange and new situation. Therefore, she is going to strive desperately, because there is no formulated plan by which she can present herself. Since there is no formulated plan, she's going to be at a loss about how to conceal her problem the way she's been concealing it from herself for a long time. Since she has got no patterns of concealment when she comes into the office, she is going to betray a good deal of her problem right then and there if you look

150

for it. After she gets acquainted with you, then she'll be able to start concealing more adequately.

The patient I saw twice, on Friday and Saturday, came in and said, "I've come a long way to see you. I've come 1800 miles. I drove halfway, and then my car broke down. Then I took a plane, even though I'm afraid of planes. I've got to go back by train. Here I am, out here in the middle of nowhere, 1800 miles away from home. I want to go home. I want to go home." That's the answer right then and there.

I saw his wife later in the hour. I pointed out to her, "Your husband isn't going to cooperate with treatment. He's already thought through how he's going to get back to Oklahoma City. He said, 'I want to go home.' He said it childishly. He said it the way a child who is spoiled says, 'I want to go home.' And he's going to go home." She pointed out how her husband was a very successful businessman. Very, very competent. He had invested a tremendous amount of money and time in the trip out here, given up a job to come out here, and that really he wasn't going to go home. Wouldn't I please have faith and confidence? She fought all night long with him Friday night, and he loaded up on highballs to have enough strength to come and tell me, "I will not submit to treatment. I wanna go, I wanna go." That's that. There wasn't anything I could do.

H: So you feel that it's partly that it's a new situation they don't know how to handle that they reveal some of the things that they wouldn't ordinarily reveal?

E: Yes. What does the good administrator do when he calls in someone he wants to reprimand or rebuke? They are very used to being rebuked, and a good administrator, what does he do? Everybody called to the boss's office for a bawling out puts his chips on his shoulder and puts on his hangdog air and marches to the boss's office. Then he has his part, and the boss has his part. Except the good administrator steps out of the office and says, "I'm sorry, I'll be busy; here is a magazine you can read while you're waiting."

A poor helpless employee comes in for the administrator's reprimand. He doesn't want that magazine. "What should I do? Should I read it?" He's got to spend some time. How's he going to spend the time? Should he throw the magazine down on the floor? Well, there it lies. Maybe he ought to put it up on the end table. No, he'll leave it lying there. It's a new, strange, alien situation. He just doesn't know what to do to handle it. And he's still struggling with it. When the administrator walks in, all of the employee's defenses are stripped because he's been trying to deal with that magazine. It's a horrible situation.

If you want an employee to quit, what do you do? You can't fire him; the union will jump on you. You can't ask him to resign; he'll defy you knowing the union will support him. So you hand him a ball of yarn and say, "While you're waiting, do you mind, as a favor to me, unwinding that in part and making two balls equal size?" It's an impossible situation. Yes, he can do it; how do you rebel against anything as idiotic as that? So you wait the 15 or 20 minutes, and then your secretary, when you buzz her, comes in and says so-and-so left his resignation. You know that he's going to resign. He isn't going to tolerate that sort of thing.

H: Well, when a patient offers you this sort of behavior when he first comes in, and you're looking for something positive you can use, what sort of things do you look for?

E: Anything that the patient actually can do. Anything that he *can* do. Preferably something that he can do in relationship to his problem.

H: What do you look for? I mean, setting that aside for a moment, what do you look for in his relationship to you? In how he responds to you?

E: Well, I'm curious about that in this way. Should he defy me, should he cooperate with me, or should he treat me as an intelligent empathizer with no personal implications? What sort of a role should I have in *his* existence? I dislike that patterned, rigid attitude. I can think of one psychoanalyst. He sits at his desk and the analysand enters. He turns, he stands, he walks over and he shakes hands. He's silent. The analysand lies down on the couch over here, and the analyst turns this way, which is slightly back of the head of the couch. Now, when the hour's over, the analyst stands, silently shakes hands. Then the analysand walks out *that* door. It doesn't make a bit of difference who the analysand is. There's no deviation in that pattern. Three months, six months, a year, three years, five years. I think Alex has gone through that routine with his analyst now for 12 long years. One of Detroit's leading analysts. Male, female, old, young, middle-aged, grade school, high school, college professor – it doesn't make a bit of difference. That same rigid routine day after day.

H: Well, let me put it this way: What do you base your prognosis on? I mean, if you do make some sort of a prognosis by the end of an hour with a new patient – both some estimate of how long it will be, and whether you can do anything for him?

E: It's a matter of their general behavior. What do they show you that they can actually do.

*   *   *

E: Well, take the selectee for the draft who could only pee through a wooden tube or a metal tube.

H: We've often wondered where you get these people.

E: He isn't the first I've encountered.

H: He isn't?

E: Oh no. But you need a willingness to inquire into their behavior. They hold it out. But what did I do? I made it a constant use of a tube, didn't I? Except since he had the inconstancy of a metal or a wooden tube, I used that and made the tube neither metal nor wood. I made it bamboo. The metal tubes and wooden tubes he used were of an inconstant length. Therefore, I made the bamboo tube of an inconstant length. Then, of course, I transformed it into the tube of his hand and then the realization he had a tube—his penis—and he constantly urinated through that tube.

H: When this first came up we were discussing the instructions you give at various times about the conscious mind and the unconscious mind. The unconscious mind will know this now, but will keep it secret from the conscious mind. One of the questions that comes to my mind is this: If they know it in their unconscious mind, didn't they know it in their conscious mind before? What happens when you say, "Now you will know it in your unconscious mind but not in your conscious mind"?

E: All right, take Bill. Bill had difficulty in his work, he had to drive down North Central to Van Buren, he worked in a car lot there. Coming down North Central he had to go past the Golden Drumstick restaurant. He was afraid to enter the bank building or any tall building, afraid to ride in an elevator, afraid to enter a drugstore, afraid to enter certain restaurants because they were too well-lighted. And he was afraid to cross Van Buren on foot; he just couldn't. He could really work up a sweat trying to cross it. If he stepped out of the lot onto the pavement, the probability was that someone would have to pick up that man because he fainted. He had tried to enter drugstores by sheer physical force and fainted. He was sick and tired of that.

I didn't use hypnosis on the matter of entering buildings, because I thought I could handle that and win his absolute confidence in me by correcting that first. Then I could employ hypnosis. So I made an appointment for him. He was afraid of girls, and I asked him how he would feel about going to the Golden Drumstick. He said he'd faint at the thought. "How would you feel about going there in company?" He'd faint even worse. Now here are various types of women: the young, naive woman, the divorcée, the widow, the experienced lady. They can be attractive or unattractive. Which was the most frightening of those four? There was no question about it — an attractive divorcée.

I told him that he was taking Mrs. Erickson and me out to dinner at the Golden Drumstick and that there would be someone coming along. It might be a young man, a divorced man, a widowed man, or an old man, a young girl, a divorcée, a widow, or an old lady. He should arrive at 7 o'clock on Tuesday. I would drive because I didn't care to be in his car when he was likely to faint. He arrived at 7. I had arranged, of course, with an extremely attractive divorcée to arrive at 7:20. I let the poor devil sit and sweat and pace the floor and sit down and jump up.

Finally the divorcée, one of these utterly charming, easily met people, walked in. I said to him, "Introduce yourself," just to make it hard. So he introduced himself. Then I told the divorcée his plans, "Bill has decided to take the three of us to dinner at the Golden Drumstick." So we went out and got in my car and I drove there and parked the car and we got out. I said, "You know, this is a nice graveled parking lot; that's a nice level spot there where you can fall down and faint. You want that one, or is there a better one that you can find?" He said, "I'm afraid it will happen when I get to the door." So we walked over to the door and I said, "Nice-looking sidewalk, probably bang you head hard if you crash." He said, "Can we get a table inside just next to the door?" I said, "We'll take the table that I pick out." So we went across – they have an elevated section – clear across to the elevated section in the far corner. The divorcée sat beside me.

While we were waiting, the divorcée and Mrs. Erickson and I talked way above his head. We told the most abstruse jokes we knew and laughed heartily at them. That reminds me, one of them was, "What is the difference between a duck?" "One leg is both the same." We told mythological riddles. "Who wrote the song 'How dry I am'?" "Tantalus." The three of us had a good time and he was out of the swim and feeling increasingly miserable. This divorcée had a Master's degree.

Then, when the waitress came over, I picked a fight with her. It was a rather disagreeable, noisy fight. I demanded the manager and picked a fight with him. Poor Bill was ready to die. Finally, in my fight with the manager I demanded to see the kitchen. We got out there and I let him and the waitress in on the secret that I was ribbing my friend. So they fell in line with it. Boy, did she slam the food on the table. Bill ate his dinner. But I kept urging him to clean up his plate, as did the divorcée. "That fat's good for you."

He lived through it, and he came home with us. I had tipped off the divorcée. She said, "You know I feel in the mood to go dancing tonight." He had learned to dance in high school a little bit. She took him dancing. The next night he picked up a friend of his. "Let's go out to dinner." They went to the Golden Drumstick. Tried out a drugstore, and so on. He didn't have to drive down North Central by driving two blocks away from the Golden Drumstick and passing it and then getting back to Central.

But when it came to crossing Van Buren he couldn't do it. So in a trance state he could. "Really I can't, I just know that it's possible, but I also know I can't." So I told him that there was one thing else that his unconscious knew, and that was that he could cross Van Buren without knowing that he was crossing it. And that he would not know when he crossed it. You see the setup there? Not even his unconscious would know it. It only knew that it was possible. I told him, "Now work it out."

He always parked his car on a certain side street. He arrived late one morning, his parking space was taken. So he drove around the corner onto Van Buren and parked on the opposite side. He crossed Van Buren and went to work. At the close of the day he went to his usual parking place, and the car wasn't there. "That's right, I had to find another parking place." He went over and got in his car. As he started up, he took a look, "Wait a minute, I'm on the opposite side of Van Buren. How did I get here? And my car is here. I must have walked across Van Buren. I left my car and crossed Van Buren, and I'm back here; therefore, I crossed Van Buren twice. But I don't remember it." In the next trance state he told me all about it. I saw to it that he got there too late for his parking space. "And I was busy cussing for oversleeping and I cussed mentally all the time while he was finding a parking space somewhere."

H: Wait a minute, who was cussing?

E: The unconscious. "I was cussing all the time he was finding a parking place."

H: He really split it into "I" and "he."

E: Of course, Bill was cussing too.

H: (Laughing) How did he get in here?

E: "But I was cussing, and Bill was cussing."

H: He developed the cussing end of it himself? That wasn't suggested to him?

E: No, I didn't suggest it.

H: Before we get away from this restaurant deal, it's like so many of your papers – we wonder why you assumed that if you took him to dinner with a divorcée and made it an unpleasant dinner he would then be able to go in there himself.

E: Listen, could anything worse ever happen in a restaurant than what I pulled on him? The worst possible thing had happened; everything else that happened would be a welcomed relief.

H: Why didn't he faint going in?

E: How could he? His fainting was done because of his neuroticism, wasn't it? And I picked his spots. And those weren't the spots that belonged to his unconscious choices. What could he do?

H: He couldn't pick another spot?

E: I kept him too busy.

W: You were always a step ahead of him.

E: I was just a step ahead. I picked out the spots.

H: Did you pick a spot you thought he would pick, or did you just pick at random?

E: Oh I just kept him busy reacting and rejecting *my* spots.

W: He has to fall down in *his* way for *his* purpose.

*   *   *

E: I've got a little cartoon here that I like to use with women who are tremendously inhibited sexually. To open them wide open. (He shows a cartoon of a young doctor with a stethoscope around his neck who is pressing his ear to a lady's breast. The nipple of the breast is caught in his ear and he is saying something like, "Help, I'm stuck.") They know you listen to the heart with a stethoscope and that you listen to the heart with the ear, and here the nipple gets caught in the ear, and he can't get it out. (Laughter) Then I ask them, "I wonder what he did do."

H: What do they say?

E: Well, I wait a few seconds, a long enough pause, and I say, "Of course, that's just a cartoon." (He turns and puts it away.) "Now, what about your sexual inhibitions? Can you tell me about them?" A patient I had last week said, "You know, I should talk to you about my sexual inhibitions, but please don't ask me. I can't. And if you try to discuss it, I can't control myself, I'll have to walk out of the office. And I don't want to. I'll never be happy, and my husband will never be happy, unless I do talk about that. But, please Doctor, don't." I said. "Well, let's introduce a note of levity," and I handed her the cartoon. "Of course, it's only a cartoon. What about your sexual relations?" "Why am I so tired every night when we go to bed that I can't have intercourse?"

H: How did you pick that particular cartoon? What's in it that you thought would open them up?

E: I don't know. The patent absurdity of it. The fact that a man does like to put his cheek on a pretty breast. The fact that there is an oriface there, and a phallic structure does enter an oriface. And it is a man, and it is a woman.

W: An awful lot of "is and isn'ts" tied in there, all framed by the fact that it's just a cartoon.

H: It's only a cartoon, only fiction.

E: I'll give you another example. I tried to write this up for publication, but I'm rather dubious about publishing it. Grace was 35 years old and a little bit more than pleasingly plump. She had a plain face but decidedly attractive face. She really had a pleasing personality. A friend saw her and said, "Good God, Milt, why doesn't she wash her face and her neck and comb her hair and put on a dress instead of a gunny sack." I had known Grace for some time. She came to me hesitantly, saying, "Dr. Erickson, I want psychotherapy. I'm 35 years old. All my life I've wanted to get married and have a husband and children. The nearest I got to it is to be a psychiatrist in a children's clinic. I can't get a date. I know that I've got an attractive personality. I know that I'm slightly overweight, but not too overweight because men do like plump girls who are slightly overweight. There is no reason. I'm intelligent, I'm cultured, I'm interesting, and I want psychotherapy. I want it fast because I am getting desperate. I'm 35 years old."

So I told her, "You want psychotherapy, you want it fast, you're getting desperate. Do you want me to give it to you in *my* way? Do you think you can take it? Because I can give it to you rapidly, thoroughly, effectively, but it'll be a rather shocking experience."

Instead of quoting from memory perhaps I can find that paper I had begun. (Reading) "She sought psychotherapy and explained in a prim, rigid, impersonal fashion that she was horribly wretched and frustrated. She explained further that therapy would have to be rather rapid since she had accepted a position in a distant city where she was determined that she would either be different or give up. She wanted hypnosis employed; however, she expressed with utter finality the idea that she could *not* be hypnotized. Therefore, it would be the writer's obligation to employ some drastic and rapid procedure that would break down her resistances completely and thus force her to accept therapy without delay or procrastination. Furthermore, her funds were limited and she knew of no one else from whom she was willing to seek therapy. As for consulting a stranger, she knew she couldn't force herself to seek therapy from someone unknown to her. Since the writer knew her well professionally, he was personally aware of her personal rigidities. Her statement that drastic therapeutic procedures would be necessary in a short time was readily accepted. She was told to think the matter over for three days. During this time she was to decide whether or not she wished therapy and to decide if she wanted therapy sufficiently drastic to benefit her. Also, she was assured that she could be benefited greatly, but that it would require a tremendous amount of personal strength to withstand the therapeutic assault that would be necessary under the conditions she proposed. She returned in three days stating that nothing short of murder could deter her. Also, she felt rather hopeful because she believed that only shock could ever change her behavior."

W: May I inquire if "assault" was your actual word?

E: That's right.

W: I assumed it was; I just wanted to be sure.

E: (Reading) "Concientious employee, cold, impersonal, her behavior seclusive, withdrawn in her habits, had only two friends – a professor and his wife. With them she was a charming conversationalist, a very intelligent person with a wide range of interests. Except for monthly visits with them she limited herself to her apartment. Her employer kept her only because of the excellence of her work. She wore steel-rimmed glasses and no makeup, wore clothes that never fit and were of clashing colors. Her color vision was normal. Her personal habits were untidy despite the orderliness and efficiency of her work. Her hair was never well combed, her ears were always dirty and so was her neck. Frequently her fingernails were similarly dirty. Many efforts had been made to mention these items to her, but she could freeze anybody that looked at her fingernails. She would be utterly cold and impersonal.

"She was assured that therapy would be sufficiently drastic to shock her into changing and she was told that before therapy could begin she would have to promise absolutely not to discontinue it, and to execute fully every task assigned to her, no matter what it was. However, before being asked for the promise, she was told she should think over all possible implications, especially unpleasant ones, of what had been said to her.

"Three days later she returned, declaring that her established mode of living was intolerable and that any change would be for the better. Therefore she promised to absolutely meet all the demands placed upon her. A prolonged session was held with her, and it was initiated by a direct inquiry, "How much money have you got?" She stated that since her mother's death she had saved $1,000. and was prepared to pay that amount over at once. She was instructed to place $700 in a checking account with a full expectation of spending all of that amount on herself in an unexpected fashion.

"She was then presented with a mirror, a tape measure, a scale, and weight chart. For about three hours a comprehensive, completely straightforward critique was offered of her weight and appearance, with all possible proof. Certainly I examined each fingernail and described the amount of dirt; her fingernails were in mourning, this one, this one, and this, and this. Holding a mirror I had her describe the dirt, the lines of perspiration. A couple of mirrors were used to get her dirty ears, her uncombed hair, her misfitting dress, clashing colors between her blouse and her skirt. Just as you would do a physical examination.

Her neck and ears were dirty, her teeth were in need of brushing, her hair sloppily combed, her steel-rimmed glasses, her lack of makeup. All these things were discussed as things she could correct without any help from the therapist, for which she herself was totally at fault, and which were expressive of willful self-neglect. 'I don't care what you want to say about my psychotherapeutic techniques; it's the results. But I said an assault, didn't I?'

"Thereupon she was handed a washcloth and instructed to wash one side of her neck and then to view the contrast between the washed and the unwashed sides. The interview was concluded with the statement that she was a sorry looking mess, but that she was to make no purchases until she was so instructed. She was merely to continue working, but to think over the truth of everything that had been said to her. Also, her next appointment would be in two days and it would be equally long and quite possibly even more devastating.

"She appeared promptly, embarrassed and hesitant, without makeup but otherwise remarkably well groomed except for the poor fit of her dress and the loud colors of the cloth. Systematically, the previous interview was reviewed and the changes she had succeeded in making were discussed for her, still in a cold, impersonal manner. She was then told to perpare herself for a new, highly important, but hitherto neglected, unrealized and disregarded matter of the greatest importance to her, as a living, sentient creature. This matter was no longer something she could neglect or disregard, nor could she ever again repress awareness of that something which was apparent and recognized by everyone with whom she came in contact. Once she was stripped of her repressions – 'Once you are stripped of your repressions, your own awareness of what had been so horribly repressed would be continuously present in your consciousness and would compel you to behave normally and rightfully with a pleasing and satisfying self-awareness.' What this was would be disclosed as she took her departure.

"She was given an appointment for three days later. As she left the office, she was told, as she left the door, 'Now go home, undress completely'"—oh, this is a falsification of it because I was thinking of putting it in print—what I actually said was, "Grace, this is the kind of thing you've got to be aware of. You have a very, very pretty patch of fur between your legs, now go home and think it over. Undress, get in the nude, stand in front of a mirror, and you will see the three beautiful badges of womanhood. They are with you always and wherever you go you cannot forget them, ever again." "Grace, you have a pretty patch of fur between your legs."

"She appeared for her next appointment promptly, exceedingly embarrassed in manner. Without any preliminaries she was told, 'You have $700. set aside for some special purpose. You have an additional $300.; you have a paycheck coming in. Go to the XYZ department store—they have a beauty counselor—go to her as you were when you came to see me. In a straightforward fashion tell her that you are a sorry mess, that you know nothing about self-grooming, and that you want to hire her to teach you all you need to know, that you have $700. and more if absolutely necessary. Have her outfit you completely. You'll find her a charming, warm-hearted, sympathetic, understanding woman. You will enjoy knowing her, and she will find it thrilling to teach you what you need to know. Additionally, there is to be a dance in a few weeks for all your fellow employees, and you will be routinely invited. You are to go. In preparation, you

are to go to a dance studio and learn well and rapidly to dance. Also, have the beauty counselor select the
material for a formal dress to wear at that dance. You
will take the material selected to Mrs. W, who is a
seamstress. Explain that you wish to engage her services merely to supervise you in making the dress. She
is to help you in cutting out the pattern, putting it
together and fitting it. The sewing, whether by machine or by hand, will be done entirely by you. You
know what you have to do. Go do it. Your next appointment will be when you are on your way to the
dance'."

She walked in, and she was really dressed. Embarrassed, blushing, flushing, I'll bet her belly muscles
were doing a dance. Beautifully, tastefully gowned.
And it was almost completely handmade. She'd lost
excess weight; animated, vivacious, and charmingly
self-conscious.

Three months later, after assuming her duties in
her new position, she became acquainted with a college professor. A year later they were married. Grace
has four kids – happily married. She'd worked her way
through college and supported her invalid mother the
whole time. And she – I presume – had a pretty patch
of fur between her legs.

W: Well, I assume that if you said so your assumption was
sufficiently real so that it was certain.

E: Yes. It was all the raping that was necessary.

W: That plus the amount that was going on in her mind.

H: It was interesting to me the way you made her next appointment with you contingent upon her going to the
dance.

E: Well, certainly.

H: She couldn't back out at all if she was going to see you
again.

E: She'd given me an absolute promise. She had to go to

the dance. She had to do everything that I said. She could engage a seamstress to supervise. To use your word, I really had her in a bind. And she could never forget that pretty patch of fur. And she never could. Stand in front of the mirror and see the three beautiful badges of womanhood. Womanhood! Grace is still my friend. She wanted drastic psychotherapy; she wanted it rapidly.

H: She sure got it.

E: Now how many binds would it take to analyze all those things that were touched upon.

W: It would take a whale of a lot. I feel like what she got was both more than she asked for and less somehow, and that's what was going on.

E: Grace later told me that she had come to me with the realization in her mind that if I thought it necessary to seduce her she would have yielded.

W: Yes, at one level you did that and more, if it can be stated that way.

E: And to see the three badges of womanhood – and she was a virgin. Of *womanhood*, after I told her she had a pretty patch of fur between her legs. See the badges of womanhood – I had raped her, hadn't I?

W: In that sense, you had raped her.

E: Because she couldn't look at the badges of possible womanhood; they were already the badges of womanhood.

H: Well, she got what she came for.

W: A little differently.

H: Well, her appearance changed to that of a woman who had been successfully seduced, which was really what you were after, wasn't it?

E: That's right. And it had been really a verbal rape – patch of fur. Imagine that prim and rigid girl standing there and hearing that.

W: The association it brings to mind is your case where the girl wanted her breasts developed, and you had her buy different sets of falsies and think about which one she should wear when she came to see you, and what might you be thinking about her as she sat there.

E: Mrs. Erickson was recently in Detroit and went up to see the girl's father. And the girl is a very, very happy girl. I really rate in that family.

H: One of the questions that bothers me in so many of your cases is: How did you know that this woman would react to this kind of a treatment and not get panicked and run away, or something another rigid woman might do? Was it her motivation when she came and her own statements about wanting drastic treatment?

E: As for consulting a stranger, she knew she could not force herself to seek therapy from someone unknown to her. She knew that husband and wife, and she knew me, and in that rigid, impersonal way she just knew her work. There was nobody else in the world.

W: Do you somehow just know, do you think it out, or does it just come to you? I think of this sort of thing over and over again when we read your work.

H: We read your papers, and you do something, and after you have done it and it has worked, it seems an obvious thing to do, and we wonder how you ever thought of it.

W: Obvious is not quite the right word—it seems very appropriate. Very appropriate but not at all obvious is the way I feel about it.

H: The couple you had kneel and urinate on the bed.

W: Our place was in an uproar for a week after that paper arrived.*

E: I was listing my papers, my secretary was making the list, and she made a mistake, a typographical error—

---

*Cf. "Indirect Hypnotherapy of an Enuretic Couple," in Jay Haley (Ed.) *Advanced Techniques of Hypnosis and Therapy, Selected Papers of Milton H. Erickson*, New York, Grune & Stratton, 1967.

the "ruination" paper. I had really ruined that urination, hadn't I?

W: Well, it did seem like a perfectly appropriate thing to do.

E: But there it is set up as a situation for me. They were so sincere, and so simple and straightforward, and so honest. Good heavens, when you get a person like that, run them out on that limb.

W: Yes, this is somehow hoist by his own petard.

E: This girl, she knew only one person. Well, she's stuck with him.

W: If you wouldn't do it, who would?

E: That's right.

W: So you said, "All right, I will make an assault on you."

E: Then that physical assault, examining each fingernail, and every one of them was in mourning. That was a pretty painful physical assault, wasn't it?

H: There must have been an anticipation in her about how much more was going to be examined, all the time.

E: That's right. And looking at her neck in the mirror and then washing one side of it, viewing the contrast. Of course, she had to go home and take a bath thoroughly, and she had to show up the next time well groomed — because I approved of the washed side of her neck; therefore I approved of her bathed body.

H: But somehow, one of the things you do is very sharply focus upon some kind of a bind problem, or ambivalent problem, so that it is dealt with very directly. You set up a conflict, or a situation, between you and the person, and you use that right to the hilt for a specific purpose.

E: You use it as a wedge.

H: Yes.

E: And effect a terrific cleavage.

*   *   *

E: This 26-year-old girl, weight 254 lbs., came in. Her statement was essentially this, "I'm too fat. *You* can see that. I always react to stress by eating. I've got two sisters and I've got one brother who's living. I'm the youngest by 13 years. I live with my mother; my reasons are inadequate. I seldom date. I go out with friends. Married friends. I'm interested in politics. That is, my mother and I are interested in politics. But my mother can't understand me because I dig rock-and-roll *and* Bach. I've got my prejudices; I'm absolutely tolerant of religion and race. What does that mean? I'm militant. I idolize my carousing father."

Now every one of those statements is made to me in an absolutely challenging fashion. Two years of college, excellent vocabulary. With all of that challenge, all of that emphasis, all of that absolute assertion on her part. Erratic criticism. Absolutely tolerant of religion and race. Militant. And very harsh condemnation.

I asked her immediately, "Why are you so defensive? Why?" She immediately picked up the "why" and never disputed the defensiveness. She said she didn't know why, unless it was because she was so lonesome in the family. She let her mother dominate her because she was the baby of the family. And she didn't want to hurt anybody. This time it was a much softer statement, not a challenge of me. Then, all of a sudden, she said, "You know, I started getting fat when I was on the farm. I worked hard. I ate excessively. Mother always cultivates everybody, and I'm awfully lonesome at home. I think that I need help."

Well, when she said, "I think that I need help," I spent the rest of the time literally wasting the rest of the hour. (Laughter) It was casual, social; I picked up an awful lot of information which I forgot about. Whereabouts she lived. Every inconsequential, meaningless thing that I could think of. I didn't inquire about any of her life, or anything of that sort. Pure casual wastefulness.

Here is a 254 lb. girl who comes into the office challenging, literally threatening, demonstrating that she can give all the answers. Then I hit her hard with that, "*Why* are you so defensive?" All of the emphasis on the word *why*, so that she will pick that up and not dispute that word "defensive." She gives some more information, ends up with that pitiful, "I think I need some help." Now here's 254 pounds of militant, authoritative, dictatorial, dominating patient, laying everything out to me—reduced to a pleading creature, "I think I need some help."

What do I do? If I offer help right then and there, I'm catching her at a very, very weak moment and letting her know that I recognize her as a very, very weak person. Therefore, I immediately start wasting time so that she can recover her sense of poise, her sense of self-confidence.

Just before she left, I said, "Before I see you again," and I gave her an appointment, "there are a number of difficult things I would like to have you do, but I'll only assign one. I think it'll trouble you a lot. You're not going to believe it when I assign it to you. I'd like to have you tell me when you come in next time: Why do you hate your mother?" She said, "I don't." I said, "No, of course you don't know that," transforming her statement, "I don't," into, "Of course you don't know that." "But that's the problem you're going to work on between now and your next appointment."

She came in at the next appointment and she burst into laughter as she sat here in the chair. She said, "Do you know how much I've hated you for the past week?" I said, "I hope plenty." She said, "Do you know that I arrived early. I parked my car in a street away from here, and I debated and debated and debated whether I would come and see you this morning. Of course, I knew I would or I wouldn't have gotten up and driven those 20 miles to be here at eight o'clock in the morning. I hate to get up in the morning. Well, I sat there parked in the car, and debated — because I got here plenty early — whether or not I would come and see you. Because I spent plenty of time hating you. In fact, I suffered from insomnia all week. Lying in bed hating you."

I said, "What else did you accomplish?" She said, "Well, I don't know if it's an accomplishment or not; it's only a week — no, it's two weeks. I've lost 15 pounds. This dress that I haven't worn for a year, that I like so much, I'm wearing it today." I said, "All right, now you hated me and you hated me plenty. You stayed awake, you missed your sleep just to hate me. And how much do you hate your mother?" She said, "I hate to admit it, but I hate her plenty."

Now, why did I feel so comfortable about that girl that I would prognostically assign that very, very drastic task?

H: I don't know why. What told you?

E: There's a girl that showed me her strength right away, and then showed me her weakness right away. Then when I was sufficiently courteous, when I didn't take advantage of the weakness and just proceeded to waste the rest of the hour, she didn't do anything at all about it. She didn't run out, and she didn't emphasize her weakness. She started gathering her forces and putting herself together. A good prognostic outlook right there. She wasn't broken down by her sudden unexpected display of weakness. She wasn't overwhelmed by it; and then I hit her with that question, the assignment to speculate on her mother hatred. Her ready acceptance of my misuse of her utterance, "Why do

you hate your mother?" "I don't." "Of course you don't
know." No effort on her part to dispute that – she's an
intelligent girl. All of the interview gave that. Her
statement that she weighed 250 lbs., and she started
eating excessively. At least I could have talked about
that; but I didn't, you know. You see, that was obvious. (Laughter) Extremely obvious. Why discuss it?

H: Well, then, one of the ways you judge prognosis is how
willing they are to show you their strength and their
weakness.

E: To show their strength. To show their weaknesses. Now
the man I described to you, he promptly started emphasizing his weaknesses. What a great big daring
thing he did. To come 1800 miles. "I want to go home."

W: Now he was only emphasizing one side?

E: Only one side, because to a man who had been in the
armed services as he had, you don't brag about coming 1800 miles. You don't brag about driving your car
all the way to Oklahoma City from Indianapolis, taking a plane from Oklahoma City to Phoenix. You start
bragging about that when you are – what is it, 36
years old, and you've been in the serivce? You haven't
got very much to brag about. You're displaying a
horrible weakness and nothing but weakness.

W: Now looking at this fat girl in a little different way.
What did you accept?

E: She was so emphatic and so authoritative. She laid out
her problems so emphatically. The interview began
on that sort of a strident, authoritative note. How did
it end? "Of course you don't know how much you hate
your mother. I want you to work on that problem.
There are a lot of unpleasant tasks I want to give you,
but I'll give you only one."

W: (Laughing) You say, if she can come in and be authoritative, you can be even more authoritative.

E: And so much more gently so. What did she do when she

came back the second time? She got up early to indulge herself (Laughs) in a make-believe, little girl fashion, to park the car and debate whether or not she was going to come in and see me. Of course she knew she was. That's the kind of indulgence I would like to have a patient have. They're indulging all their fantasies and still measuring up. You recognize that, don't you? Not the least bit ashamed of telling me, "I've been a bad little girl, but here I am to measure up." And to tell me that she hated me. Then I told her I hoped she'd done a good job, and what else had she accomplished? I've forgotten the other things she had accomplished. Of course, she lost the 15 pounds of weight, the 14 pounds of weight. One of the other things she mentioned was that she had not worked or looked for a job for a year and a half. Well, she's got a job.

H: You use the initial interview, then, as a kind of a testing situation.

E: As a testing, as a diagnostic situation, and as a prognostic situation.

H: Do you tend to use any particular behavior on your part to put stress on the patient?

E: "*Why* are you so defensive?" That's my behavior. But it's a reaction to hers; it's an appraisal of hers.

H: That was your first statement to her? After listening to her?

E: I'd been listening to her. She had been in charge of the interview. The only real questions I asked her were her name, her age, her address, her telephone number, her educational background, her religious background, and whether or not she was married. Then, "What do you want to say to me?" Sometimes I do that immediately when I'm not certain about what the patient is like. Sometimes I take that information at the middle of the hour, and sometimes at the end of the hour.

On rare occasions I take it at the next interview, wherein I put an appointment in my book with an X mark. (Laughter)

H: You don't even ask their name?

E: That's right.

W: In what sort of a situation would you do that? I'm sure you'd have some particular reason with a patient.

E: It's always some highly individualistic reaction that the patient shows.

H: Someone who was terribly proud of his name and his address would really be put down by that, wouldn't they? (Laughs)

E: The girl likes her job. She's been off to two political meetings. She's got a job with the State Department. She's the only girl in that office of 14 girls who doesn't smoke. What was the purpose of that communication?

H: I don't know.

E: She's a pretty extra special girl, isn't she?

H: Militantly extra special.

E: She's the girl who is telling me, and drawing my attention to the fact, that of all the 14 girls she is outstanding. Then I realized that at the previous interviews she looked very, very carefully at the ashtray, and then repeatedly searched my desk. You know, neither of us smoke. Now she's identified with me, and I'm identified with her, and she's done it so sweetly. Then consider that other communication; she likes this dress very much, she hasn't worn it for over a year. She likes it very much. This dress she likes very much she's wearing today in the office with me.

H: You had quite an effect on her all right.

E: Yes. And those two literally simple utterances: "Why are you so defensive?" "I'm going to assign a number of unpleasant tasks, only one to work on before the next appointment." Have I intimidated her? No. I made her want to please me, and she's tested my goodness by telling me that she debated coming in to see me. Then she's tested my goodness by telling me that she hated me, and I told her I hope she did a good job.

H: You made it that there were a large number of unpleasant tasks to make it easier for her to do just this one of them?

E: That's right.

W: So you were being hard on her and good to her at the same time.

E: Hard and good at the same time. I told her that I hoped she did a good job of hating me. That's right. How vulnerable am I as a therapeutic figure in her eyes?

H: She was exploring you all right.

E: She explored me, thoroughly, competently, and in the way that little children do—how do little children have such remarkable insight? But they do explore you so thoroughly, and she used that little child's attitude of threatening.

H: So, you not only classify them by their strength and weakness but by how willing they are to reveal their strength and weaknesses to you, and then what reaction they have after they have revealed their strength and weakness to you.

E: Yes.

H: Well, when you look for something they can do, what do you settle for? I mean, how do you know what's going to be useful? Obviously they can do something —they can talk, they can sit in a chair, and so on. But what do you prefer that they can do?

E: Well, for that girl, anybody who wraps herself up in that quantity of blubber and who expresses some ambivalent feelings toward her mother—what does she need to do? A girl who lays out her problem so thoroughly—what does she need to do in a reality situation? Something in relationship to her problem.

H: Well, what did you see that she could do?

E: Consider this matter of her hatred of her mother. In other words, "If you can come into this office and outline your problem to me, you've come to me as a psychiatrist for help. I, as a psychiatrist, ought to specify some area in which you need help. What are your mother hatreds? Examine them."

W: She's a positive outliner; therefore, you send her home and outline this area positively.

E: Well, certainly.

W: So, it is like the case of Ann where you picked up on the inhibition and utilized it. Here you pick up on the aggressive outlining of things, attacking things.

E: The aggressive, intelligent outline. She stayed awake nights hating me because of the thinking I made her do about her mother, which was a beautiful way of telling me that she'd done a lot of thinking about her mother hatred. That she was doing something about the hatred of mother by transferring the hatred to me, and I'm not very vulnerable. At least she's finding that out at the very beginning of the interview. Then I can ask her what else has she accomplished? What else? A weight loss. The wearing of a dress she hasn't been able to wear. A pretty dress, a dress she likes very much. In other words, a beautiful statement to me, "I like therapy."

W: Just before we came down, I was reading your recent paper on utilization techniques in hypnotic work, and this was about accepting things in a similar sort of way.* One of the things that struck me there was that sometimes it seems that what you focus on accepting is the most immediate level of behavior. Like the man who paces up and down in your office, and you get

*"Further Techniques of Hypnosis-Utilization Techniques," in Haley, Jay (Ed.) *Advanced Techniques of Hypnosis and Therapy, Selected Papers of Milton H. Erickson, M.D.*, New York, Grune & Stratton, 1967.

him to pace on instruction. Whereas at other times you don't pay any particular attention to the immediate behavior but you hit a more general level of functioning and accept and begin to direct that.

E: Now take that man who paced back and forth here. This is a very small office, yet he paced back and forth. All of that tension, all of that anxiety, a tremendous tension. How could I focus any attention on any deep, underlying thing? Perhaps if this office had been larger, less cramped, and he could have had more room in which to pace, I might have directed attention to something lying underneath. But I doubt it, because he had so much tension. I think he'd show the same degree of tension in an auditorium or an office.

W: Then this was a case where this was so immediate that there wasn't really any other place to start, practically.

E: Yes, and that was what he was making the office interview. A pacing. He'd been kicked out of other offices because he wouldn't cooperate. He told me this interview is going to be a pacing interview. (Laughter)

W: Who told who?

E: Well, he'd been kicked out of other offices. Would I kick him out? Thereby, he told me, "This is going to be a pacing interview. Are you going to kick me out?" Therefore, it was up to me to take charge, literally, of that implied question by having him pace.

H: This you would consider formally similar to preventing the inhibited woman from telling you the risqué stories that bother her. Setting up an inhibited situation that she is inhibited.

E: Yes.

H: Well, there's something about this that strikes me as terribly obvious when I try to write something about your work, and that is that you treat psychiatric cases in the same sort of way as you treat resistant hypnotic subjects, that the same sort of pattern is involved.

E: You see, the patient comes in to you – whether he's a hypnotic patient or psychiatric patient on whom you're not going to use hypnosis – he comes to you to the best of his understanding because he cannot get along in his immediate reality situation. He doesn't come to you to have you explain a childhood situation. He just wants to live today, happily today. He'd like to be free of today's tension. In fact, he'd like to be free of this moment's tension. He's urgently asking that. Therefore, I meet him at that level. Yes, we can correct this immediate moment of reality, which then makes it possible for him to accept the reality of five minutes from now, the reality of five days from now, the reality of five years from now.

H: That's a big extension of this moment.

E: I know.

H: Well, we'll get to extending that moment a bit later, but what I wonder is if you see any difference – suppose you're going to hypnotise somebody in a stage demonstration. You're not going to therapute him, and this is a resistant person. Do you see any formal difference to the ways the person resists you and tries to control the situation?

E: Well, let's go back to that San Francisco demonstration. You were there, weren't you? With that woman psychiatrist? No matter what she said, how did you feel about it?

H: What do you mean, no matter what she said?

E: What I did with her.

H: I thought you were accepting whatever she said.

E: Yes. How did she feel about it?

H: I think she had very mixed feelings about it.

E: Very mixed, yes.

H: Both more desperate and pleased at the same time.

E: More desperate and more pleased. Why more desperate?

H: Because she couldn't handle you.

E: In spite of my accepting behavior.

H: Because of it, let's put it that way.

E: Yes. And pleased that she had met a match.

W: You're also offering her something for the future all the time, aren't you? I seem to recall various references to something about what was going to happen in her office at some time.

E: Yes. Now at my last seminar another woman physician volunteered as my resistant subject. Afterwards, several of the seminarians with good insight said, "How did you measure letting her top you each time by such a narrow margin?" (Laughter) They said, "You let her top you every time. Each time you made it more and more difficult for her to top you, but each time she succeeded by the narrowest of margins."

H: Of course, you set that up so nicely to begin with when you ask them to demonstrate resistance for the audience.

E: Except this woman came to me the first morning and said, "You list on the program the handling of resistant patients. This is my first seminar. I would like to be your 'resistant patient.'" (Laughter)

H: I volunteer to resist you.

E: Yes. Therefore, what did I do? I wondered, and as soon as I got her on the platform I knew I would let her top me. I had to let her top me every time. I also had to let the audience see, but not let her see, that I was measuring things very carefully and always deliberately. Letting her top me by just so much. One of those who came up and discussed it with me said, "I've always tried to put patients in their place, and I didn't know you could put them in their place by letting them put *you* in your place."

H: It's the controlling the control all right.

E: Yes. And of course she had her handkerchief. (Laughter) She wiped the perspiration from her brow each time, but she had such a triumphant smile. Everybody could see it so beautifully.

H: Well, do you see any formal difference between resisting you when you're hypnotizing someone and the way a person tries to deal with you when you're trying to remove their symptoms?

E: It's essentially the same sort of thing. Frequently, the patient has a more centralized goal.

H: In what sense centralized?

E: When you can resist me, it would be between you and me. But if you were the patient, you would have in your arms some treasure, a little object here that you'll be turning yourself this way to protect while you resist me. Do you see? You feel yourself as yourself and your problem as a burden, or another entity of some kind, that you have to shield from me.

H: Well, isn't the burden used to shield the person from you though?

E: Well, it might be. While with a resistant subject, that's between man and man.

H: Well, do you think that implies, or applies to, the fact that when you're dealing with a patient the symptom is not only involved with you at the moment but also used outside of here?

E: Yes. It's another entity. You see, that's one reason why with a patient, as soon as I've got name and address and all that statistical data, I sometimes ask the patient, "Now what can I do for you?" If I choose that opening, the patient says, "I have a problem." I watch the way in which they say, "I have a problem." I tell them, "Well in order to handle your problem I'll have to know all about you, but in giving me an account — this is only the first interview, you know — I would like you to be extremely careful to withhold from me everything you feel disinclined to tell me." What have I said? This is only the first interview. In this first interview, withhold all the material you are disinclined to tell me. In other words, this is a free and easy situation with no pressure, no compulsion. At long last you've found an easy, free situation, so take advantage of it. I've had more than one say at the end of the hour, "I came here anticipating tremendous difficulty in talking to you. I was very, very certain that it would take me weeks and weeks before I'd ever dare to tell you these things. And here I've already told you, and I'm glad." My answer under those circumstances is unexpected, "Well, you know, so am I; but I'd like to have you bear in mind that you undoubtedly have a lot of unhappy repressed memories that didn't come to mind, and those will have to come out later." So I told them they have withheld, and they can't be disappointed by being too informative in the first interview. They're comforted by the fact that they have withheld.

W: Those will have to come out later.

H: There's another thing going on here too. When a patient comes to you, he's at a disadvantage because he needs help. But he has one advantage and that is that you need information, and he can withhold it from you. Now, when you instruct him to talk and also to withhold, you've got him going in both directions. But if at the end of the hour, after you've told him to withhold, he says, "I didn't withhold."

E: He's disobeyed me.

H: Then you've got to go around again and say you have withheld. (Laughter) It's this sort of a struggle going on here.

E: Well, why do you call it a struggle?

W: It's just sort of cooperation going on.

H: A working out, let's say, of a relationship.

E: And a defining of the relationship, always accurately though.

W: Accurately but with a positive emphasis.

E: Yes.

W: How did you ever develop the ability to get such a view of the positive side of a whole lot of things that everybody else would probably be considering difficult as hell?

E: Well, it's this way. Somebody wants to learn psychiatry, so they start reading Freud, and they're absolutely fascinated by Freud. He is so instructive and so informative. But they never looked at the rest of the books on the shelves. They actually absorbed themselves in Freud as if that was the only book that was ever written. You read Freud, and you read Freud with the utmost of interest and pleasure and satisfaction. You also ought to wonder what Jung and Adler say about it, and what would Westermark say about it?

H: How is this relevant to the positive attitude?

E: Then when a patient comes into your office and presents you an awfully negative thing, you're always looking at this side of it, and that side, above it and below it, beyond it and in front of it. Because there's always obverse and reverse to a coin.

W: You might also say that we can rely on the patient to give us the negative side.

E: Almost always you can rely on them (Laughter) to give the negative side.

H: Well, we have one example of what you feel can't be accepted. This man who came to you and wanted to go home. You thought there was no way to accept this and utilize it.

E: There's no way of utilizing it that I can see. He had already defined the distance, his wants, the fact that he was going to go home by train. I can't see him all day long. I've got him for an hour. He's done all of that thinking before he comes for the first interview. I just haven't got any time. He's got everything defined. He's closed his mind. Then, instead of dealing with it, he said, "I want to go home." What little boy is speaking? He tells me his plans in a man's tone of voice; "I want to go home" in a little boy's voice. If I want to discuss it, I have to discuss it while he talks to me in a man's voice. Periodically he will interrupt in a little boy's voice. He came to see me on Friday. The second visit was on Saturday. The next possible appointment is going to be on Monday. He's got all day Sunday in which to execute his plans for going home—period. I'd better recognize that reality. He's going home by train. There's no possibility of difficulty in getting a train seat. He came by plane. He's in a hurry to get home; he tells me he's going to travel by train. He's an ex-GI who's been overseas. He knows all about traveling. He wants to go home with childish eagerness. He takes that slow train. Sunday is coming up. A plane you might have to wait for a seat.

W: Suppose you would have, on the first day, put him in a trance and sent him home?

E: 1800 miles?

W: Well, that's not so far for you.

E: Oh yes, I'd like to add the other additional information. They arrived, and he insisted on spending the first night—I've forgotten what motel—and then checked out so they could find another, which, of course, was vital information.

H: How was that vital?

E: The patient comes to see me from out of town and checks into a motel. He was planning to see me. His doctor recommended three weeks. So before he comes for the first appointment, he checks out of his motel. He's got no place to return to in Phoenix, which, of course, I just automatically added into the picture he gave.

W: The picture then is one in which he's cutting himself loose all the time before he even really gets here.

E: He's cutting himself loose before he came to see me.

H: Well, what other things do you face that you feel cannot be accepted and utilized?

E: Suppose I get my schedule. (After looking at his schedule) Fifty years old, a high school business education. "I'm an alcoholic; even Alcoholics Anonymous failed me. Besides, I'm mean to my mother. When I fall in love, it's always with some no-good married man. Every time I do something I do something to hurt myself, even if it's no more than having a temper tantrum. I hate living on the ranch. I live with mother and my brother. My brother is an alcoholic, and he hates my mother too. I hate him and I hate my mother. You ought to see the way she wastes her time making stinking little plants grow in the yard. I live a purely parasitic life. I take a joy in aggravating my mother. I'm a completely worthless person. Why are you wasting your time? Don't you think it's rather stupid of you to waste your time on a worthless creature like me? Here I am 50 years old in a psychiatrist's office. I went to Dr. B. I told him what I'm telling you, and he kicked me out of the office. I went to Dr. D., and I told him the same thing I'm telling you. He wouldn't have anything to do with me. They're pretty smart men. They know I've got a wealthy brother-in-law. They know that my sister will pay any fees. You know how they like money. You know it. You know what their reputation is in Phoenix. They kicked me out of the office, and they like money. Don't you think you're stupid to deal with me? Let me tell you, I did have a car. My brother-in-law bought it for me. So I got drunk and speeded and then I beat up on the cop. I got thrown in jail. I lost my driver's license. I lost my car. When I lost my driver's license, I just took that car and I sold it for a small sum of money instead of what it was worth. Then I drank up the money. I went home and I laughed at my mother. I'm depressed. I hate myself. There isn't a solitary thing. Here I am 50 years old."

That was my initial meeting with her. I said, "Well, do you feel happy or depressed?" She said, "Naturally, I'm depressed; can't you see it?" I said, "Yes, I can see that you're depressed, but what else?" She said, "Do you want all of the rest of the sordid details?" I said, "No. I'm not interested in sordid details." "You're a psychiatrist, aren't you?" I said, "Yes." "Why aren't you interested in sordid details? For example, my sexual life? I've lived with this man, that man. Especially married men. They're all no good. Never seen a married man, no matter what walk of life, that was any good. They're all stinkers. Now, what one of my affairs do you want me to tell you about?"

I said, "Well, I'm not interested." "Well, what are you interested in?" "I just want you to tell me one little thing. You are 50 years old. Mr. X is a very, very wealthy cattle owner, a very, very wealthy rancher. He married into a family – that would be your sister. It's a rather talented family. You're 50 years old. The little thing that I want to know is, before you reached your present state, age of 50, and your present state of being my patient, what was just one of your accomplishments? She said, "Good or bad?" I said, "I'm not interested in the sordid." She said, "I built up a ceramics business." Just one little detail.

Let's see, when did she come to me? That was October. She didn't come back until May. She saw me off and on, not very frequently. (Reading schedule) Let's see, May 25th, May 29th, June 1st, June 4th, June 8th, June 12th, June 15th, June 25th, June 30th, July 7th, July 10th, July 13th. On June 30th, I mark,

"Very slow improvement." July 7th, "Much self-pity."
July 10th, "Improved." July 13th, "Much self-pity."
She canceled out after July 13th. She said that things
were absolutely hopeless and that there was no sense
in coming to me further. I said, "Of course things are
absolutely hopeless. That's why you've got to change."
(Laughter)

She was in to see me in September. Do you ever
want to meet a high pressure, successful business-
woman? Allan went to the fair, and he was asked what
impressed him most about the fair. He said, "I learned
something. There was a woman there that had a booth
selling a self-relaxing machine. I think she's also selling real estate. I don't know what all. But the way
that woman handled everybody at that fair – she had
her booth surrounded by people." A patient of mine
went to the fair. I said, "What was interesting at the
fair?" "The woman selling a reducing machine. She's
got a lot of other interests too. I wish I could be like
that woman." A third person told me the same thing.

She was absolutely hopeless. Much self-pity, of
course. There wasn't anything too big or too small.
The petunias, the St. Augustine grass, the lipsia. No,
that isn't the correct name for it; I can't think of the
correct name. But I'm doing the same thing I did with
her. She told me about the stupid thing her mother
was doing, that stupid thing of planting those stupid
little pieces of grass that grow only so high and make
a permanent lawn. Yet I stumbled all over the name.
I couldn't pronounce it. I couldn't spell it. I still can't
think of it.

H: It's dichondra.

E: All right. I brought in that special grass they're using
    in Pennsylvania for eroded areas. She was discussing
    it for me. I mispronounced it, and I tried to spell it.
    She told me I was stupid. But all that self-pity meant
    that she was really running out.

H: Now wait a minute, you're getting shifty here. What does your being unable to recall or spell the name of this stuff have to do with what?

E: What does it have to do with it? There's nothing too large or too small for her to find fault with. All of her relationships with mother, all of her relationships with her brother, her relationships with her sister, her brother-in-law, with all the psychiatrists, with me, with everything. That's the sort of thing. She told me all about the ranch her mother owned. All the work her brother did.

H: All right, but how does your behaving inadequately in some way get into this?

E: All right, when she wants to find fault with her mother putting in a new lawn, dichondra, then in spite of the fact that she gives me the name, I mispronounce it, and I get it confused with some other grass, then I can't even spell it. What have I done? I've given her some more things to find fault with.

H: You mean, if you can get her to find fault on your terms . . .

E: On my terms, and over and over again. "But what's wrong with you, why are you so stupid? I told you last time my brother's drunk when he's cultivating the *cotton*. Where did you get the idea it was corn?" I'm stupid.

H: If you can arrange for her to call you stupid, it's good for her?

E: Yes, it's very good for her.

H: Particularly if she would be doing it anyhow.

E: Oh, she was going to do it anyhow.

H: Well, that's another example of how you can accept anything. You can even accept that. It raises another question. When you accept something of that sort, you behave inadequately so they'll behave like you're inadequate, how do you keep them coming to you?

E: In the first place, they wouldn't come to me if they

thought I was inadequate. They wouldn't come to me if they thought I was stupid. But if they want me to be useful to them, I'd better be useful in a way that meets their immediate needs. Now she needed to call me stupid.

H: So, that would keep her coming to you because you were meeting her needs?

E: That's right.

W: She needed to be critical.

E: She needed to be critical from the very beginning. She showed how she needed to be critical with large things and small things. So she was critical about the dichondra. Then I pointed out to her that she didn't even know the different kinds of weeds that grow in the pasture where the cows were, the weeds that were using up the irrigation water. That's really hunting for something to find fault with. The water that's used up by the weeds growing in the pasture where the cows feed. Why didn't she take a hoe and go and chop down those weeds? She's calling me stupid. She's chopping down a married man. "All married men are absolutely worthless." Why doesn't she chop down worthless weeds; they're stealing the water away from the grass that should feed cows to produce milk.

W: Now this is beginning to get toward the thing that was puzzling me. I can see the aspect of accepting her criticalness. What I haven't seen in this one yet is how the transformation takes place.

E: You finally run out of things to criticize when you're trying to criticize things to somebody who keeps directing the way in which you criticize. It's the same thing as that obsessive-compulsive woman who said, "Oh yes, that's a staple." Remember in my "Utilization Techniques" how I kept passing out things until I would delay her in naming it as a pencil, pencil holder, pencil. You see, as soon as that particular woman became dependent upon me to show her things to name – then she was my patient. As soon as this patient became dependent upon me to name the things that she should criticize . . .

H: Oh, I see.

E: Well, of course, you realize, do you not, that the plantain has a much shorter root than the mullein? And the mullein is going to take the water that soaks in deeply. The plantain is going to absorb the water near the surface. I think you ought to chop down the mullein weeds first. (Laughs)

H: Now, were you working out some oedipal drama on this? I mean, with married men, and the cow that doesn't get to take the food, doesn't give the milk, and so on?

E: Was I working on an oedipal drama? No, I don't know what I was working on.

H: I just wondered if it was deliberate in some way.

E: No. Now she's going to come back to see me once a month. I think from now on. Her statement is, "Any woman my age, with my ability, made a lot of business successes in the past. Of course I always break them up. I think that I'm old enough now to know that I need some good advice. Now and then. Once a month I think will swing it for me, so I'll get back to see you once a month. Of course, I'll probably sell you a little real estate, and a few things like that." But you see, that's only a sop to her vanity.

One of the things that is intriguing her is this question, "Dr. Erickson, would you please tell me: How did you see anything worthwhile to salvage in me? I've inquired, you never asked a question of my brother-in-law. You never asked a question of my sister. You never asked a question of my mother. How did you see anything worthwhile to salvage in me?" I said, "Well, you know, you're underweight, you look your age, you've got a history of affairs. You gave me a history of promiscuity; certainly I didn't see sexual appeal. You've seen my wife. I didn't see sex appeal in you, at least not for me. I must have seen something in the way of brains and personality and ability." (Laughs) I *must* have seen something in the way of brains and personality and ability. She asked me again, what did I see? I said, "Oh well, let's call it personality." She asked me again. "Oh, let's call it brains." The next day, "Well, let's call it ability." I'm never going to answer that question. See, it's wrong to answer that question.

W: If you answer anything specific, she will go out and disprove it, won't she?

E: That's right.

H: Well, why did you eliminate sex appeal?

E: Well, I'm a married man.

H: Oh, I see.

W: So this would fall right into the old history if she's been getting involved with married men all the time and thinking that she and they are no good.

E: I'm not going to have her waste her time with me. Why should she waste her time with me? She's already told me *all* married men are no good. Now, let's close that question. Let's close it rudely, emphatically, painfully, but let's close it. "At least not for me."

H: Well, that's another example of what you're accepting; do you have another example of what you cannot accept? And utilize?

E: Let me give you an example of what Allan did in high school. Allan was driving along in the Nash one night. I've had the same experience happen to me. My secretary has had it. It's a common thing in Phoenix. At night some hot-rodder breezes up alongside of you and challenges you to a drag race. Or are you chicken? If you don't measure up to the situation, you get your fenders marred at the very least. Or you get a terrific tongue-lashing. Anyway, it's a most unpleasant thing, because you don't know what – they may run alongside of you for a few blocks and try and run you into the curb, mash your fenders, get behind you and jolt you. You'd better accept their challenge.

A couple of hot-rodders pulled up alongside of Allan at a red light and gave him a preemptory challenge. Allan looked at them (acting strange and laughing); they looked at him in absolute horror. That braying laugh of a teenager, that completely asinine – you have to have heard – that braying laugh of a stupid teenager. They just drove on so glad to be free of that idiot. You've accepted it; you've placed a reinterpretation on it in a completely acceptable way. It's displeasing to the other person; they have to accept it. Those hot-rodders (laughing), "Let's get out of here." Instead of trying to make Allan run, they wanted to run. You see? With your psychiatric patients you bear that in mind. I don't care who calls me stupid. He wouldn't be here if he didn't have a need to do it.

H: Well now, the crucial thing that we keep trying to understand is what about after you have accepted what the patient offers. Merely accepting isn't enough. If you just go on accepting what they're doing, maybe it is enough; I don't know. What about a situation where a patient tries to handle you by being inhibited? And you accept their being inhibited, and are a little inhibited yourself? Now, at some point there has to be a change, or a shift, on your part.

E: Yes, but when you are absolutely positive that the other person is as inhibited as you are, and won't go any further than you'll go, it's awfully easy to go along. Because you start relying on his strength to aid you in inhibiting. You know what he has told you, "Now you can think these things; but you withhold everything

that you don't want to tell me, and be sure to withhold them." Now and then patients start some things,
and one word possesses a double meaning, but you
know it's going to be an innocent comment. You say,
"Just a moment, think over what you started to say."
Then you repeat, and they become aware of that other
meaning. They know they can trust you, that you're
not going to take advantage of their unwariness. Actually, of course, they came here to tell you.

H: Yes, that's the point.

E: That's the point. And you're inhibiting them to their disadvantage, and they want their advantage.

H: Well, then at some point you have to shift, don't you?

E: But you see, when they become aware of the fact that
you are inhibiting them to meet their wishes to be inhibited, but it's to their disadvantage, they better do
something about it. So then they decide to tell you
this. And they find out that you survive. Then they
tell you a bit more. And you're still living.

H: Well, you have to stop inhibiting them at the point
where they begin to decide to tell you this then?

E: When they start releasing, I always review the inhibition on some unimportant item. If the girl is disclos-
ing a traumatic affair, and she starts to tell me what
the street address is at which it occurred, well, naturally, I don't want to know the street. You see?

H: (Laughing) You mean you continue to inhibit, but you
shift from inhibiting the major things to minor things?

E: To the minor, the unimportant things. The patient
wants inhibition; but the patient wants freedom too,
you know.

H: Well, typically the patient also wants to inhibit the major things and not the minor things.

E: But the patient is coming to you to get rid of those major things; therefore, you let them keep the inhibition,
and you let them get rid of the major things that are
troubling them.

H: Now, that's a case where you don't shift inhibiting them, you shift the content in some way.

E: Let me give you an example. "Dr. Erickson, you remember me. I was your patient a long time ago. There's a new situation, and I'm very glad that I've got you to come to. I'm absolutely horrified by my behavior. I'm also somewhat amused, in fact quite amused. I don't know whether or not to tell it to you. I don't know how much to tell you. I would like to have you help me tell you the right amount." That was a patient on which I used inhibition technique, oh, back in the '50s, the early '50s. "I'm certainly horrified, amused, somewhat amused, quite amused, horribly distressed, horrified."

My statement was, "All right, so you're horrified by your behavior; and you're amused by it. I wonder how well you understand the behavior if you've got those contradictory attitudes toward it? I don't know which you want to tell me, the horrifying aspect or the amusing aspect? Or a little of both?" In spite of her experience, she didn't know what I was saying. "A *little* of both" implied withholding a large part.

She said, "I think I'll tell you a little. I went to college last year. I enjoyed my course immensely. The teacher was very, very helpful. I was most enthusiastic. I suppose I formed a student's crush on the professor. I enrolled this year in a different course, different professor." Long pause. I said, "Are you enjoying this course as much?" She said, "Oh yes, it's a different course." I'm trying to pause to duplicate. "Well, let's see, what you're trying to tell me is something about last year's professor." She said, "Yes. This year's professor, in this other course, doesn't discuss things as well as last year's professor. I was wishing that I could get last year's professor to discuss it. As I came out of the classroom I saw him, went over; I told him how much I enjoyed being in his class last year. How much I had gotten out of it, how much I wished I were in his class this year. That I was having difficulty comprehending this year's course adequately, and I wondered if he would discuss it with me? He said, 'Why don't you come to my office? I've got a little time now.' I said, 'Well, I've got to go up to speak to someone, but I'll be up shortly.' I didn't really have anybody to speak to. But he went up to his office, and I went to the woman's room and I thought things over. I had the feeling as if I were going there for a rendezvous. It took an awful lot of courage. I went up and I apologized to him for taking his time. He told me he was glad to give me time. He took the textbook, and he inquired about the chapter, and he gave me a very, very nice discussion. He talked about the various things associated with it. He was so nice. All the time I kept thinking, this is really a rendezvous. I kept telling him, 'I mustn't take your time.' He began looking at me in a rather queer fashion. I felt I ought to change my seat, and somehow or another I put my chair around alongside of him. I told him I mustn't – take his time. (Laughter) Finally it finished. He said, 'Really now, what is on your mind?' I said, 'I've lost my head.' I said, 'I like you an awful lot. I'm awfully grateful to you, and I shouldn't talk this way to you because I'm a married woman.' He said it was a very painful situation for him, and then he said, 'You know, I'm glad you came up, because I'm tremendously attracted to you. If you don't mind, I would like to kiss you.' I put my arms around him and I said, 'But I'm a married woman, and I can't let you kiss me on the mouth.' I don't know how I did it, I had a low-necked dress on and I had him kiss me here." (Laughter) I had told her to tell me "a little."

H: That was a little?

E: But you see, I told her to tell me a little. She was a patient I had treated before. An inhibited patient who had learned that she could tell me a little. But that's how a little builds up. The situation is amusing, but she's horrified. How could she go back to see him? That was her question. And what should I answer?

H: Well, did it stop with a kiss?

E: She's an inhibited person. She doesn't know how she managed.

H: She managed a little.

E: Yes. Shall she go back to see him?

H: Well, what did you advise?

E: I said, "You're thinking the whole situation over, aren't you?" She said, "Yes." I said, "You know, it seems to me if you can think the whole thing over, the professor can too. I don't even know who he is. He might have some questions too. I can't answer *his* question. Your question is only half of the situation." Because I'm not going to be hung for my answer to her question. If I give the wrong answer, she can use me as a scapegoat, isn't that right? If I say, "Yes," she can blame me if she does go back. If I say, "Yes," and she doesn't go back, then I've disclosed the fact that my advice is faulty. If I say, "No," and she goes back, I've disclosed the fact that my advice is faulty and I'm wrong. If I say, "No," and she doesn't go back, it's *I* who barred her. I stand to lose on any answer I give.

H: That's not atypical of the situation you get into with advice.

E: That's right. Therefore, I point out that I can only answer a part of it, and it's not the correct answer or the full answer, the adequate answer. But look, when I do that, she has to consider the professor. Now she's got to consider the professor, and she is a married woman. At the purely personal level, knowing what I know about her husband, why shouldn't she go back and have an affair with the professor? That husband has never hesitated to take every cruel and selfish advantage of his wife imaginable. Everything they have is something that he wants, nothing that she wanted. He has a spinster sister who is rigid and reared in Europe in one of these matriarchal-patriarchal types of families where the eldest sister who isn't married takes mother's place and dictates to all the other members of the family. The husband is bringing that sister into his home. The girl knows what's in store for her. Her husband really worked for a year bringing that situation about.

H: Well, now this started on the question of whether you have to make a shift or not, as I recall.

E: Yes.

H: Now, in your utilization technique, you accept what they do and encourage what they do to the point – I mean, one way you make the shift is you encourage what they do until they begin to wait for you to direct them. Then you direct them in a different direction. Now in this inhibition you continue to accept the inhibition, but displace it from something major to minor. Are there others?

E: She was going to tell me a little, and what did I shift from? From wondering whether the amusing, or the horror, is what she wanted to tell me. It was contradictory. I shifted from helping her to inhibit to a receptive attitude, isn't that right?

H: Yes.

W: You mean, when you made the reference to contradictory, that was inhibitory, and then you changed to say really any aspect of it, or some of both, would be acceptable?

E: Yes. So then I shifted from an inhibitory to a receptive force. She started pouring it all out. Then she asked me the question, and I avoided that by defining it as a part of the whole. And then what type of thinking did she think he was doing, and how did that reflect her type of thinking, and what did she really feel? And what was her attitude toward her husband? What's her home situation? Can she think freely about her own emotional desires, and how does she think her emotional desires fit with her personality structure?

Before the hour was over, she said, "You know, actually, emotionally I would like to go to bed with him. I'd like to make love with him. I'm pretty certain he'd like to do that with me. But when I consider my childhood, my lifelong experiences, my religious attitudes, I don't think my personality could take the actual physical experience. What I'm really going to think about – I'm not going to hesitate about recognizing to the fullest degree exactly what my emotional attitudes are." I said, "What do you mean, to the fullest degree – your emotional attitudes?" She said, "You know what I mean, because with emotional attitudes you get physiological responses too. I'm going to recognize those." Yes.

She means she's going to think about the professor. She's going to notice certain erotic responses in the erogenous zones, and she's not going to be ashamed of them or hesitant. But she's not going to put any of her thinking into action until she is convinced whether or not she, as a personality, can tolerate it. She isn't going to feel that she ruled out action because of fear; if she rules out action, she'll have the feeling she ruled it out because of willingness to consider it fully and freely. In getting patients to resolve problems by examining all of their thinking, and separating it from action, and then in accordance with their understandings, whether positive or negative feelings, determining their actions.

CHAPTER 8

Failure,
and What is
Essential for Change

1959. Present were Milton H. Erickson, Jay Haley, and John Weakland.

H: When you get someone who's failing or defeating himself in some way, and you accept this, how do you make a switch on that? I mean, are there other ways besides delaying until he's waiting for you?

E: Now, here are a couple of patients I'm failing on miserably. I'm settling in the one case for a less destructive goal. That's all that I can see that I can accomplish with him. Let's see, for eight years he has been going to college. Really capable. He hopes to complete his junior year in June after eight years. His goal was to become a Ph.D. in psychology. Well, if it takes you eight years to complete the junior year, and you've got chiefly D's and C's and repeats with C's, you're never going to qualify for a Ph.D. degree. Isn't that right? So he's going to graduate with a B.A., and then possibly – he isn't going to take a Ph.D., that's settled – possibly become an accountant, possibly go on to become a real estate salesman. I'm settling for that lesser goal instead of trying to make him a Ph.D. He's beautifully qualified in endowments. That horribly destructive attitude toward his mother. His mother's horribly destructive attitude toward him. He's certainly getting even. His mother and father were happily married. They had a very, very nice home. He adored his father, and he adored his mother. Then his father died; I think it was from cancer. After about a year's period of grief, a friend of his father started comforting the mother. They have never bothered to get married. The boy wanted the man to marry his mother. He's wanted his mother married all through high school. Today he's 28 and he still wants it. But they won't do it. Mother and her lover both want him to graduate with honors.

H: They want him to be legitimate even if they don't want to be. I wasn't thinking of examples of you failing, I was thinking again of this shift . . .

W: Though we had that on the list as another topic.

H: We do have on the list what failures you've had and what you've thought about them.

E: You see, with that failure, I've got to go along with him.

H: That's a pretty mild failure, a B.A. instead of a Ph.D., isn't it?

E: Yes, but he isn't going to use any of his actual abilities. He'll get a clerical job; he'll sell real estate. Any high school kid could do that. He'll function at that level.

*   *   *

E: I had a patient who said, "What will you say if I tell you I'm going to commit suicide right here in your office?" I said, "Well, I ought to call the police *before* you do it. Honestly, I really ought to." She said, "A psychiatric interview is confidential." I said, "Suicide never is confidential." I did call the police. It took the sergeant and two patrolmen about two hours to talk the girl into going home. The girl came to me for one definite reason, "Either you do an abortion, or you refer me to an abortionist, or I'll commit suicide right here." That's what took the sergeant and the two patrolmen so long, that fixed, rigid demand.

H: You had them haul her out of here and take her home?

E: Oh, I turned the office over to them and let them talk to her. Fortunately, she was my last patient in the afternoon. She'd come in as an emergency. She said there was an emergency situation—could she come right in and see me? Then she told me the psychiatric interview was confidential; suicides aren't.

H: How come you didn't try and manipulate her out of it in that situation instead of bringing in the police?

E: Because she was a university student over at Tempe, and her roommate knew that she had called me. If that gal committed suicide or went to an abortionist, where would my professional standing be? The only thing to do is protect myself. Get the police in. The sergeant was smooth in handling the girl. He said it was one of the toughest cases he ever had to handle, and he was literally sweating. She wanted an abortion, or the name of an abortionist. The police told her the same thing I did; under no circumstances could they give her the name of an abortionist, even if they knew a thousand.

W: What became of her?

E: I don't know.

W: Didn't see her any more?

E: I know the police were trying to persuade her to marry her boyfriend, who was on his way from San Franisco, wanting to marry her. I know the police got in touch with the girl's mother.

H: Well, when was the last time a patient managed to disturb you?

E: When I know a patient is going to go and deliberately give up.

H: What do you mean "give up"?

E: When the patient says, "You know, I've been very grateful to you. I've been off of liquor for over two years. I've got no desire for it, no hunger for it. I'm getting along all right with my job. I'm well adjusted with my wife. I've been thinking about it for some time, and what the hell is the meaning of it all? I thought I'd better drop in and say goodbye to you. I've said goodbye to my wife. I'm going downtown and get plastered." It's a very distressing thing to have happen to you. Because what does it mean? Well, you know where they're headed then. Skid row. There's been some sort of slow, insidious cessation from that normal happiness, good adjustment. "I want none of it."

And I've had patients come in and resign from the process of happy living. I had a patient come in and say, "You know, since my wife and I saw you we've been living happily, getting along. The kids are happy; but I met a prostitute the other night, and I'm going to move off with her." You see that in everyday life all the time. The careful automobile driver one day, for no reason at all, opens it up to see if it will go 130 over the wrong kind of a road. You'll see the drug addict, who's been off drugs for five years, saying, "This is silly, this is ridiculous; but I want to have some horse tonight." He knows exactly where he's going to wind up.

A patient, a new one I got recently, said, "All through World War II I was an overt homosexual. I reenlisted for two years over in Italy so that I could remain in Italy where the kids were so numerous and would do anything for you." He said, "My last homosexual experience with a kid was two years ago. I haven't been tempted. I have often gone hunting with a 16-year-old. I'm a welcome visitor to his home. But the other day I thought to myself, what the hell, so I went down on him, got him to go down on me. Then

I went down to South Phoenix; I picked up some more, knowing all the time that I wouldn't go back to my wife, my mother, my brother, or anybody. I'm going down to skid row." That's what he's doing. "How can I go down to skid row," was the question he put to me, "more safely?" What does he mean by that? So that he can get a long sentence on a relatively minor crime.

I think that if you make a searching enough inquiry in a lot of patients, you'll find a long period of adjustment, and then some nut comes loose. Some screw comes loose. They go haywire. You see these people who are perfectly wonderful people, and friends; and they hit the age of 25, and they cease to be nice, likable, friendly people that you want to associate with. Each half decade wipes out some people; even though their bodies remain alive, their personalities have died.

*   *   *

H: Well, granted that you accept the patients' behavior and that you direct them differently and such, what do you think is crucial for producing a therapeutic change? I mean, some people have the idea that a patient has to have some insight, some people have the idea he has to ventilate his feeling, and so on. But you obviously have a different idea. What is it you're after that you think is essential to produce a change?

E: I think it's the same as in the matter of teaching a child in school. It isn't enough to explain to the children two plus two equals four. You can explain that and argue it, and deduce it, and everything else that you want. But you do need to have the child start *doing* something. He does need to put down one, and another one, and draw a line, and put a plus sign, and he learns one plus one equals two. It is his sense of doing something.

Whenever you work with a patient, if you're dealing with an oedipal situation, you want that patient to do something about the father, whether it's to write him a letter or not to write him a letter. You want the patient to write the word "father" on a piece of paper. You want him to draw a picture and label it "father." You want him to crumple the paper up and put it in the wastebakset. It isn't sufficient to have the patient just simply say, "My father did this, my father did that," and free associate endlessly. A patient who has free associated on father extensively, and informatively, and with insight – it is still an incomplete process until the patient has actually done something.

In therapy, the first thing I want to do with a patient is to get that patient to do something. When inducing the hypnotic trance, one of the first things I want the patient to do is to participate in some way. I ask them to take a comfortable seat, and they are sitting comfortably. Then I point out that they haven't shifted and I want them to. Do they mind moving the right foot one-fourth of an inch to the right, to the left? I want them to *do* something. If they still refuse, then I want to know if it's all right if I move their hand slightly. They're still not doing anything, but I'm very likely to move the hand so that it rests in such a way that the weight of it causes the hand to tip slightly over. (Laughter)

H: So they've got to do something?

E: They've got to do something. The patient I had for the first time this morning was going to be quite passive about it. She was *not* going to let her eyes close. I asked her a couple of times. So then I told her, "Now hold your eyes open after I say, 'close them,' for a while." You see, she had to hold her eyes open, but she was doing something. She had to close her eyes also, and that way, when she resisted, I got her to do two things: the one she was going to do anyway, and the other she had to do to stop doing the thing I asked her to do. (Laughter)

H: When you say you want them to do something, what you seem to mean is that you want them to do something under your direction.

E: Yes. To do something under *my* direction. Just as the teacher says, "Now take your pencil and your paper out of your desk and get ready to do *your* lesson." So under the teacher's direction they initiate, and they do *their* lesson. So I want my patient to do something as a measure of initiating his performance of the things that he himself needs to do.

H: It just isn't enough that he do something under your direction; he has to do something which you mutually define as "voluntary" on his part?

E: As voluntary on his part, and as relating to his problem. Now sometimes it isn't necessarily a tangible act. I want you to *think* over *your* thoughts on this matter. That is doing something too. It's an assignment of a task, but it's merely initiating the task that he himself must do. Because *I* want you to think over *your* thoughts on *your* problems. While I'm telling him what to do, yet all the thinking he has to do is *his* action. And it's in relationship to his problem. So it's an intangible act, but nevertheless it's a participation.

H: You would define doing something as some overt piece of behavior, or thinking something, or feeling something?

E: Yes. In addition, over and above, what are the ordinary events of the therapeutic hour? The patient comes to tell you about his problem. He expects you to talk about his problem. He expects you to give him some advice. He expects to receive some advice. But you put in another task. This patient I saw Saturday who said, "I can't talk. Can I write it out the next time I come here?" I told her, "Yes, but could you tell me some of the things by name that you might write about?" She tightened up her mouth and shook her head. I asked her if she could talk. She shook her head. Complete blocking, verbal blocking. I asked her if she could write for me. She shook her head. I told her I was sorry that she couldn't talk, I was sorry that she couldn't write. But I was glad she could shake her head. And I was very glad she could hold a pencil, and I handed her one. I asked her to hold it in her *left* hand. She looked at me with some question and held it in her left hand. I said, "Of course, you are right-handed; but after you've held it in your left hand, I want you to hold it in your writing hand. You really can't write yet, can you? Not until you get home. I wonder how you feel about not being able to write here now in the office? Do you think you'll be glad to be able to write at home for me?" And she started in talking.

H: Can you explain that?

E: Yes. She shook her head. I was glad she could shake her head. She's here in the office, you know. She shook her head. She was a school teacher; shaking her head was a communication. I asked her to hold a pencil. I asked her to do more than communicate. I asked her to do the wrong thing in relationship to a pencil. She was right-handed. It's wrong to hold a writing pencil in the left hand. Do you see that?

H: I see that, but I don't see the significance of that.

E: I was asking her to do something wrong in relationship to communication. Do you see that?

H: You mean you were asking her to do what she was doing anyhow?

E: Oh, yes, the wrong thing in relationship to communication. (Laughter) Then I shifted the pencil to the writing hand and asked her how she felt about it.

H: That was telling her to do the right thing in communication?

E: To do the writing. The "right" thing really, because I

called it "the writing hand," not the "right" hand – "the writing hand." I asked her how she thought about it. Whereupon she started verbalizing. She was doing the right thing about communicating. Just by getting the patient to do those things, we had quite an extensive talk. Did I think she was schizophrenic? Did I think her prognosis was bad? Did I think she hated her husband? Did I think that she wanted a divorce? Was she afraid to face her own thinking? The amount of material that came out was very, very extensive. But it would have been so very, very easy for her to sit here with her mouth all tightened up, pursed up, and shaking her head violently. But here's an intelligent woman, a school teacher.

H: Well, why didn't you want to accept her saying she'd write it the next time?

E: She came into the office fully prepared to talk to me, and then she blocked so completely. If I allowed her to go home after an hour's silence, or allowed her to go home right away, that would have taught her it is useless to be in the office. I'd better teach her that a tremendous amount can be accomplished in the office. By getting her to participate in that little way, approving her shaking her head. Well, I'm glad she can shake her head. I'm glad that she can communicate, even if it is negatively. Then the pencil in the hand. For a school teacher, it's of tremendous significance. But putting it in the *wrong* hand is a very *safe* thing.

W: It's safe but yet it's something that she will want to correct.

E: That she will want to correct; she's a school teacher.

H: (Laughing) Well, that's a nice example of something – I'm not altogether sure what.

W: Of several things.

E: But you see, it's simply a recognition – she is a school teacher. She'll want to correct that. She recognizes a pencil in the hand is a means of communication. She's blocked and she can't talk. She's blocked and she can't write. She wants to correct it. I speak about the right hand as the writing hand, but I only ask her how she feels about that.

W: Then her questions. Really, the things that she wants to talk to you about are related in a way, in that they're all so much, "Is there something terribly wrong with me?"

E: That's right.

W: You've taken her shaking of her head and said even this is good.

E: I said that is good. She felt distressed because she shook her head, "No," in a situation where that was wrong. But I was glad she could shake her head, and so I got participation. It's so vitally important to get her to do something. But it's getting the patient to do something that fits into the situation. Now suppose I'd had her on the psychoanalytic couch, and I could have comforted myself for an entire hour by thinking what beautiful resistance. I could have explained to the patient that it was resistance. I don't think it was resistance. I think it was much more terror, fear, uncertainty, and I wouldn't really call it resistance at all.

H: There's something awfully slippery in that. It may not be resistance in the sense of resisting her own ideas. It can be seen as a way of handling you.

E: I know, but why call it resistance? Because here's a patient horribly afraid of the self, the ideas.

H: Yes, and of you.

E: Why of me? Not necessarily. I don't think I'm the least bit important in her life. I think this horrible idea, "Am I psychotic?" is tremendously important. "Am I schizophrenic? Do I hate my husband?"

H: She doesn't stop someone on the street and ask him

that. She asks an authority that. You're important enough to be an authority to her.

E: Yes.

H: And she comes to an authority and is unable to speak to him.

E: Why? Because that authority may confirm her suspicions – not the person. She isn't afraid of *me*. She's afraid that maybe her ideas are right. That's what she's afraid of. Not of the therapist. Maybe her ideas are right, and she's afraid of discovering that her ideas are right. So it isn't really resistance to me as therapist.

H: There must be some of that involved, or after the shenanigans with the pencil she wouldn't start talking to you. You didn't relieve her fear about whether her ideas were right by this business with the pencil.

E: No, all I taught her was that she could do something. I taught her that she could do something in relationship to what she, as a school teacher, understood as communication. Everything that I did there was centered around the fact that she was a school teacher. I could have handed her chalk; I could have handed her an eraser, a pencil, a pen. I *wouldn't* have handed her a box of paints and a paintbrush. She's not an artist.

H: You put a great emphasis on vocation as a part of character.

E: I put a great deal of emphasis on speaking English to the English-speaking patient too. I would prefer to speak Spanish to the patient who speaks only Spanish. You try to speak to the patient in terms that are familiar to them in a matter-of-fact, everyday language. Because in presenting things in matter-of-fact, everyday language they tend to accept it casually. How do you explain about childbirth to a first-time mother? As surely as you explain in medical terminology, she wonders if it is as bad as that. (Laughter) When you explain to her about uterine contractions, "You know, the uterus is a muscle, and you know what muscle contractions are," so you demonstrate with your biceps. The patient begins to think about the uterus as a muscle, and it contracts.

H: Well, you have a way of getting the patient to do something. Then is it necessary to make a shift so that the idea gets across that they're doing something on their own volition?

E: Suppose I take the example of this morning. This woman came in this morning, and she said, "I've got a very bad sinus. I know that's correct. My face is aching, and my face is hot. I've got a horrible headache. And I don't think I've been behaving very well. My sexual behavior has been pretty bad. I don't think I am improving at all. I think I'm slipping. I think I'm going backwards." I don't know what it was in her tone of voice, but this frank, and open, and ready negative attitude; I said, "Well, what do you really think?" She said, "I wonder if I'm in pretty serious shape?" I said, "You're wondering if you're in pretty serious shape. Do you want to repeat that question again but change it slightly?" She said, "I'm wondering if I'm going crazy?"

I said, "That's not your question at all, and you know it, and I know it. I think it's about time that you stopped all of that pretense. I've been trying for a long time to get you to face the facts. You've been afraid. You wouldn't do it. You've gone in every direction. And you know your headaches have been increasing. Your body pains have been increasing. Everything. Now go ahead and ask that question." She said, "All right, is my husband an alcoholic?" I said, "Would you ask me that question if he weren't?" She said, "No." "So what are you going to do about it?"

Then, when it came to leaving the office, I said, "What about your headaches, what about your body aches? You haven't got arthritis, you haven't got a backache, you haven't got migraines, you haven't really got headaches. You really haven't got an ulcer of the stomach. You haven't got any of these complaints. There's nothing wrong with your heart, nothing wrong with your blood pressure. But for a long time you have been refusing to recognize your husband. What did you do yesterday?"

She said, "I did some sewing." I said, "Yes, you did some sewing. What did you do yesterday?" She said, "I counted his drinks for one hour and a half. Seven double shots of gin in one-and-a-half hours. I didn't pay any attention to the drinks before that, and I didn't pay any attention to the drinks after that; but I knew that last Sunday, and the Sunday before that, and the Sunday before that, and the month before that. I know I can't stand to have him make love to me. I don't want a drunk to make love to me."

So before she left the office, a woman with that long record — even before she came to me — of arthritis, backaches, bellyaches, headaches, neck aches, arm aches. Now, suddenly faced with that particular problem of full recognition that her husband is an alcoholic. What is she going to do? In the past I couldn't get her to face his alcoholism, even in a trance state. I was afraid to. She was an excellent hypnotic subject. She wanted to leave the office with the statement, "I suppose I'll have to go home and face my headache." "My heartache" was really what she meant by "headache," but she was saying "headache."

I told her, "Sit in the chair and cross your legs, relax." She looked at me and said, "Are you sure you can hypnotize me? Because I don't think I want to go into a trance." I told her, "No, you don't want to go into a trance. You don't know what you want to do. You've got to do something, and I don't like the idea of you having physical complaints. You resent your husband making love to you drunk. You are a very reserved and shy person. Now I'm going to bully you. You're sitting there, and I want you to sit quietly. And I can reach over and pat you on the knee, and that's something you don't like. You couldn't possibly like it. You have rather rigid ideas about ethical conduct."

After she went into the trance, I apologized for bullying her. I had stated that I was going to bully her, and I pointed out that she could think through regretfully, without headaches or physical aches, but with emotional heartache, the problem of what she was going to do with an alcoholically sick husband. She's a nurse. And she left free of those physical complaints. She won't have any. Why did I use that word "bullying"? How did she sit and sew and watch her husband for an hour and a half while she counted, and then that resentful statement—she didn't know how many drinks before and how many drinks afterward. But seven double shots of gin in an hour and a half. How much of a bully is her husband?

H: Well, what's she going to do about his drinking?

E: She isn't going to be able to do anything about her bullying husband. She's simply confronted with that malignancy in the family relationship. Her husband isn't going to come in for any therapy. Her husband is a dentist. I had to put her in a trance once so that she could go to the office and have her husband do some simple work on her teeth. There was no way for her to get to the office; she couldn't bring herself. She said she was so phobic regarding dentistry.

Today I asked her, "Remember that occasion on which I had to put you in a trance to send you to the office, and that tremendous phobia you had for den-

tistry?" She said, "Yes." I was very respectful of her
statements about having a phobia, not telling me the
truth; she was awfully surprised with her answer. She
said, "I wasn't a phobic. My appointment was for
Saturday afternoon at 1 o'clock. That's the time when
all the office help leaves. I didn't want him working
on my teeth after having taken a drink. I'm afraid to
know if he drinks while at work." When I put her in
the trance, I told her, "For some reason or other, instead of getting there at 1 o'clock, I want you there
at least one-half hour early, even though your husband has told you to come after the girls leave." Her
husband won't take a drink at the office while the girls
are there. I don't think I could have gotten her to go
to the office. I could not have corrected her "phobia,"
if I had told her to arrive there at 1:15 or 1:30. I don't
think I could possibly have gotten her there. Where
did I get onto this question of her husband's alcoholism? Her tremendous fright reaction about the neighbor next door. He was an alcoholic.

W: You mean the next-door neighbor was also?

E: Was an alcoholic.

W: And she brings this up somehow?

E: She brings it into the therapeutic hour. I learned quite
a bit about a number of alcoholics that she had met.
About her husband not going into the same office
with another dentist because that other dentist drank
at work. Really an irrelevent bit of information so far
as those father relationships, mother relationships,
and those intensely bitter brother relationships to
which she was trying to attach her headaches and her
backaches, leg aches, and joint aches.

W: How did you tell that this particular day was the time
for this move? You apparently had been seeing her
over a period of time, and this particular day you say
to her, "Now tell me this differently."

E: There was that desperate note in her voice when she
spoke about her face aches and her sinus. Haven't you
ever heard somebody speak irritably, and you know
this is it, they've had all the aggravation that they can
take? How do you recognize that?

W: They've had all they can take; they'll get down to cases.

E: Yes.

H: Well, on getting them to do something: If a patient
comes in and starts by doing something voluntarily,
he does it on his terms, which are not the best terms
in the world. So you get him to do something on *your*
terms, but then there's a shift to where he thinks he's
doing something on *his* terms.

E: You know the biblical phrase is, "As a man thinketh,
so he is." What am I having this patient do? She's going to, I hope, open a special savings account, and
she's going to abstract a dollar bill here, and a five
dollar bill there, and she's going to start a special savings account. Economically it's a good thing. Emotionally it's tremendously important. Her resentment
about her husband making his deposits with the bartender. She's making her cash deposits with a savings
account. So often these patients decide, "Well, my husband is an alcoholic, I might as well pour it in too,"
and many a nice person goes downhill that way. I'm
going to let this woman join her husband in an out-
lay of cash in relationship to alcohol. For every ten
dollars he deposits with the bartender, . . .

*   *   *

E: A woman wrote me a letter saying it would take her
some months to get up enough courage to see me, but
she would. She finally did. I pushed her into a corner
pretty thoroughly. She gave me the impression that
I could do that. And she said she had very little self-

control. And that her mother had always found it objectionable to take care of her because of the odor. Her emphasis on the word "odor" told me that it was passing flatus. Now she couldn't really talk about that, so as the therapeutic approach I launched into athletic contests. "You know, to be able to hit a golf ball three hundred yards, now that's something, isn't it. To hit a home run over the fence, that's really something. To swim a long distance, that's really something. A weight lifter who can pick up 200 pounds and (grunting with the effort) lift it up, that's something." (Laughs)

You see where that girl was right then and there? That grunting. And then I told her the body's muscles had the privilege of feeling that they had contracted hard and forcibly and effectively. That the muscles of the forearm, the muscles of the upper arm. That there really was a satisfaction in biting down on hard candy. That every child has learned in some way the absolute delight of swallowing a whole cherry and feeling it go down. She could recognize all those, and she thought it was a very charming dissertation I was giving her. And she thought that every child should have the experience of swallowing a cherry. She mentioned some of the things that she swallowed with particular delight.

Then I spoke about respecting one's feet by wearing proper shoes. She agreed that one should respect the feet and the eyes and ears and the teeth. Then I said, "Of course, you know that tremendous satisfaction that you have after a good meal when you really feel well stuffed." She was rather plump; she did like food—one look tells you that. The stomach deserves to be pleased, and didn't she think it would be fair and honest of her to recognize that her rectum could really be pleased by having a good bowel movement? All the foregoing discussion had been accepted; it was just the foundation. "And what should be the consistency of bowel movement? On a hot day in summer on the desert, and you run out of water, a bowel movement ought to be rather hard and firm due to dehydration. Now a bowel movement after a cathartic ought to be rather watery, because the intestine knows what it is doing. The stomach looks at the food it receives and selects that which it can digest, which is taken from what the stomach digests, and so on throughout the intestines. The bowels should look at the cathartic and recognize, this needs fluid and removal."

Then she went into the question, "But gas, what is that?" I gave her a dissertation on the intestinal floor and how it's a symbiotic thing, that the bacteria in the intestinal tract aid in disgestion, and they aid in digestion by virtue of their own digestion, and there has to be some putrefaction, and therefore there must be the release of gaseous substances. And of course, using technical words and stopping to explain them really put it on a high scientific level. "The rectum should take pleasure in a large firm bowel movement, a large soft one, a long liquid one, or a gaseous one. And one should recognize that there's a time and place for various things. You may eat at the table, but somehow or other – not because it's against the law – you don't brush your teeth at the table. You leave the table. You can wash the dishes at the table, and in a country kitchen where there is no sink, you do wash the dishes at the table by putting the dishpan at the table. Perfectly all right. But when there's an opportunity to wash them in the sink, wash them in the sink. When there's an opportunity to brush your teeth in the bathroom, brush them there. Time and place, and a good time and good place, for the good function of the bowels. But it must be recognized that the bowels' needs supersede those of the person. You may be driving a car and need to go someplace, and it is urgent that you as a person get there, and you get some

sand in your eyes. You'd better park the car and tend
to the needs of your eyes. Never mind yourself as a
person, attend to the needs of your eyes. And one attends to the needs of the various parts of the body,
and repeats those attentions until one gains the
amount of control necessary."

She elaborated on that herself. She went home and
cooked herself a big meal of beans. She said, "You
know, it was fun. I spent the entire day making little
ones, making big ones, loud ones, soft ones." Her sexual relations with her husband had been very difficult.
He insisted on sex relations; she abhorred them because she might pass flatus. Now she has a baby.

W: I'm very struck by the beginning buildup of control,
more and more control. Reminds me of the paper in
which a man had some sort of a tic, and you showed
him it could be increased, and if it could be increased
it could be decreased.

E: Yes. She really had a good time. She enrolled in college.

W: But first the acceptance.

E: Now, this batting a home run, this hitting a golf ball,
so far removed that foundation of sports, and then the
weight lifting (he grunts). I was talking about sports,
wasn't I? Or was I?

W: The answer is yes.

E: But whether she understands, in that sense, the nuance
was there. Not any direct attack upon her bowels, and
yet there was that nuance of meaning, the weight
lifting.

W: She gives you the nuance cue in that little reference to
odor.

E: Yes.

W: You build up from nuance.

E: I'm going to go out and see her baby.

*   *   *

E: The girl I just interviewed is very much depressed. She's
   one of these quiet girls, thoughtful girls, rather intense girls, who feels her emotions very strongly but
   does not express them too much. She took a certain
   position in the chair. She's been married several years,
   seven years, and has a six-year-old child. She took a
   certain position in the chair which made it imperative
   for me to ask her about her premarital affairs. Some
   day I'm going to run across a woman who takes that
   particular position without having had premarital affairs, or who has not been stepping out on her husband.

H: Well, what's the position?

E: (Demonstrates) A little bit more than that, but the
   knees are differently placed. There's a certain position
   of the hands, of the shoulders, a certain position of
   the head. Of course, the girl was amazed so tremendously because I wanted to know about the premarital affairs. I think too she stepped out on her husband,
   but there was something very special about the premarital affairs – something very special about them.
   She looked at me rather amazed and said there was,
   that the one premarital affair entered into her present depression. She didn't know that. I made use of
   the trance state off and on. I asked her a question and
   told her to let her unconscious answer it. I worded it
   for a "yes" or "no" answer. She is very much . . . well,
   she was not in full recollection of all of her answers,
   and she has a tremendous conscious feeling that her
   unconscious is giving every correct answer. It amazed
   her because she didn't know some of the answers.

H: What you've done then is noticed this position before
   and then found out there were affairs, so now you assume it's correlated with the affairs?

E: I'm looking for the time when I see that sort of thing
   in all the body position, and there's been no affairs.

With this girl today, I was tremendously hesitant, seemingly uncertain, tremendously gentle, over and over again changing a word in a sentence. Now the rapport that I established with that girl—she just didn't want to walk out of the house. Just didn't want to walk, and she told me how for three months nearly every day she sat down at the phone and sat there with a hand on the receiver looking at my name and phone number in the phone book. Should she call me or shouldn't she? For three months. Every day. And she almost didn't get here. And the rapport with her was tremendous. I was so utterly taken by that girl as a hypnotic subject. I told the girl, "I asked you about your premarital affairs, and I asked as if I knew all about them, and that rather startled you." She was sitting something like this, and I said, "I asked that because your unconscious mind had done something that told me you'd had premarital affairs, and she said, "Why, I thought it was just a question." (Demonstrating changing her position) (Laughs)

H: She shifted her position?

E: And put her feet right back, and changed her body position and her head position. (Laughs) "Well, I thought it was just a question you asked me." I said, "No, it's the acuity and the capacity of your unconscious mind to understand and to answer." You should have seen that beautiful smile on her face, and that glazing of the eyes as she went into a trance to accept that thank you. Now, therapy with her is going to be done where even I won't know what part of the time she's in a trance and what part of the time she's out of a trance. But I do know that I have all the rapport in the world that I could ever ask for. And you always look at patients when they come in to see you, what sort of positional evidence they give you.

H: It's one thing to see it, and it's another to be able to interpret it.

E: Some day I'm going to see a woman who takes that posture and who hasn't had an affair, and then I've got to figure out why that posture.

(Interruption for a surprise visit from an ex-patient)

E: Periodically I have private patients, some as long ago as 25 years, come back and check up on me like this. That grandmother in Boston. It was a marvelous experience. I was lecturing and she came in to greet me. Still a good hypnotic subject. It wouldn't take long to put her back into a trance.

H: What was this girl's (the visitor's) problem in the hospital?

E: Oh, that was some peculiar type of stuporous withdrawal.

H: It wasn't schizophrenia?

E: No, it was a psychotic reaction, as I recall it. At first sight she looked like a catatonic schizophrenic, and as you got acquainted with her you wondered what the diagnosis was. It wasn't manic. It wasn't a depression. But it was a tremendous psychotic reaction with much fear and uncertainty. I don't remember enough about it. Oh, incidentally, what do you think I wrote on that picture of me? (He had given the visiting patient a picture of himself.)

H: I don't know. I wondered.

W: I think I got a look at it. From what I gather you thanked her for coming to see you.

E: That's right. You saw the tremendous emotional reaction. For me to give her my best regards would have been a horrible thing to do, isn't that right? But I thanked *her*. Where does that put her values in her own eyes?

W: This makes her very important.

E: Yes. It hasn't detracted from me one particle, but it's increased her importance in her own eyes, increased her own respect. It elevates me at the same time it elevates her. She's got a tremendous motivation, and I have given her my best regards. She's paid off. Should I write it across the face of the picture, or across the back of it? And when will she find *that* out?

H: When will she find what out?

E: Find out that I wrote it across the back of it rather than the face of it.

W: She knows it, but she doesn't realize it.

E: Yes. She is Spanish, isn't she?

W: Yes.

E: What is she going to do with that picture? She's going to frame it. The picture is for all to see, but the message . . .

W: The message is for her.

E: It's for her. That's when she finds that out. (Laughter) Because I hesitated, I thought about it.

W: Not a public message, it's a personal message.

E: Yes. I thought it over, hesitated, and then I put it on the back. Of course, she can get these frames where you slide out the back.

W: She can get another look at it.

E: That's right. But it's her personal message. And she's going to find it out just as soon as she gets it framed.

*   *   *

E: This reminds me of another patient who came in. Her name was, let's say, Mary. I didn't recognize Mary. Mary had gotten up in the middle of the night, and she didn't want to awaken the children, so she had taken a healthy swig of cough syrup from a bottle in which she had carelessly placed some lye.

She reacted to her hospitalization, and her terror, and all the damage she had done, by developing a very severe psychotic state with a profound withdrawal. She had been committed to Arizona State Hospital. Her normal weight was about 110 pounds. They had put a stomach tube in to feed her, to build her up, so that they could eventually operate on her esophagus and build a new esophagus. She'd been there about six months getting 4000 calories a day. Profoundly depressed, passive, schizoid, apparently hallucinating. Taking 4000 calories a day, and her weight was slightly over 80 pounds.

So when I joined the staff at Arizona State Hospital, I ran across her in the hospital. I didn't like that history, so I took over the feeding of Ann. The tube feeding. I reduced the intake of food to 2500 calories; that's enough for her to gain. It's just a waste of time to ask her body to try and digest 4000 calories; 2500 is enough, she weighs 80 pounds. Let's see, I think one of the first things I did was get some nice fresh horseradish. I explained to Mary that before I fed her I was going to put some horseradish in her mouth – you see, she couldn't swallow at all – and to chew it.

W: But she could smell and taste and chew?

E: That's right. At every tube feeding, chewing gum, catsup, tabasco sauce, cinnamon bark, cloves.

W: Something to stimulate.

E: Something that ordinarily initiates the process of digestion. Mary built up to 110 pounds very rapidly. Then she was discharged, sent to a general hospital for an esophageal repair. By the time she got out of the general hospital, I had left the Arizona State Hospital and gone into private practice here. About three years later Mary said that she just couldn't stand it any longer. She had to look up that doctor. We discussed her social adjustments, her marital adjustments, her family adjustments, and her adjustments to the operation. Then we took up the question of food, and all the talks I'd given her while handing her gum or cinnamon bark. She had really gone into cooking with her kids to teach them to enjoy food.

But you see the simplicity of handling her? Calories wasn't the answer. Getting the patient to chew gum, that smarting horseradish, the biting, burning horseradish. Here's a very, very passive patient, months of experience being passive. Therefore, I started the procedure with something I was dead certain she would spit out. But she would taste it. I made certain I'd get my patient to *do* something. I wanted her to use her mouth in relationship to her tube feeding. You are going to use your mouth when you get a mouthful of nice, fresh, strong horseradish. (Laughter) And you're being tube fed at the time. Instead of that passive role of letting it be poured in, she was being very active with her mouth, which is connected with her stomach. Then, of course, after that I could give her anything else, and if she showed any tendency to be passive about it, I always had something that would bring action. The nurses, of course, thought I was foolish until they saw the patient beginning to gain weight. But you see that manner of participation—*doing* something.

CHAPTER 9

Some Psychotic Problems

1961. Present were Milton H. Erickson, Jay Haley, and John Weakland.

H: John's got a problem that we might bring up. He's got a mute schizophrenic boy that he's been struggling with.

W: I'm struggling with the whole family, and the boy is essentially mute. I've heard him say a few words, and he is reported to talk a little bit to his mother or to his father separately. Never when two people are there in hearing range together. My feeling is that the parents have been making some visible changes in how they deal with each other, but the boy is still just as mute as ever. He looks a little more with it, but that's about all I can say.

H: He's 16?

W: He's 17. And he's a long-standing case. He's been in bad shape since he was a little kid.

E: And he's catatonic then?

W: Yes. I'm told there is a question about getting him to be more expressive, complicated by the fact one of the main themes of the parents has been to get him to talk by any means. This also has the implication – get him to talk and leave us out of the picture.

E: George had been in the hospital about six years. He was in his twenties. He had never been known to utter anything except neologisms. Usually a neologism or a meaningless phrase. "How old are you today?" "Two and bear." "What day is it today?" "Up one and down brown." Then sometimes just noises.

So I sat down with George, and I very carefully asked him dozens of questions and wrote down his replies. There was no pattern to them at all. So I got a great variety of possible replies. Then I started duplicating them, paraphrasing them, until I had a thousand or more. Then one morning at 8 o'clock I sat down beside George, and I said, "Good morning, George." He gave me an idiotic reply, so I replied in kind. So he replied in kind. So we had a steady conversation. Up until about 11 o'clock – complete nonsense.

And finally George said, "I'm getting tired of this." I said, "So am I, but I don't mind." He said, "What do you want to know?" I said, "I'd like to take a history of you?" "Square holes and barefoot." So I replied in kind. A few minutes later he said, "Why do you want to take a history of me?" I said, "Because I'd like to get all the information I can from you." He said, "Why are you talking this nonsense to me?" "Because it seems to be the sort of stuff that *you* enjoy talking." (Laughter) He said, "Well, if I give you my history, will you leave me alone?" I said, "Certainly, until I want the mental examination. I don't know when I'll take that." So George said, "All right, after lunch I'll give you the history."

He interrupted his history several times with nonsense, so I joined in. But I got the history. A few days later I told George I was going to do a mental examination shortly. I got the nonsense replies, to which I replied. George and I became very close friends. He cut out his nonsense talking. I was able to send him home. I was able to have him get a job. But you sit there and talk that idiocy.

H: Are you suggesting that with a mute boy you should sit there and be mute with him?

E: No. I was thinking what I've done with the mute ones. Looked them over and said, "Let's see, your name is Raymond. No, that's not right, it isn't Raymond; it's, oh yes, I wonder why you wear brown shoes? Your name, of course, is Harold; but that isn't a red shirt, that's a blue shirt. Oh no, that's right, your name isn't Harold."

Have you any idea how absolutely irritating that sort of thing is to one of those mute patients? Sooner or later he's going to say, "My name is John, and this is a red shirt, and those are black shoes." But you're softspoken, almost apologetic at times, because you correct your error. "Of course, it's rather early in the morning to be talking to you, but wait a minute, is this early in the morning, or is it early yesterday, or is it late next week?" You really don't know. They try to shift their attention away from you. But you know there's something awfully morbid about a normal person, the doctor on the ward, sitting down and pulling that stuff, and their attention gets dragged back again and again.

Phillip had been in the hospital ten years and had not spoken a single word. He stared straight ahead. So I sat down beside him with a great big pad of paper, and my statement was, "I want to take your history. I want to find out a lot of things about you. I've got plenty of time to do it. So I'm going to ask you questions, I'm going to write them down. Then I'm going to write down any answers even if I have to give the answers myself. Now your name is Phillip Jones. Let's see, Phillip is spelled 'Y-t-u-w-x-z.' Now let's see, Jones, that's a hard name to spell, 'I got a look from you.' Your age? Let's see, I know you're older than my baby boy. You're not as old as my father, so you must be 103." I wrote it down. And he finally grabbed the notebook from me and the pencil and said, "Don't write any more nonsense." It's a very painful thing. Phillip and I later became very close friends. I could walk in, sit down and chat with him, and discuss a lot of things. Phillip's explanation was, "There's nobody around here worthwhile talking to except you."

W: What you do, then, is take their refusal to give you information as a license to be wrong. I mean, they're keeping you from being informed . . .

E: Yes, and therefore I have informed them of the fact that I'm completely uninformed. I am completely uninformed when you try to spell Phillip with a "y" and a "z" and a "w." But you're recognizing that they *aren't* going to give you any information. You recognize that you've *got* to make a *record*. You'd better make that record because that's your obligation. But you make the record without information because they didn't give you any information. And "W-x-y-z-l-k" doesn't spell "Phillip," so there's no information about his name there. But you're frustrating the patient's own symptom.

H: A mute patient has so much power.

E: But he doesn't.

H: If you see him with the family he does.

E: Within the family, yes.

H: With anyone else who tries to get him to talk he immediately has the advantage.

E: You see, whenever you violate, effectively, a patient's system of symptomatology – Herbert stood in a corner in his nightshirt. Had been standing there six months, night and day. He had to be tube fed. I asked Herbert why he had to be tube fed. He said he had no stomach, he had no bowels, no throat. I asked him what happened to the tube feeding. He said, "Haven't you ever seen these stage magicians? Dr. Hause is just pulling a magic stunt on me. He pretends to tube feed me." I said, "Well, Dr. Hause is discontinuing you and he's turning it over to me. I'm going to tube feed you." He said, "Oh yes, you'll tube feed me the way they all do. I haven't got any stomach, no guts. You go through the motions of tube feeding me, but you won't tube feed me." I promised him that I would tube feed him next week, and he himself would offer me the proof. The proof that he had been tube fed. Each day that week, every time I saw Herbert, I reminded him about next week. The next week, of course, I tube fed him. How would you tube feed him?

W: I think I've got this one. You're giving him an emetic?

E: Oh no.

W: No? Wouldn't this do it then?

E: No. I fixed up a tube feeding of raw cod-liver oil, vinegar, baking soda, and milk, eggnog. When he started belching raw fish, rotten fish, there was the inner proof. I got him with rotten fish. The emetic he could take as an assault. I told him, "Now I think that belching of yours is proof that I fed you. Of course, you don't have to be satisfied with it, but I'll see to it you belch every time I tube feed you." He finally said, "Don't tube feed me anymore with that rotten fish." Then he ponted out that tube feeding wouldn't do him any good because he had no colon.

W: He was really asking for it.

E: I told him I thought he had a colon. I was positive, but I'd let him get the proof all by himself. All by himself. So I slipped a cathartic in his tube feeding one night, locked him up in his room and put him in restraint in the bed. The cathartic was scheduled to work about 6 a.m. He was restrained in bed. He didn't mind that— until 6 a.m. the next morning. I was down there, and when he yelled to be taken to the bathroom, I pointed out, "But you've got no colon." I fed back statements until he finally crudely told me what was going to happen if I didn't believe he had a colon. All the way to the bathroom I kept asking was he sure.

Then he said he could be tube fed and he could move his bowels, but he couldn't eat solid food and he could not put a glass of anything up to his mouth or feed himself. I told him that I was willing to bet that next week, on Monday morning, he would be pounding on the dining room door asking to be allowed to go into the dining room. That there would be a glass of milk on the table awaiting him when he finally got in there, and that he would drink it. Well, he just jeered at me. But the next morning at 6 a.m. he was really pounding on the dining room door. When it was opened there was a glass of milk there. He went in and drank it. In tube feeding him the night before I put plenty of salt in him to dehydrate him in a most gosh awful fashion. He was literally dehydrated. He was dying of thirst. I had all the bathroom doors locked, so the only source of water flowed through the dining room.

Herbert came out of it. He was discharged from the hospital and hired by the hospital. Years later he was still working in the kitchen. To teach Herbert to eat food, I sent him out on the hospital farm in mid-winter to get cold. Then I brought him in and stood him in the kitchen right where he could smell all the nicest kind of food. Then I had the cook, who really liked to eat, sit down beside him and feed her face. Without inviting him. Until finally he demanded to be invited to have something to eat.

That's manipulating, maneuvering. That's taking the patient's own symptom and handling it. He called that place in the kitchen his punishment corner. Smelling all that nice food that he couldn't eat. I argued it wasn't a punishment corner. As long as a man can't eat, the least you can do for him is give him some nice odors.

W: That's real benevolence.

H: Yes, that is.

E: Herbert had one other thing. Herbert had a lifetime history of gambling, and he was an expert at cards. To get him to participate in ward recreation was literally impossible. There were four badly deteriorated patients who played cards all day long. One played bridge, one played poker. It was primarily a matter of picking cards up and dealing them out, and tossing the cards in and saying, "I win the pot, that's my hand." Whoever spoke first got it. They each kept their own scores, all day long. So I stood Herbert behind one of them so he watched the game. I told him I thought it was interesting. Herbert said, "That's torture watching those men do things like that with cards." I said, "There is only one way out of it. Teach so-and-so how to play a game." So Herbert taught another patient a new game of cards. But that was horrible, to stand there all day Sunday watching that card game.

*   *   *

E: I put John and Alfredo on the same bench. John knew he was Jesus Christ, and Alfredo knew *he* was Jesus Christ. (Laughter) John would say, "Listen to that crazy guy; he says he's Jesus Christ, and I am. You know it and I know it." I'd step over to Alfredo, and Alfredo would say, "He says he's Jesus Christ; that man's crazy. I'm Jesus Christ." We'd talk, and, "Yes, that man's crazy; he claims to be Jesus Christ." I'd step back to John, "Alfredo there *claims* he's Jesus Christ and you know damn well he's crazy, and Alfredo knows damn well that you're crazy, because you *claim* to be Jesus Christ." (Laughter) That went on day after day, with me wondering, "Now John, you say that you're not crazy, and I hear you saying exactly the same crazy things that Alfredo says."

Finally, one day John said, "You know, I've been thinking it over. He claims to be Jesus Christ, and I know he's crazy, and you know he's crazy. Only he doesn't know he's crazy; that's why he keeps on saying he's Jesus Christ. I'm saying that, and he thinks the same way about me that I think about him. It looks to me as if we're both crazy." I said to him, "That's the way I feel about it; that's the way every nurse in the ward feels about it. You know, Jesus Christ wouldn't have to claim to be Jesus Christ. But John, you have yelled it and screamed it and shouted it. I don't think that's very Christ-like. I think that's just plain crazy behavior."

So John said, "Well, there's one test I'd like to make. Will you take me to the library? And we'll pick out a book." He looked through it, and he said, "Let's see now, there's a capital T and an h, there's an o, and there's an r, and there's an n – T-h-o-r-n – and there's a t, and an o, and there's an n. That's my name, Thornton. And there's my name on that page, too. So this book is written about me." I said, "Well, let's see. There's a capital E, there's an r, there's an i, yes, a c, and k, and s-o-n. E-r-i-c-k-s-o-n. I think, John, the book's written about me." "Somebody's crazy. It isn't you. Let me think it over awhile."

So John discarded all of his delusions. He became the hospital librarian, and then he went out and got a job. Four years later he was still gainfully employed, no delusions. Now and then he'd visit the hospital to see how Alfredo got along.

Yet doctors would criticize me horribly when a patient would tell me, "I'm framed, I don't belong here,

I'm not crazy," and then I would ask him if the other patients were crazy if they were locked up, and who should be locked up. "Crazy people." "Are you locked up?" "Yes. But wrongly so." "If you were crazy, would you *know* it? "No." "And you don't know that you're crazy, do you?" Yet I was accused many times of being harsh and unsympathetic. Always avoid the issue: "The Institute of Euphemisms," The Hartford Retreat. Now and then a patient goes there and just blows his top, "I am a patient, I'm not a guest, and that *is* a nurse, not a psychiatric aide, and this is a hospital grounds, not a campus." Yet the staff there very carefully tried to educate the patients in euphemistic living.

H: It's a very insidious kind of thing.

E: It's damned profitable. (Laughter)

W: It's profitable in other fields too.

E: I got horribly condemned the other day — I think I mentioned telling a woman to get out of town with her kids.

H: No, I don't think you mentioned it.

E: I was *royally* condemned because I told a doctor's wife, "From what I know of your husband, and I know a lot, you came here because you're worried about him. I think you've got reason for it. I think you ought not waste any time. You've got your car, you've got the kids. Get the hell out of town. Get out of the state." She took my word for it, and she just beat it. Later her husband came in, after getting sympathy from some others, and he complained about *my* sending his wife out of town. He came in and cussed me out. The next day he showed up and said, "What shall I do with that revolver? I loaded it. I was going to kill her, and the kids, and myself. I think I've come to my senses."

H: Whew!

E: Now he's not going to go around and tell people he criti-

cized me too. I could have sent her home and kept my
mouth shut when the corpses were found.

*   *   *

H: We would like to know how you treat the ambulatory
schizophrenic. For example, how do you handle the
schizophrenic who is hallucinating and has delusions.
Or, for example, the patient who comes in and says,
"The neighbors are shouting at me, and everybody
says the neighbors aren't shouting at me, but I know
they are."

E: I had a patient come in who was plagued and pleased,
annoyed and delighted, about those nude young men
who floated about ceiling height above her as she
walked down the street.

H: (Laughter) I'll be damned.

E: Half a dozen of them. They talked to her, sometimes
discussing art, literature, music. Sometimes they talked
crudely on the subject of sex, sometimes even horrifying the patient on the subject of sex. They were
nude. Sometimes they had erections, and sometimes
they didn't. She came in here. How would a prospec-
tive employer feel about those? What are the neighbors going to think? What did I think? She walked
in here, she circled around, and with great difficulty
she sat down on that chair. She wanted me to define
the situation. Why did I keep a bear trap there that
was set? She described it to me. A great bear trap set
ready to spring. I told her that it was a rather involved matter that couldn't be explained in just one
session. She kept looking over in that alcove there,
and she asked me if I didn't feel it was rather un-
professional to keep half a dozen nude dancing girls
in my office when I was interviewing patients. She
didn't like the way her young men were looking at my

dancing girls. (Laughter) She objected rather strenu-
ously. But I told her if she could have young men, I
could have dancing girls. What did that do?

H: I don't have any idea.

E: My rights are to be respected; her rights are to be
respected. It validated her hallucinations; then she
could view *her* hallucinations in the same way I could
view *mine*. (Pause) Isn't that right? And if I could take
a *good* view of *my* hallucinations, then she could take
a good view of *her* hallucinations. She could take the
same view of her hallucinations that I could take of
mine, but she didn't recognize where that would lead.
Because my view of the dancing girls was quite different from her view of her dancing boys. But I had
it established right there. I promised her that my
dancing girls would be faithful to me, that they *would
not* become involved with *her* young men. I had to tell
her why — because they belonged to me, they were
mine. Besides, the young men were only interested in
her; they had no eyes for my dancing girls.

H: You began to treat this like a trance hallucination to
take it over?

E: Yes. And let her have her wishes. She didn't want to
share those young men with any other dame or dames;
they belonged to her. And I established her right. I
established my right to the dancing girls.

H: I gather you wouldn't interpret the bear trap in any way
to her, such as she was a little worried about what you
were doing in the office.

E: No. When the telephone rang, I stupidly, thoughtless-
ly, started walking into that bear trap. She leaped to
her feet, put out her hand and pressed me back. Thereafter I walked in and out of the office, when she was
there, *around* the bear trap. I didn't explain to her for
many interviews that bear trap. I told her eventually
I'd remove it. But my purposes were mine, and I didn't

feel accountable to her how I ran *my* psychiatrist office. Again defining me as a psychiatrist. I slowly raised with her the question of when she would want those young men floating along over her. All the time? At least I didn't think they ought to go into the bathroom.

H: You treated that like you would any of the symptoms? Like a neurotic symptom?

E: Yes. Then, I didn't allow my dancing girls to go out in the living room. No reason why they should trouble Mrs. Erickson. Those were *my private* dancing girls. "What do you do with them when you have other patients?" "Patients who won't appreciate them? I have them out of sight." For the patients who won't appreciate them, the dancing girls were out of sight. And she felt that was a good idea. Many people are so unappreciative of things. Why try to force them to appreciate that which they cannot? Which then gave me the opportunity of wondering if she wanted those young men to go into the offices with her where she wanted to apply for work. I kept the dancing girls out of sight for people who wouldn't appreciate them. It wasn't long before she thought it would be a good idea to leave them here. She applied and got a job, but she was at liberty to come here every day if she wanted to and enjoy her young men. They didn't mind staying here, and she discovered that the dancing girls had no eyes for her young men. That they really liked only me. And sometimes I'd banish the dancing girls, so that just she, the young men, and I were in the room. Then sometimes I'd banish the young men too. They are still in that closet you know. (Laughter)

She taught school for four years, a high school counselor. Now and then she came in to check on her young men. She is out of the state now, holding a good secretarial position. She is catatonic schiz, always will be. Periodically she'll write me a letter, wrap up a lot of catatonic symptoms in it, and send it to me to put in the closet along with the young men. They are there and she can come back here any time she wants to, and the young men can come out of the closet. She's a chronic catatonic.

H: With her you just try to make that as easy as possible on her?

E: She writes me her letters and she wraps up her symptoms. When she first became my patient she was some $3,000., some $4,000., in debt. She paid that off, paid me off; she has accumulated savings. I don't know what the eventual future is going to be. I think that by the time she reaches 40 or 45, she'll break completely. But I think she will have had a reasonably productive life from 27 to that age.

H: One time when I was here there was a blond girl who had just gotten married and you said she was an acute schizophrenic the year before.

E: Yes.

H: I gather she had a better result?

E: Oh yes.

H: How did you treat her?

E: From earliest infancy her mother had hated her. Her mother used to take advantage of her father's absence to spank her as an infant. She got punished all along the way. She told her that she was hideous and homely, that she had no future, that her father was no good, that he was selfish. Her mother kept insisting that she, the mother, was once a beautiful girl but that this miserable child had ruined her looks for her. My problem was to teach her to recognize the fact that she was a pretty girl. And that she did not have to overeat. That layer of fat — I was so curious about the beautiful thighs inside that wrapping of blubber. And that's what I called it. Her thighs were horribly fat, her hips

were horribly fat. She was definitely overweight. I
was curious about those pretty thighs, those pretty
hips, and that pretty belly, with all that wrapping of
blubber.

H: What kind of symptoms did she have?

E: Withdrawal, with that vague sort of fantasy formation,
apart from this world, never fully described, wherein
she lost her sense of reality. Trying to find out where
the arm of the chair is, feeling it, and looking everywhere to see the arm of the chair. But no coordination of the tactile sensations with the visual. Where
is the arm of the chair? She can feel it, but she can't
find it visually. That sort of defect. And I was so interested in finding out what that pretty girl was underneath that wrapping of blubber.

She's married, happily so. She's going to have her
baby this summer. She married a very nice young
man of whom I approved. Her wedding? The mother
and father separated. The girl asked me, "Should I invite my mother to the wedding?" I said, "Your mother
will come to the wedding. She'll throw a very weepy
scene; then she'll throw an hysterical scene. Then she's
going to denounce you, your bridegroom, and the
groom's parents, and your father. Yet you feel you
ought to invite your mother." You see, her mother had
been over to see me and I knew what she was. "You're
going to tell your mother and lay it on the line for her.
Tell her to sit down, to shut her trap, and to listen to
you. Then, with absolute intensity, you explain to
your mother that she is welcome to come to the wedding, and to be *your* definition of a good mother — well
behaved, well poised, and courteous." The girl really
did lay it on the line to her mother. And the mother
was terrified, and did behave, and she acquitted herself in magnificent fashion.

The girl had one difficulty with her husband about

nine months after marriage. A student – he began neglecting her sexually – too tired. So I had a long interview with her – what to do with her husband. A brief one with him. The girl proceeded to recognize that she had sexual rights, and she was going to execute them, and that she was going to get every sexual pleasure that she wanted, and as much as she wanted, that she enjoyed it so much that he would find it impossible not to enjoy it. And she seduced him into very adequate sexual behavior.

H: When you dealt with her, did you discuss her parents with her, and their behavior with her?

E: Oh yes, what I insisted on when discussing her mother – I called her a flat slob – I asked her why in hell her father shouldn't go screwing around, with a flat slob of a wife like that, who yelled and screeched and beat up the product of what should have been a very happy sexual relationship.

H: How did the girl react when you criticized her mother?

E: I tensed her up; then, of course, I would distract her, and ask her, "Is your elbow comfortable on the arm of that chair?" Then tell her, "Yes, you can't really find the arm of the chair, except with your elbow, and since you can find it with the elbow, you can really enjoy it." So less and less of that visual searching. Then I started in, "You can't find the arm of the chair; it's just your arm, but your arm can find the arm of the chair and you can find your arm."

H: Why did you distract her at the moment she tensed up, when you criticized her mother, rather than let her tense up?

E: Merely to mobilize her emotions. I didn't want her to get her emotions roused up and then try to dissipate them in her own way. I could mobilize them, distract her, and her emotions were right where I wanted them. Then I could offer another criticism of her mother, intensify her emotions, distract her again, and then come out with the idea that if her father wanted a mistress, when his wife denied him sex, I didn't see why it wasn't all right. I had her emotions and her father's rights. After that I told the father to separate from his wife, and live in a different place.

H: You did tell him that?

E: Oh, he would now and then, because his wife would get agreeable, go home and have sexual relations with her. It didn't take the daughter long to find out about that. So I told the daughter it's all right for her father to go outside the house and find a piece of tail, and if he happened to walk in the direction of XYZ street, that was all right too. And if he wanted to walk in L and M street, that was all right too. And all her emotional intensity went into the right of her father to have intercourse, with any woman he chose, including her mother. Actually, of course, the father had *never* stepped out, but the mother had taught the daughter to believe that he had. And building up her emotions and then starting to attach them, by immediate mention of her father's rights, so she became protective of her father and favorably inclined towards his rights. At the same time it gave me an opportunity to let her father really make up for her mother.

H: Did the father and mother go back together?

E: I don't know if they formally reunited. But I do know that he's been staying a week, two weeks, a month at a time with her. The mother is an excellent golfer, likes outdoor life, a marvelous companion, but her husband accepted my statement that if his wife picked a row with him on the golf course, he could *think* of some other place he wanted to go immediately, turn on his heels and leave her there. I've seen the mother here a number of times. They live in California. Time and again I get long telephone calls from the mother.

The mother soon learned to use me as some sort of a father figure that would talk harshly but impersonally to her, so when she'd do something wrong she'd call and tell me about it, and I would whip her over the phone.

H: Why did you want the daughter to get concerned about the father's rights?

E: With whom did the daughter identify? Pretty difficult to identify with her mother except in fatness, in all the wrong things. But her father was a good man, and when she started defending his rights, she started to identify with all the good things about him. You start defending my rights and what happens? You become my ally. You become part of me.

H: Did the mother make any attempts to take her daughter out of therapy?

E: Oh yes.

H: And how did you handle that?

E: The father brought her here. He stayed the first week to see to it that his wife didn't come to take daughter home, and I did everything in the world to build up the rapport between daughter and me. I used light hypnosis on her just for the rapport, and in teaching her the goodness of her body underneath that wrapping of blubber. I could praise her body, tell her how attractive it was; it was still completely wrapped. It was covered not only by her clothes, but by a layer of blubber. She hadn't seen the beauty of her body, and I was talking about it, and so it was rather a remote thing about which I could talk freely. I gave her a good narcissistic appreciation of her breasts, her belly, her thighs, her mons veneris, her labia, the soft inner skin of her thighs underneath that layer of blubber. And her mother had impressed upon her that she was a fat, hideous, undesirable child. The mother's raucous laughter at the little girl when the little girl

stood in the bathtub to take a bath, and the mother
raucously laughing at that hideous child.

H: Did the mother really do that, or did the girl just think
she did?

E: The mother did it. Because I wondered if the mother
had, and as I told you I had the mother here, and she
justified it on the basis that when she got pregnant
against her wishes her husband ran out on her.

*   *   *

E: This great, big, six-foot, fat colored woman marched
furiously up to the nursing station and said, "Fust I'se
gonna just yell, fo' bout 15–20 minutes, and then I'se
gonna break the bones of everyone around here." She
had a history of being violent and disturbed. So the
nurse called me, and she also notified the male supervisor, who sent a half a dozen men up. The colored
woman sat down in a wheelchair, and she said, "White
folks, keep away from me. I'se got my yellin' to do,
I'se gonna do it, and then I'm gonna break your bones."
So I promptly asked her, "Do you mind if I sit in this
chair about this close to you?" She said, "White boy,
as long as yo' mind yo' own business and lets me
scream, you can sit there." So I called the nurse over
to me and told her, "Get me a syringe and put about
twelve grains of sodium amytal in it, dissolved."

The colored woman was really raising the roof with
her screams, taking a nice deep breath and then scream-
ing at the top of her lungs. I signaled to the attend-
ants, "Keep away." As she was taking a deep breath,
I said to her, "Do you mind if I go about my business,
doing what I should do?" "It's all right, white boy, so
long as you don't touch me, but don't talk too much
to me." I waited until the next deep breath, and said,
"If something else touches you, as long as I keep my

hands off and nobody around here touches you, will that be all right?" "Just so nobody tries to tie me up with nothin'." So I said, "Go ahead and scream, really get it out of your system." Holding that syringe, I waited until she threw her head back, opened her mouth for a nice scream, and I squirted the sodium amytal into her mouth. (Laughter) She said, "White boy, I don't understand it." I said, "Go ahead with your scream." She swallowed it.

Finally, when she asked if there were 15 minutes gone by, I said, "Well, I don't think so and I thought it was going to be 20 minutes." She kept on scream- ing, and yawned. Yawned again. She said, "White boy, what did you shoot in my mouf?" I said, "I didn't touch you. I asked your permission to go about my business, and you told me I could, as long as I didn't touch you, and I didn't." She yawned a few more times and said, "White boy, did you give me some sleepin' medicine?" I said, "Yes." She turned to the assembled group and said, "You folks, there's a doctor as knows his business." (Laughter)

She was a psychotic patient. My assault on her was an utterly ridiculous assault, wasn't it? Literally, at a psychotic level, because you don't give medication by squirting with a squirt gun, do you?

H: It's remarkable how it was all right as long as you said what you were going to do, and as long as that was what she said she wanted done, within her limits.

E: I defined my limits, and her limits: a clear understand- ing. Charlie was a disturbed patient, and he stated that anybody that came into his room would be beaten up. I pointed out to Charlie that he had to be put in restraint, and apparently I would have to do it. I said I was coming into the room, and he knew very well he wouldn't have to hit me to knock me down. He could it it with his little finger. I repeated it enough times to know he understood me, and I walked in. "As long as you can do it with your little finger, it won't be necessary for you to hit me. You only want to hit and knock something down, you're not just interested in pushing them down. You want to knock them down, and with me it's a little finger." So I walked in. Charlie said, "I don't understand that. (Laughter) But if you want to put me in restraint, put me in and let me think it over." I put Charlie in restraint quite a number of times. When I was off duty it was a six-man job.

H: That's a peach of an instance.

W: Let me think it over, too. (Laughs)

E: Because I was a man, I was the doctor in charge, and yet you can't knock me down—you can just push me down.

H: You meet the patient's needs.

E: I proved to him that I couldn't possibly meet his needs in knocking somebody down. (Laughter)

* * *

H: We begin to suspect that one of the purposes of schizophrenic symptoms is to top in some way. That he can put his mother or his family in their place very nicely if he does it in a psychotic way; they can't handle this.

E: But he can't get any satisfaction out of it. With the schizophrenic, the parents top the patient, or the patient may top the parents; but neither one of them gets any satisfaction, any real satisfaction, out of it.

H: Yes, I think that's true.

E: While in the hypnotic situation, no matter who tops, *both* get satisfaction. In normal life situations both get satisfaction out of topping.

W: Yes. That reminds me of the story about my patient,

"G." He used to sit on the ward and do nothing. One day the ward doctor finally decided he should get out, so when they took the ward group out they urged him out the door. They got him out on the grounds, and the whole group was moving along, including him, so they figured, "We'll let go of his arms at least." They weren't going to drag him any further. So they let go and he kept walking. He walked absolutely straight ahead in the line in which they had last been directing him until he walked into a tree and bruised his head. Now that certainly seems to be a case in which he topped them in a way in which nobody got any satisfaction out of it. Carrying out what he was apparently asked to do to the letter to such a degree that he injured himself and threw the blame on them.

E: Yes, and nobody was satisfied.

W: Now I wonder what is the difference, the essential difference, that determines whether everybody loses or whether some satisfaction is obtained?

E: The satisfaction that can be derived from dissatisfaction.

W: What determines one or the other?

E: I think it starts in the learning process. The teaching of the child to learn to enjoy satisfactions. When you deprive him of the opportunity to learn the joys of satisfaction, then when he strives for satisfaction, he hasn't learned to enjoy it.

H: How do you prevent him from learning to enjoy satisfaction?

E: I don't know if this is pertinent or not; I'll find out if it is. Mother Kincannon, or Ma Kate as I called her, and others, was my landlady, 70 years old, illiterate, unable to read or write. She took in university students and school teachers as roomers. For some 20 years she'd been trying to get school teachers to teach her how to read and write. School teachers undertook to teach her. I watched the last two school teachers work with her. They used a classroom technique, such as you would use with a little child. Ma Kate was 70 years old. I could see nothing really wrong with the teachers' approach except it didn't apply to Ma Kate. After one whole semester, the teachers gave up. Ma Kate got very weepy about it. I told her I would teach her to read and write in three weeks' time. The teachers jeered at me.

So I told Ma Kate to take the pencil "and hold it any old way you want to, make any kind of a line you want. Now make another one" (demonstrating). I said, "That's the way a pencil writes." I said, "Now, here's something else you can do. You can make a straight line, straight up and down. You can make a line that way. You can make a line that way (in different directions). You can make a line that way. You can make a circle, you can make a half a circle, you can make the other half of a circle, you can make the top half of a circle, you can make the under half of a circle. You can make two straight up and down lines. You can make three, you can make any number of them. You can make a straight flat one, you can make three, you can make any number. You can make slanting lines, any number of them, slanting in any direction. Now go ahead, Ma Kate, fill up a couple of pages with those, because you're learning to write."

She really enjoyed it. I said, "You can make a straight line this way, and you can make a straight line that way. In fact, you can make a straight line that way too (demonstrating). You can make a straight line that way. That's the letter 'E.'" We went on another page.

Three weeks later she was reading the *Reader's Digest*. I didn't teach her, really. I just let her use what she knew. She already knew straight lines, slanting lines. Was Ma Kate delighted to find out the letter "A" was two slanting lines, one slanting one way like the side of a roof, the other slanting the other way like the side of a roof, and a straight line. She started in making words. "L-a-t" didn't spell anything. Two short lines can become "c-a-t." Her construction of words was utterly phenomenal. In three weeks' time she was reading the *Reader's Digest*. Those teachers haven't forgiven me yet. Ma Kate had topped them in all of their efforts—to her disadvantage. All I did was to teach Ma Kate to enjoy the satisfactions that she already possessed.

W: You put them together.

E: She could make a straight line up, and a flat straight line. A slanting line.

W: Something here about putting them together differently.

E: She had all the satisfactions of being able to make pencil marks and to enjoy them.

W: Well, now, if I could take "G" and do something so he could put together differently the satisfactions he gets out of going ahead and out of resisting going, then he would live very differently. He uses them backwards in a sense.

E: You try to get him to learn to enjoy his satisfactions.

H: Well, the schizophrenic seems to get mad when he starts to enjoy his satisfactions. At any rate, this patient I've been working with has discovered that when he begins to enjoy a meal, when he finds he's getting some pleasure from eating, he gets mad.

E: Well, I think that if I had started out trying to teach Ma Kate to read by this method, I would have come up against a stone wall. If my schizophrenic patient gets mad if he enjoys the pleasure of eating, I would teach him the pleasure of a clean plate. I'm thinking of the patient who had been tube fed for six months.

So I got a glass pitcher. The satisfaction I wanted that patient to develop was the satisfaction of seeing the quantity in the glass pitcher decrease. Not the satisfaction of being fed. But the satisfaction of the emptying of that glass pitcher. Then I doubled it by taking two pitchers half the size. And gave him twice the satisfaction.

H: Is that a distraction technique?

E: No, it's a teaching technique. The satisfaction of being fed. Along with which I told him the old Joe Miller joke about the Chinese, presumably Chinese, cultural pattern of burping after a good meal. And a good loud burp. Of course, in tube feeding him, pouring out the fluid into the funnel and letting it run down the stomach tube, I'd allow it to start down and the tube would start to get empty, and then I'd pour in some more and put a bubble of air down in his belly. (Laughs) So I got my burps. I didn't ask him to enjoy the satisfaction of *eating*. It was the satisfaction of burping. Actually, of course, a burp is a reverse when you eat. If you can enjoy the reverse, you can enjoy the obverse. Because his reverse did depend upon the obverse. But that was a safe way to teach him to enjoy his satisfactions, centering around eating.

H: Now, it was also safe in that you weren't demanding that he enjoy eating.

E: Yes.

H: His mother could have taken the way he ate as a statement about her, so if he didn't enjoy his food, it was a statement he didn't like her. To avoid that problem is safe, all right.

W: It seems to me that the original question is not necessarily so much one of — originally at least — learning to enjoy, but how a person learns *not* to enjoy what you would naturally expect anyone to enjoy. If enjoyment of eating gets to be something that you have to do to please mother, then it gets in the way of enjoyment.

E: You can lose a learning so quickly, so suddenly. I'm thinking of the army officer who doted on eels. Stationed in Texas. A friend flew in a shipment of eels to him. He ate them with great satisfaction, and then discovered they were rattlesnakes. He can't look a plateful of eels in the face now. A sudden idea and he lost all the learnings about eating eels.

W: It reminds me a little bit of a story I once heard about an intern in residency in Bellevue in New York. He had friends who were fond of milkshakes, and he would make them up a milkshake. After they had had the milkshake and expressed their satisfaction with how good it was, he would tell them he made it up from the mother's milk supply of the hospital. And quite a number of them vomited.

E: And thereafter avoided milkshakes.

W: Presumably they did, yes.

E: I was discussing that point with a psychologist in Chicago last week. His father and mother, during the war, always had cream for their coffee from the hospital supply of mother's milk. They let some of their friends in on the secret, who still after all these years can't take cream in their coffee. We were discussing that problem of a suddenly violent learning.

H: Well, the violence of that is in the betrayal, isn't it? The deception? You're told it's one thing and it turns out to be another.

E: The betrayal, the deception; but it can certainly cover a whole range of behavior.

*   *   *

E: Have a cigarette.

H: I've got one, thanks.

E: Have a cigarette.

H: You want me to take one?

E: Would you like one? (He offers the pack and takes it away, offers it again and takes it away as if accidentally.)

H: I could see what this would do if I didn't know you were illustrating something.

E: That's right, what would it do?

H: Well, it would be exasperating, but you wouldn't quite feel right about being exasperated. You'd feel you were missing something.

E: That's right. They are bound to reach out and take it. It's an exasperating situation. They've got to do something. I used this technique once in front of a group. I was sitting this way, in relationship to the chair (on right of chair and to one side) and I had arranged very carefully that a young man there didn't have any cigarettes. And he was practically a chain-smoker. I took a cigarette and then extended the package to him. And I had Paul and Hugh and Dave primed. As I started to extend the package, and he started to extend his arm, Paul said, "But Milton," and I turned (turning to his right away from the subject and pulling the package away with him). I answered the question, and then I remembered and extended (the package again). Then Hugh called me (he turns away, again pulling the cigarettes away). Then I put the pack in my pocket, remembered, extended it again. Dave attracted my attention. The chap was without cigarettes, nobody was sitting around near him. It had all been arranged. He wished for a cigarette. After about a half dozen extensions of the cigarettes and taking them away, he just shoved his hands in his pockets and continued listening to the seminar and discussion. After about 15 minutes someone asked him, "Did you get that cigarette from Dr. Erickson?"

He said, "What cigarette?" He said, "He extended his package to you." "No." Every effort to get him to recall that half dozen times I'd extended it and jerked it away—he had no memory of it at all. Spontaneous amnesia.

W: I notice you have "Balinese Character" here.* It strikes a note in relation to that. Where mama says, "Come here, come here." The child comes to her, and she looks away.

E: Hmm. And furthermore, he didn't want a cigarette to smoke. Until finally Paul went over and sat down beside him, and after a while he accepted a cigarette from Paul.

H: Would this have worked, do you think, if he had known you were doing this?

E: If he had known that I was doing something like that, he would have said, "Hand me those cigarettes, you lug." It was carefully worked out as an experimental procedure.

H: He had to believe that you were benevolent and just overlooking it.

E: And through no fault of mine, too. He has to do something; he has to make allowances. And you see my statement to Dave and Paul and Hugh and Joe was that I would induce an amnesia for a literally unforgettable incident. And do it in the course of just a few minutes. And even though everyone in the seminar declared I had done it, he still had no memory of it.

H: That's extremely significant somehow. What would that produce besides amnesia? I mean, you seemed to assume or know that that was going to produce amnesia. Would that kind of thing produce anything else related to it?

---

*Bateson, G. and Margaret Mead, *Balinese Character: A Photographic Analysis*, New York, New York Academy of Sciences, 1942.

E: Well it produces rejection.

H: Rejection of the cigarette. Which is equally important. When Paul first offered him a cigarette did he take it?

E: No, not interested. He was too interested in the seminar discussion, much too interested.

H: Then Paul tried it again and it took several times before he took one?

E: You see, Paul took a cigarette, offered one, smoked it; later Paul took another, offered it, and he turned it down. I think it was three or four cigarettes that Paul offered before he accepted one.

H: If that isn't therapy I don't know what is.

W: Yes. He was very interested in something else.

*   *   *

E: Since this is our last session, how about you . . . I guess you'd like to ask questions.

H: All right. Maybe we'd better start with a big one. The more we think about it, the more we think that example of yours when you offered the cigarette to the guy and then "inadvertently" turned away so that he had amnesia and a lack of desire for cigarettes is the most pertinent thing we can think of for what we think is involved in schizophrenia. In fact, that alone would be worth the trip down here, I think. Are there similar kinds of situations that involve an offering that isn't an offering but that isn't your fault?

E: I've played around with variations of that cigarette deal. But right at the very moment I can't call to mind . . . there are at least a half dozen or a dozen others.

H: Can you think of what more they produced besides amnesia and the lack of desire?

E: Amnesia, lack of desire, loss of interest. Which now reminds me of one. That is systematically planning to bring in a book for someone to read, and systematically always arranging it so they could not possibly get that book.

H: What do you mean bringing it in?

E: Picking up a book to take to somebody. You see, you can do that very easily. You can get the book from the library and keep it out, and yet let your victim know that you have gone to the library each day to get the book. You know darn well where it is; you've got it locked up. And so the book is out. The chap knows that you have laboriously tried to do that favor for him. On one occasion I did it for three weeks, and toward the end of the three weeks he said, "What book?" And I saw to it that he had proof that I went to the library.

H: I see. Is there confusion about remembering the book or the cigarette, or is it just simple amnesia in the sense that it doesn't bother them at all?

E: It's annoying and they tend to forget it.

H: Then when it's brought up to them and they don't remember it, do they seem confused? Or do they just not remember it?

E: They remember vaguely – yes, you did talk about some book to them.

H: Well, on that first example of the cigarette, when Paul asked him if he had been offered a cigarette, did he look confused or did he just not remember it?

E: He just didn't remember it. But that damn trip to the library, that is reinforcing the memory but killing the interest. And very definitely killing the interest.

H: What did you have in mind when you did it? Was it just an experiment to see if it would kill the interest?

E: Find out what would happen.

W: Suppose then you wanted to recharge the interest.

E: To recharge the interest? Drop it for a while and then you can pick up the book in their presence, call their attention to an interesting thing. And you build up enough affect in them so that they are willing to accept the book. Otherwise, *they're* likely to put it down. And you see that in kids all the time. I can think of one doctor's kid – he promised to take them out for a drive every Saturday afternoon, and every time he got some housecalls. The kids wouldn't even let their mother take them out after that. Father also promised that some Sunday morning, next Sunday morning without fail, he would fix up that train table. Six months went by. I got disgusted with him and I told him I'd brain him if he didn't fix up that table. The kids were all through playing with the train. They did help him fix up the table, and then walked out. When he asked me about it, I asked him if he hadn't cultivated that action. After a couple of weeks I assigned him the task of going into that room Sunday morning and playing with the train himself, until the kids got their interest regenerated.

H: Hmmm. Now it would be quite a different situation if you offered the cigarette and the book and they got any idea that you were deliberately withholding.

E: Then it would be just sheer resentment. I know how Paul and Joe and Hugh and Dave felt when they saw me pulling that; they got mad at me – and yet they knew it was an experiment on my part. Yet they were angry about it; they couldn't help but react with anger.

*   *   *

E: What is the basis of the anger the target shooter shows, or the golf player, when he knows that his score was less than such and such? And unexpectedly improves it? The need for altered adjustments. I'm thinking of one of my patients who went out on the golf course early one morning to shoot nine holes of golf; he played alone. He had never broken 80. He just hoped to hit 80; he'd do an 85, 90. And that particular morning he hit a 72 or 73. Something like that. He was so furious that he broke his favorite club. He mentioned it to me later. Another of my patients hit a 67 and came to me and asked me, "Why did he get so mad?"

H: Why did he?

E: His need for an altered adjustment to himself. He need not think of himself as a 73, 72, 71, 70, or 69, he could think of himself as a potential 67.

W: This means if he is more successful he can do better, and that also means . . .

E: An altered adjustment.

W: It also means an altered adjustment with everybody with whom he is in contact, cooperation or competition.

E: But nobody else knows it.

W: Yes, but he knows it'll be different.

E: He knows.

W: If it's different when he's out on the golf course, it may be different when he is in contact with anybody else in any context whatever.

CHAPTER 10

Ordeals

1959. Present were Milton H. Erickson, Jay Haley, and John Weakland.

E: You accept whatever your patient brings you. For heaven's sake, accept it and use it. If he wants to be resistant, you accept it.

W: That's one of the things that has struck us repeatedly in reading your papers. But it's hard to make the transition from reading it to *really* grasping it.

H: There is a question whether you *really* accept it. That is, if by accepting it completely you don't negate it.

E: I accept it completely, knowing that a minute later, or 10 seconds later, I'm going to reject it. Now I can pick this up (he gestures with an object) and really hold it up there knowing I'm going to put it down. But I am holding it there. But it's going to be in the future that I put it down. Therefore, I accept it completely, even though I know I am going to reject it later.

H: You have the odd situation of an actor who can be weeping in despair and yet perfectly well aware whether he's being upstaged. But he really feels despair.

E: That's right. Now to illustrate communication in another way. Burt was home on leave. I was sick and Burt stayed home that evening to keep me company. We lived just outside of Detroit. Burt was gabbing with me, entertaining me. He started reminiscing about our summer vacation a few years previously up on Lake Huron. He talked about the swimming and the fish and the albino frog we found. And the frog legs we ate. And the blue sky, highway, and the woods and the wind in the woods, and the trimming of that tree in the yard, and the poison ivy we dug up. And I had a sudden urge to say, "Burt, why don't you take the car keys and go for a drive." But I suppressed it.

Burt kept on reminiscing, and then all of a sudden while he was mentioning the food we had at summer camp he said, "That reminds me of Aunt Bertha's scalloped potatoes and ham." Then he started talking about visits to Aunt Bertha in Milwaukee. And Allen's behavior in bulldozing his food, and all my sisters and my parents. Again I got a sudden urge to suggest he take the car keys and go for a drive.

From Aunt Bertha's, and Allen bulldozing his food, because Allen put his plate up and just shoved his food in, he shifted to Allen's curiosity about the chickens on my brother's farm. And Allen's question, "How does the mama chicken nurse her baby chickens?" And Betty Alice's remark, "Allen, only mammals nurse their young." I got the third impulse to say, "Why don't you take the keys and go for a drive," but then I recognized it. In a little while he was finishing up about Betty Alice's erudition, and I said, "The answer, Burt, is no." He looked at me and grinned and said, "Well, you'll have to admit it was a nice try, Dad." I said, "Well, really not a nice try; you let me catch on."

H: All that was a maneuver to get the car and go.

E: Yes, he had talked about things that had occurred at the end of a long car trip. Beautifully done, but I caught on to it. "Well, you'll have to admit, it was a nice try, wasn't it, Dad?"

*   *   *

H: One of the things we're curious about, and I don't know whether you can phrase it or not, is you assume that you know exactly what a person should do and a large part of the problem is engineering them to do it.

E: No, that's not quite right. I assume, first, that they should do *something*. Second, I am willing to make an assumption as close as possible to what they should do. Then it's up to them to do the thing that I'm approximating, but the thing that fits them, which I can only approximate.

W: Well, I think that sort of fits in with what we were approaching with patients that are better able to tell us. The patient can be fairly communicative; sometimes you can get him to tell you something that he ought to be doing and isn't doing, because often he knows, and then that can be fed back into an instruction. Some of these people are very much aware of something that they ought to be doing, and they've been putting it off every day.

H: So that in general when you tell them something to do, it's not something they are going to find agreeable. (Laughter)

E: It would be inspirational to find something that's agreeable, that's desirable. It's just inspirational rather than agreeable. (Laughter)

W: I hadn't noticed that most of the things you were getting people to do were particularly agreeable either, Jay.

H: That's right. I tend to see it as in the nature of the psychiatric population of cases; it's very hard for them to do something that's both good for them and pleasant and that they enjoy and that they're successful at.

E: Well, they'll fight against that.

H: Yes.

E: Therefore, you inspire them. (Laughter)

H: One of the things I'm curious about at the moment . . . I had a woman who had anxiety attacks to the point where her hands were constantly wet with perspiration. I suggested she get up and scrub the floors in the middle of the night and realize what a good home she was making for her husband while she did this — every time she was more anxious during the day than she wanted to be. That perspiration just *vanished*. She got over her anxiety attacks almost without — I don't think she scrubbed the floors once.

E: You see, those punitive measures depend upon the nature and character and personality of the patient.

H: Milton, I also had a 17-year-old boy, and I think he's now cured. I had him take a two-mile walk every night when he wet the bed, and he carefully clocked two miles with his automobile and faithfully took his walk. He went from wetting his bed every night to once a week to — the last I heard it was once about every three weeks. But he was eager to get over it.

E: Let's see. Where was that rehabilitation camp during the war? They had 600 bed-wetters there. The army sent the major in charge of them up to see me. (Laughter) I told the major what to do. I said, "Is there any possibility of moving the latrine a couple of miles away from the barracks?" He said he had full opportunity of doing it. I said, "You'll have to play ball with these boys, because if you pull brass on them they won't like it. At 11 o'clock, full-pack, you too, march down to the latrine whether you need to or not. At 2 o'clock, full-pack, march down to the latrine and back. At 4, march down to the latrine and back, full-pack. And explain that this separates the bed-wetters from the non-bed-wetters.

*　　*　　*

E: You can use the concept of energy with your patients. You can say a person is very much like an automobile. You wake up in the morning with a full tank of gasoline, or a full tank of energy, and just running through the day uses up your energy. You go to sleep at night, and you fill up on energy for the next day. You can carry only so much energy within certain limits. Then how are you going to utilize that energy? "You use it all in worrying," I pointed out to a patient who had a ritualistic, phobic, panicky reaction to his television broadcast. Forced panting, breathing, and for 15 minutes he would stand gasping, and gasping, and choking, and his heart would pound, and then they would say, "You're on," and he'd broadcast over TV with the greatest of ease. But each day he became increasingly more miserable. At first it started with a minute or two; by the time he came to see me it was built up to 15 minutes. He was looking forward to 20 minutes, 30 minutes, an hour; and it was beginning to interfere with his other work at the station. I gave him that concept of so much energy a day after I found out what his sleeping habits were. As you would expect, rather ritualistic. Always in bed at a certain hour. Always up at a certain hour. After I got that concept of energy pounded into his head, I pointed out to him, why not use up that energy that he spent that way? (Demonstrating panting.) How many deep squats would it take each day?

H: You mean in the morning before he went to work?

E: That's right. (Laughter) I told him that I didn't know how much energy it would take, but that I thought he ought to start out with 25, even though I thought at least a hundred would be requisite. But he could start out with 25. Have you ever done 25 deep squats?

W: Oh my.

H: I don't want to.

E: No, you don't want to.

W: I got to where only a few is more than enough.

E: And his lame legs. You see, I said 100. I thought that would be a requisite number, but we'd start with 25. His lame, sore legs all day long convinced him that he had used up plenty of energy. He had none left over for that. (Demonstrating panting.)

W: So with something that would make him lame like this, you got it out of the way beforehand, but yet he had a reminder all through the day.

E: His tendency was to reach down (Laughter) to those sore legs of his.

H: You make it seem so simple, Milton.

E: I know. I make it seem so simple. Was it simple the way I looked over that obese woman?

W: No.

H: No.

E: Yet it's so simple.

H: I'm not saying it *is* simple. I'm saying you make it seem so simple.

E: Yes, but there's an awful lot that you do.

W: You give these little instructions, or these little analogies, and they look so simple; but they're covering about five different things all at the same time. Like the idea of energy. He gets it out of the way early in the morning, but he's got something so that he hasn't forgotten it when the time comes that he's going to gasp. He's still got the reminder that he's carrying with him.

E: Oh, I'll finish with what that chap did. He liked that use of his energy. He built up his knee squats, deep squats, as a health matter to reduce his obesity. Then he began going down to the gym to exercise, and he began to enjoy that daily ritual of going to the gym. He came back to me and said, "My trouble is recurring. I really like those squats and building up my body and reducing my weight and putting some muscles on me instead of fat. I've got a lot more energy." I said, "How do you feel about it psychologically?" He said, "It distresses me psychologically, but I'm having a recurrence. I noticed the other day I took three or four deep breaths, and the next program I increased the number, so it is starting to build up. Now what are you going to do, because doing the exercises won't work? I've got a lot more energy."

I said, "It's a profound psychological reaction you're showing." He said, "Yes." I said, "Well, suppose we work on it at the psychological level. Now I know your sleeping habits. You sign off at 10 o'clock. You go right home. You just summarize the day to your wife and then you go right to bed. You sleep eight hours. You're a sound sleeper. You enjoy your sleep. You're a regular sleeper. After four hours' sleep, get up and do a hundred squats." He said, "That I would really hate." I said, "Yes, you can really use up a lot of psychological energy hating that idea. How do you think you'll feel psychologically every night when you set your alarm, as you always do, realizing that you can take up a lot of psychological energy panting in front of the microphone and the television camera? You can take out an awful lot of psychological energy in two ways: one, setting your alarm for the regular time, and psychologically considering with a great deal of intensity of feeling how you don't want to get up in four hours' time to do deep squats." That analogy worked—for a while. He came back.

W: That's a tough customer.

E: Oh yes. I said, "So you have got an excess of energy." He said, "That's right." I said, "Now tell me what has been your lifelong ambition?" He said, "To own my own home for my wife and my child." I said, "It will really make you sweat, won't it, to buy a home and mow the lawn." He said, "My wife has been after me for years, and I flatly refused to budge, but we're buying one this month." He's had no recurrence. He's got a home. He's got a yard. He's using up all his excess energy.

W: He's got a practically inexhaustible reservoir of demand there.

E: There, yes. And his lifelong ambition. Yes.

H: You don't worry about recurrences of symptom particularly then?

E: No. You meet them. With the patient coming back it wasn't particularly alarming; let's see what was developing.

H: But what I wondered is how far this can go in producing a change? Have you ever had a stammerer go through an ordeal every time he stammered?

E: The stammerers are so darn hard to handle because they do insist so flatly and yet so absolutely that they want to talk correctly today and now, and on an entire sentence. Once you can get them to be content to stutter on 999 words in return for saying *one* word correctly, you'll have very little difficulty with those stammerers because they get over it. When they go through those terrific ordeals of physically twisting, grimacing, waving their feet and the back of their head, and their shoulders and their hips, which is a horrible ordeal.

I can think of Joe — sitting in the chair, he would wave both hands and both feet. He'd twist and grimace and wiggle his entire body when you asked him, "How old are you?" I told him to sit very quietly and lean back in the chair and listen carefully to what I said, and that I was going to ask him a question shortly. What he could do instead of waving both feet and both hands and his entire body, he could lift his foot this way. When I asked him, "What number comes before two?" "One." (Brings foot down) There's your physical activity. You can hear it, you can feel it, and you can do it. So I could ask him quite a number of questions—"Two," "eight," "nine." (Putting foot down, or tapping it) Took his mind off of *this* type of activity, but he was still going into activity. But it was a purposeful activity. It was a required activity. It was an unnecessary activity so far as saying "one," "two," "eight," "nine," "21." It had no part in the utterance of the number, of the reply. From numbers we went to "yes" and "no" and so on.

H: I've just been seeing one of those intermittent stammerers, and it's a lifelong deal. I was thinking of setting up some sort of an ordeal she had to go through each time she stammered, to see what would happen. I was wondering if you've ever done that? She doesn't stammer on every word or every line, but she does hit a word every once in a while and then she goes through a facial contortion and gets it out. I was wondering about the possibility of setting up some sort of an ordeal that she has to go through each night if she has stammered once during the day, or twice during the day, or whatever she decides on. I wondered if you'd ever done that?

E: I'm awfully wary of setting up ordeals for the stammerer.

H: Why is that?

E: They punish themselves so terribly. They punish other people so terribly. Now there's no punishment involved in that sort of thing, is there? Neither of you nor me nor anybody, no punishment there (stamping foot).

H: What if the punishment is good for them, productive?

E: The stammerer has so much punishment in his soul; he punishes you by making you listen and wait and wait.

W: But isn't the same thing a good bit true with most people with severe symptoms? They punish themselves, punish other people?

E: They punish themselves; but, you see, speech *always* requires two people. The other person has to wait while they speak. A lot of other symptoms – they can have their symptoms, like claustrophobia, all by themselves. They can have their claustrophobia and it doesn't touch the other person. It may *annoy* the other person. But in this matter of defective speech, the other person gets it in the ear.

W: Well, I see that in some ways it's more direct; but certainly, it seems to me, and I think to both of us, other symptoms can be pretty powerful in influencing and disturbing people that are involved with the patient too.

E: Yes, but you see, the neurotic person who is late, they make other people wait for them. But they're late to the show that they're going to attend all alone, and the theater doesn't mind. They may arrive after the last show has begun; they're late – the theater doesn't care. They may arrive at that choice restaurant just before it closes up. Of course all the choice dishes have been exhausted. They have to take what's left over.

W: Well, I think that the next day they would tell somebody about this rather vividly in such a way that they provoke a reaction.

E: That may be, but then it isn't the restaurant. It's the owners who are the remote unknown background.

H: It's pretty hard to have a symptom without its . . .

E: Indirectly influencing others.

H: Of any sort. Because it's always some kind of extreme behavior, and you can't live with somebody with extreme behavior without being tied up in it. But you're kind of uneasy about putting a stammerer through a punishment ordeal?

E: Yes.

H: Have you ever done it?

E: I've thought of it, and I've tentatively approached it, and felt otherwise about it.

W: Did you ever ask one to stammer?

E: Oh, yes. "You see, I really don't know exactly the pattern of your stammering. I'd like to get the pattern so I know what labial and dental and palatal sounds are involved, if any. Whether it's consonants or vowels. So will you stammer for me?" They know that I'm treating them as a physician would treat them for an ulcer. He'd examine the ulcer to find out. There is nothing insulting or punitive about it. But they never really like it.

H: They sure don't.

E: They don't want you to know the labials. They don't want you to know the palatal sounds.

H: Well, it's a part of speech therapy now to encourage them to stammer a bit. I'm not sure how much good it does; I've seen only a couple of stammerers, three, and all of them had been through speech therapy, and none of them have benefited by it. I don't know who does benefit by it.

E: Have you ever encountered a patient that has benefited by the speech therapist?

H: No.

W: No. I had a stammerer, and I had a woman who was a big, mature woman who had a little tiny girl's voice, and they had both been through the routine and it hadn't worked. But it's a flourishing institution.

H: It is. Graduates people every day.

CHAPTER 11

Substituting Symptoms, Puzzles, Passing Examinations

1959. Present were Milton H. Erickson, Jay Haley, and John Weakland.

W: We have one question about hypnosis. Can you really, directly suggest away a symptom? If so, is there any real evidence about whether a substitute takes its place or not?

E: You see, that's an awfully silly superstition that if you remove one unpleasantness it must be replaced by another. It's the most unthinking, bitter superstition that I know. The whole practice of medicine is based on symptom removal. You go to the doctor because you hurt, so he gives you something so you feel better. You don't deliberately go out and get a worse hurt. You break a tooth so you go to the dentist and he corrects it – so you go out and break a leg? No. If you suggest to a patient directly in a trance state, "I want you to stop smoking cigarettes," he may accept that. He may stop. Anytime that he has a need for a replacement for that thing, what does he do? He smokes Luckys instead of Camels. He goes back to the same thing. You don't go to the trouble of learning a brand new thing; you go back to the old, the true, the tried, the familiar. You may modify it by trying Luckys instead of Camels. One of my patients said, "I've smoked every variety of cigarette that has ever been manufactured. That will give you an idea of how many times I've quit smoking."

H: This is such a deep idea in psychiatry that one of the things we've been tempted to do is to persuade a medical school, a psychiatric department, to get a grant to just suggest symptoms away. There is such an idea that this can be done but shouldn't be done. In my experience it is very doubtful that it can be done—just banish a symptom and have it go.

E: You can suggest it away only when the symptom has become . . . well, you have to do more than just suggest it away.

H: I know. But there is this belief.

E: You can ask a person to lose his headache. Now when you stop to consider, what happens to the headache? You lose it. You can suggest that he lose it now instead of three hours from now. If he goes to bed and sleeps for an hour, he'll lose his headache. He can go into a trance and you tell him to lose his headache; he comes out of the trance with his headache gone. Three hours later he's not going to develop it. But if you'd left him alone in the ordinary waking state, he would have kept on with his headache until it came time to lose it.

H: This is such a common idea.

E: I have heard it said, "Cured of smoking, took up eating; cured of eating, took up drinking; cured of drinking, took up heroin; cured of heroin, took up a depression." Well, of course that's a fabricated history and it's false. The patient would have returned to smoking.

H: But you do feel that there are some symptoms that are just about ready to leave anyhow that could be banished?

E: Yes. I can think of one retired soldier, aged 70. At age 56 he had developed tic douloureux. He had a couple of operations – I saw the scars – and he described the alcohol injections with ganglion . . . what's the name of that ganglion? For tic douloureux? That was when he was 56. Every time his face healed up, he had the operation; and the alcohol injections would last about six months. Then his tic douloureux would start.

As the man sat here, I had a pole light in the corner there and I watched his eyes. As he was talking, explaining how he had that pain almost continuously, the stabbing pain, I noticed his pupils dilating, contracting. I noticed the catch in his breath when I would see the dilation of the pupil. I noticed the twitching in his face on the right side. That accompanied the dilation of the pupil and the catch in his breath. So when the man said he was suffering pain, I thought he was. But in the trance state, I explained to him that I thought the pain he was suffering was a habitual misinterpretation, a rhythmical, habitual misinterpretation of the ordinary sensations of the face. That he was a victim of body learning, a conditioned response. I suggested he lose the pain. When he died seven years later, he was still free of that tic douloureux pain.

H: That's not quite just banishing it.

E: No, but I gave him a chance to understand that he had a habitual misinterpretation. Once he got that understanding, he could direct his attention against pain development. As he said, his nose didn't seem to belong to *him*. His face didn't seem to belong to him. Then very shortly everything felt normal.

* * *

E: A girl came to me who was constantly bathing, and she had to dress a certain way in order to read her mail.

She could sit only on certain objects and live in a certain apartment. An exceedingly rigid, limited way of living. Sometimes she bathed as much as 19 hours in a single day, with that tremendous anxiety. She came to Phoenix and stayed here. One of the first things I did to her was let her tell me what utterly, utterly intense anxiety she had to get herself clean. I let the girl impress that upon me until I was thoroughly convinced. She sold me a bill of goods to the effect that she was completely absorbed and all wrapped up in this tremendous anxiety.

As soon as that story had gotten across to me in a thoroughly and most convincing fashion, convincing to her, presumably convincing to me, I pointed out that, absorbed as she would be in this awful, awful, awful anxiety while showering, she wouldn't mind if I watched her. That really jarred her, practically loose from her teeth. That confronted her. She didn't want me to see. She had to admit that she just couldn't have me there. And I pointed out, "But you'd be so absorbed in your anxiety that you wouldn't know I was there." I pointed out to her that it wasn't that bad, that she could be so absorbed that she'd be unaware of me watching her. I was willing to bet that I could rattle the door of the bathroom and she'd notice it.

W: You didn't even have to rattle it, did you?

E: I didn't even have to rattle it. Then I began to just wonder if I would come over and rattle it. You produce a change in a phobic response in the trance state, not as a means of correcting the phobia, but as a means of teaching the patient that the phobia can be removed. The person with a phobia has an absolute conviction; "This is the way life is; it's unchanging. I'll always, always, always have this fear; and nothing can change it. I'm helpless. Everybody else is helpless. There is nothing I can do."

Your therapeutic efforts run up against that brick
wall. In the trance state, in some circuitous way, you
circumvent the phobia, and then the patient says,
"But I am the same person and I can be free of the
phobia." Then they start looking for and accepting
any therapy that would correct the phobia. But previously, because of their absolute belief, they wouldn't
do it.

Take one thing I do with these paranoid type of
people: They tell me that this is the only way you can
view certain things. So I let them educate me to that
effect until they are absolutely convinced that I understand there is just this one view possible. And then
I raise with them the question of planting 10 trees in
five straight rows, four trees in each row, and they
promptly tell me five straight rows, four trees in each
row would be 20 trees, and so I merely arouse their
antagonism and make them go way out on a limb
proving that, and thinking I'm all wrong. And then,
having done that, I point out to them there's always
a different way of viewing anything, no matter how
absolute it is. Then I diagram how you *can* have five
rows of four trees each with only 10 trees. Well, that
is established with the same absolutism as their paranoid ideas. Then they have to view their paranoid
ideas from a different point of view.

H: You wouldn't, with a phobia then, give a posthypnotic
suggestion that would carry for a while to relieve the
phobia.

E: Oh yes, I'll do it *this* way. "You have this phobia, but
it's going to surprise you that some time next week
between a couple of hours on the clock—it may be between 1 and 2, it may be between 11 and 12—you're
going to feel a sense of freedom from your phobia. It
will surprise you. I don't know how long it's going to
last. Of course, the phobia will return, but you will get

that sense of freedom." Then you've used a posthypnotic suggestion and you've used a hypnotic freedom to further enhance their realization that it's not an absolutely perfect thing.

*   *   *

E: First of all, a few comments on the patient I just finished seeing. He's got to take the state board medical examination. He has flunked it twice. It's absolutely imperative that he pass it. He completes about two-thirds of it, does beautifully, and then he gets uncomfortable, frightened, and panicked, and he quits. Now he didn't want to see me, because he couldn't bother seeing me when I was in his home town. Now he's coming a thousand miles to see me. He's got to be back home tomorrow. He wants to pass that exam.

I let Betty go into a trance for him so I could watch his reactions. He did not like the discomfort of his lids batting, but he started to go into a trance as he watched Betty go in. He struggled very much against it. I told him to let them go ahead, but he said it was an uncomfortable habit. After I dismissed Betty, I induced a trance in him by a fatigue technique, that is, just waiting and talking. He developed a perfectly beautiful hypno-anesthesia with his right hand, and of the left thumb and the left forefinger. That distressed him terribly because he sensed *this* more than he did *this*. He became awfully uneasy and then he began to feel a little bit strange. So I let him wake up, and he told me he discovered his hand, so he corrected that right away. He couldn't stand it to have hypno-anesthesia of the hand. He corrected *this*, and I put him back in a trance, and he developed a very profound hypno-anesthesia of the left hand, completing what he had started.

He went through an awful lot of agony correcting that learning, that hypno-anesthesia. He said, "It's uncomfortable, it's uncomfortable." I pointed out to him that he came here to learn something, about which he knew nothing, that would help him. That he always got uncomfortable in the exam situation and then panicked. Now here in this learning situation, he gets a little bit uncomfortable and he wants to correct it right away, even though the discomfort arises from learning. I asked him to explain, since he is a M.D., how could that numbness of his hands constitute a threat of any kind? He said it was uncomfortable. I asked him if it was uncomfortable or an *unusual* feeling? He agreed that it was unusual, but that's uncomfortable. Am I going to get anywhere with him?

H: I don't know, are you?

E: I don't know.

W: But you did get him to complete something that he wanted to get out of.

E: Yes. He's coming back later this afternoon, and I wonder if I can, if he will make any progress in acceptance of the unusual, the unfamiliar, rather than interpreting it as uncomfortable. He also has the typical mystical conception of hypnosis.

H: Well, your goal when he panics like that on an examination is to do what? To get him to accept those feelings?

E: This is what I've done with the state bar exam students, the state medical exams, high school students, college students, and board examination students that I've treated. First of all, I differentiate for them — as soon as I get them in a light trance — differentiate between *taking* an exam and *passing* an exam. They go in there and they try to *pass* the exam with every question. Instead of carefully, thoughtfully, enjoyably writing an answer to a question, they put all the attention,

"Will I pass? Will I pass?" on each fragment of the exam. I teach them the importance of just taking the exam, enjoying recording as much as they know on *this* question. Recording as much as they know on *that* question. A feeling of ease. "This is what I know, this is what I put down. I'll enjoy putting down this, which I know," and to move on comfortably from one question to the next. That's the only way they're going to pass it, you know, if they write that exam with an utter feeling of freedom. They write question one, comfortably, "This is what I know, I'll put it down," and move on to the next.

As one of the law students said, "I flunked that state board twice. I was in a panic the first time, I was in a panic the second time. This time I wrote the answer to the first question, and I felt good about it. I enjoyed writing the answer to the second question. When I finished, I finished early, I went out and had a smoke, a beer. Then my pal came out, and he said, 'Did you pass?' That was the first time I thought about it." He had done a simple writing of an exam with never a thought of passing. Well, he did pass. His friend didn't.

W: This is like the case, you told us once, of your friend who was a golf player.

E: Yes.

W: And you had him play one stroke at a time.

E: One stroke at a time. He's a professional golfer now. That's one stroke at a time. You write comfortably, happily.

H: Well, when you suggest this to them, do you suggest it in just the way you are suggesting it now?

E: Yes. In a light trance or a medium trance, or, for that matter, a deep one. Every time they write the exam that way I find they passed.

H: Well, you make it sound so easy, Milton. Do you usually see them one session and do that, or what?

E: I did one over the telephone long distance. He paid the bill. It took about 20 minutes, half an hour. I told him to get a chair, sit down, hold the phone, lean back, be comfortable. He passed. It was after his third failure. The junior who came in had gotten a flunk on *every* final exam, passed only on his class work and his six-week test, and mid-semester tests and so on. He said he would like to get an "A" on at least *one* final exam. So all I did was say to him, "Well, it would be nice to feel comfortable when you write an exam, and suppose that this year, since you're a junior, you go in and happily write a 'D' exam. All you have to do is write enough on each question to merit a 'D.' Write it happily. Next year is another year." He got an "A" on every one of his exams. You see, he *could* write a "D" exam comfortably. He didn't have to strive, he didn't have to struggle, he was perfectly at ease. And he was only shooting for a "D." He got all "A's." Let's see, I saw him twice, two hours, in preparation. He came over after it, and he asked me please to explain. He hadn't tried to get "A's."

H: You told him to write a "D" on just one exam?

E: I told him to write a "D," a "D" grade exam, for *all* of them.

H: For all of them?

E: Yes. So he could learn to write an examination comfortably. I didn't tell him what I expected him to do. But you see, there was no overwhelming or frightening burden that he was carrying.

H: In thinking over your work, one of the things that's most obvious, and it certainly struck me when I was struggling to do a paper on your work, is that in almost all cases you tend to encourage the person to behave in a symptomatic way, and then you may add something to that, or you may have them do it under special circumstances, but in almost all cases that's what you instruct them to do.

E: Well, take this junior in college. He had been writing "F" or "D" exam papers right along. You're sure he's going to do it. You would like to have him do it comfortably. He got an "F" or a "D" in the past because he fought hard against what he was doing. All right, now let him go along comfortably with what he's doing. He's a *good* student. If he goes along comfortably with what he's doing, he's going to write an "A" exam. But as surely as he fights – so you give him the task of writing a "D" exam, which he's been doing right along. Then he doesn't have to fight against his symptom.

H: Well, it has a little bit more to do with *you* than that, though, doesn't it?

E: What do you mean?

H: I mean he comes to you for help in writing an "A" exam, and within that framework you encourage him to write a "D" exam. Now this is a very peculiar situation for him to be in.

W: This means he not only can't fight the exam, he also can hardly fight you except by doing better.

E: Well, you see, I held out for him – he was a junior – that the "A" exams could come next year.

H: But as soon as you see symptoms as a way one person handles another person, then if somebody comes to handle you that way and you encourage him to behave that way, he can't handle you that way.

E: He what?

H: He can't handle you that way anymore. He can't handle you with symptoms if you're encouraging him to have a symptom.

E: No, he can't. (Laughter)

H: I just wondered how much of your work you see that way? I'll tell you what I did. I got experimenting with this once, and I took a guy who came to me for headaches. But it wasn't headaches; it was pressure in the head and ringing of the ears. All I did was encourage that man to get worse, as an experiment. I didn't do anything else. I told him I wanted him to get control of this and the way to do this is to be able to make it more severe.

E: That's right.

H: I spent the whole time. I never once suggested it would get better, and the man progressively got better and better.

E: Well certainly. (Laughter)

H: Now, this is a point of view that is not common in psychiatry.

E: I know. Did you ever work with a wheelbarrow?

H: Yes.

E: You know how darn hard it is to push? Did you ever drag it behind you? (Laughs) That's right.

H: What's right?

E: Sometimes you can push it ahead of you, and sometimes you drag it behind you. Instead of trying to keep the load ahead of you toward the goal, you leave it behind you. But you get to the goal with it. I don't know if you include in the paper that illustration I gave about the calf. When I was a kid at home on the farm, one blizzardy day, my dad was trying to haul a stubborn calf inside the barn with a halter. The calf was braced with all four feet, and my dad was braced, and they were at a stalemate. I started to laugh at the funny sight. My dad said, "If you're so smart, *you* pull the calf in." So I grabbed the calf by the tail and tried to pull it *out* of the barn. (Laughter) You know what that calf did to me.

W: Right on in.

E: It hauled me into the barn in a hurry. So we were *all* happy. That's the way you handle patients, very often. As surely as the patient intensifies his headache, he unwittingly and unconsciously realizes, "I have too got control over this headache." He says, "Making it 120 percent painful is too darn much, 115 percent is enough, 110 percent is enough. Ninety-five is enough. I'll settle for 85," and down he goes. You don't even have to tell him to diminish it.

H: That's right.

E: All you've done is taught him to take control.

CHAPTER 12

Brief Intervention into a Performance Problem

1959. Present were Milton H. Erickson, Jay Haley, and John Weakland.

H: A man came to me for a difficulty speaking in public. He gets very anxious when he has to speak. He's arranged his life so he has to speak all the time. He's a curriculum director in a school system, and he's constantly talking to groups. Now he can talk to a group of school children without the least bit of difficulty. If he talks to a group of parents, he has all this extraordinary anxiety. Now what's the simple solution for this?

E: (Looking in a file folder) August 24th, one hour; August 25th, two hours; August 26th, one hour. An exceedingly talented concert pianist, a professor of music, could play the piano incredibly, wonderfully, anywhere except in a concert hall. An absolutely rigid . . . where is that letter? When he came out, he had exactly four hours that he could give me. He flew out and arrived on the 24th, and he had to leave on the 26th. He wanted to know what time I could give him – the four hours.

For the first hour, you see my notes, utterly frag-
mentary. The essential thing on the first day was this:
complacent cooperation only, for the trance. He closed
his eyes when I told him to, he held still when I told
him to, he levitated his hand when I told him to, and
it wasn't levitation. He did everything, and I enjoyed
myself with the hour because I've got the note here:
"Actually capable of learning." (Laughter) That sum-
marized it.

In the two-hour session I described his trance of
yesterday. As I talked about his trance of yesterday,
I really took it apart, his complacent activity. He
began wondering about that, and he went into a trance.
I got my hand levitation, I got the eyes closed; he
didn't even know they were closed, he was still visualizing me as if his eyes were open, you see? So I went
all through that, and then I told him that I felt a musician, above all others, should have fluidity in his music.
That music should be essentially a stream of melody,
a flowing stream of sound, rhythmical and fluid. Never
harsh and rigid. I hammered that home, which even
to you doesn't seem to have any meaning.

Then I developed the question of learning processes,
how they are unconscious. How do you actually learn?
No matter what it is? You get the *feel* of it. You learn
to type. You learn "a," "s," "d," "f"; but you can't really type until you've got the feel of it. The *feel* of the
typewriter so when you sit down you *feel* right. Therefore, body attitudes should be free to fit into the fluidity of the music, and the hand movement on the keyboard should not be a straight up and down, or a
horizontal. There should be rhythm in the hand movements so the finger doesn't go from note "a" to note
"b" by the process of lifting straight up from "a," moving straight horizontally to straight perpendicularly
down to "b." It should be a nice curve. A fluid move-

ment, not an angular movement. Do you follow me so far? All right. Then this matter of geometrical progression. One learns a penny's worth today, this week or this month two cents' worth, and so on.

I told him that therapy was over with except for the summary of the next hour on the 26th. In that trance state he had to take that statement, and he had to place a meaning, a tremendous amount of meaning, because his whole future was at stake. He was either going to give a public concert or his professorship at the college was going to be over. That's that. He had his orders. They put up with him and his excuses year after year, and by God, by Jesus, the Board of Regents has had enough of it. The professor is going to give a public concert or else.

So the next day I put him in a trance, reviewed everything I'd said, and then delivered the punchline. "For years you have rigidly refused to play a concert in the concert hall, and you know that music is fluid, and that it should stream not only through and off the stage and through the concert hall, but the music should stream and flow in fluid fashion through the corridors, through the doorways, through the windows. The artist is always a part of his music, and his fluid movements of his hands. There's no room for rigidities."

Well, I got my letter. His public concert was a phenomenal success. The man went back, and I had one of the most thrilling letters. He said he no longer had to practice in that little studio room of his; he could go to the concert hall and practice there and play. His students could come. And now I've got word from the doctor who sent him here about the tremendous success of that long-awaited, and absolutely demanded, public concert. The man is brilliant, very very brilliant.

H: Suppose you start over again and explain why this happened.

E: Well, his brilliance, his acuity, and my emphasis on the fluidity of the music, and then pointing out that even the hands should be fluid in their movements, that they are not angular movements. One does not do it this way, but he does it *this* way, with a curved movement, a fluid movement. No angles, no rigidities, nothing stilted.

W: You got him very committed to this idea in places where he could accept it to start with.

E: Yes. Where he had to accept it. Then that accusation. He is a musician; he told me he was. He couldn't play in public. I have put that down as the most objectionable of all things. Rigidity, angularity, lack of fluidity, absence of flow. In other words, I successfully called his stage fright bad names.

W: I can see that is what you did, but there is one thing that's not clear—how you successfully called it bad names. Because we've seen so many cases of somebody calling a bad name unsuccessfully and producing the other result.

E: But he didn't know I was calling it a bad name.

W: How's that?

E: Because at the end of the third hour, I said that I had completed therapy. I waited until the fourth hour to state that he was rigid. I had completed therapy, you see.

W: He couldn't resist it because it was already all over.

E: Yes.

H: I'm afraid that's a little too tricky for me. Apparently you told him what he already knew, that music had to be fluid, and so on.

E: Yes. I told him in a trance state where he had to listen to me. And where he kept thinking how much better he could word it verbally. (Laughter) And how much better he understood, because I confessed I was tone deaf.

W: So he was way ahead of you.

E: He was way, way ahead; but he had to sit there and listen. He had to elaborate, and elaborate, and elaborate. Now, don't you know that ethnic custom that you find all over the world, where a stranger in a country — he comes from a different country — you happen to know a little bit about his country, so you very, very courteously offer him the one insult of your culture that will seem utmost courtesy to him.

H: Why do you do this?

E: You want to insult him, you see. So you offer him the one thing in *your* culture that he can interpret as a courtesy. But which you know is an insult. You want to insult him. But it's your satisfaction in knowing that he's insulted. You don't care whether *he* discovers it or not. Next week, when he discovers that he was insulted, it's too late to feel bad about it, you see?

W: This is like the native, who when asked certain questions, replied by giving the anthropologist a list of dirty words. This has happened more than once.

E: Oh, you know the names of the many mountains and rivers that are given in native language. The explorer says, "What's the name of that mountain?" The native guide says, "Stinking s.o.b. How would I know what on earth you are talking about?" So the explorer says, "Tell me again," and he writes it down. You see, you get Popocatapetal, or whatever that mountain is in Mexico, that you can't pronounce.

H: Well, Milton, you have a way of presenting a case; you did this, and the result was achieved here. When you're pushed a little bit, then you say something more. Now, obviously it was crucial that you make a point that you were tone deaf so that he could be feeling how much better he could do this when you were giving him this story.

E: That's right.

H: But you didn't say this the first time. Now, you say it the second time. I wonder if you're pushed a little further, what else is in there that is crucial? Now, why all the business of fluidity?

E: Because he's mentioned his stilted walk onto the platform, his stilted movement is limiting. How it had been going on year after year, and he was always forced to give the same weak excuses.

W: Then, when you talk to this musical expert about the necessity of the fluidity in music, he can't say, "no"; the only way he can object to you is by going further by building it up much bigger.

E: He has to build it up, and build it up. And I am ignorant; I'm tone deaf. Then I tell him therapy is completed. It's completed with his enormous build-up. I'm still master of the situation because I will tell him when to come out of the trance. I'll give him a review, and so the next day I hit him with the charge of rigidity which has no place in music.

H: Obviously, if you deal with this man in a particular way in this room, he goes through some sort of a change which affects his life outside of this room. There is this peculiar thing about therapy that you start with a patient who deals with you in a certain way. You manage it so that he deals with you differently, and this affects how he deals with others outside the room.

E: Yes.

H: I wonder how much your assigning tasks is to get him doing the same sort of thing outside that he's doing inside, or to extend this outside the room. Is that part of the purpose in assigning tasks?

E: Yes. Because he's got to take his therapy outside of the room. Why do so many analytic patients stay year after year? Because they always do their therapy on the couch, and they don't take that couch home. They never take it to work. Therapy improvement is restricted to the couch.

H: Do you think that part of this guy doing well in the concert was a refutation of you, in some sense, or still a dealing with you, only outside the room now? Let's put it this way: Why did he do well at the concert? Why didn't he walk out there stilted as usual?

E: He had to walk out there freely, fluidly.

H: He had to in relation to you, or because of you.

E: The only way he could put me, a tone deaf person, in my place and keep me there was to prove conclusively to all the world the rightness of his elaboration of the fluidity of music.

W: Then in a sense he was proving that he knew a hell of a lot more about fluidity than you do?

E: But he was in a trance, and he couldn't make mention of it.

W: I mean, when he got out there on the stage.

E: When he got out there on the stage.

H: That is, he *had* to write you a letter and tell you he did well?

E: Yes. Oh, there's no question at all about that. He had to.

W: He couldn't write that letter unless he did do well.

E: That's right.

H: Did you also expect him to write you after that?

E: Oh yes.

*   *   *

E: Now that patient I mentioned yesterday, the pianist. I forgot to mention one important consideration, and you raised that question. He came for three days and he told me so; therefore, he laid down the law to me,

most emphatically. He placed me under horrible re-
strictions. I saw him the first day, then I saw him for
two hours the second day. At the termination of the
two hours on the second day, knowing he was coming back just one more hour, I said, "Therapy is terminated." Do you see?

H: He said three days and you said two?

E: And I said *two*. Even though he was coming back, just
for a review. Now you can call that, incorrectly, a com-
petitiveness or, what is that? One-upness?

H: One-upmanship.

E: One-upmanship, but it really isn't.

H: Well, what is it really?

E: It's a recognition of exactly how you have to handle the
situation. It's not a personal struggle. It's the need
to meet that situation so that it will develop adequately. You're using the same technique as in . . .

H: One-upmanship.

E: One-upmanship. It's the same technique.

H: It is.

E: But it isn't for the purpose of putting the *man* up; it's
for the purpose of putting the *goal* up. He came for
therapy, let's really put that goal up. Because I really don't need to enter into competition with him. It's
unnecessary. But the thing I want is therapy; the
thing he wants is therapy. We've got a common goal,
and you should be willing to use any technique to
achieve that end.

H: Well, now that's putting it in the nicest of all possible
ways. But I'm not sure any technique will achieve that
goal besides some kind of one-upmanship.

E: Yes. You're not certain that other methods will achieve
the goal?

H: That's right.

E: That's right. But you should be aware of this technique,
that technique, this procedure, that procedure.

H: But I would think, when you say that any techniques to achieve the goal, when it's a goal of this sort, that any procedure you choose would have to be one in which *you* take charge.

E: Yes, but not because it's personal.

H: No, it's not personal.

E: It's not a personal, emotional need on my part. It's a need for me to take charge to achieve that goal.

H: Well, I think it's in the nature of psychotherapy, not a personal need, except insofar that therapists have these needs.

W: With this pianist, I wonder what reason did he give when he came that he could not give these recitals? In other words, you shifted things around so that if he does not give the recital, this is rigidity. I was wondering what his explanation was originally?

E: His original explanation was that his parents set out to make him a famous musician when he was a little child, because of his unusual talent for music. They bossed him in everything. Supervision had been very, very rigid, and he had rebelled – not against the talent – but against his parents. And they weren't quite certain if they wanted him to be a pianist but . . .

W: His parents were rigid.

E: Yes. But *his* choice was the piano. While they liked several other instruments, he preferred the piano. But his parents had a preference for the violin. So in his rebellion, he just rejected personally, for himself, all other instruments. He made his selection of the piano because he felt that it was a better instrument. In his teachings he teaches a lot of instruments. He can play the violin and various instruments. But his real satisfaction is the piano. It's a personal thing.

H: He also rejected public performances. What did he describe as his difficulty in giving a public performance?

E: That he was so rigid — so stilted, I mean. So stilted and so hollow and so stagestruck.

H: You shifted it to "rigid" after making rigid an unfortunate thing for a musician?

E: Yes. Because it didn't fit in with fluid music. Now, the therapy was primarily oriented to the future, without any real analysis, or real consideration, of the dynamics of the past. Over and over again you have that sort of thing.

H: Now, you always tell a patient to do something. What did you tell him to do? The way you described him, all you had him do was listen to you.

E: Well, you see, he had to do a lot of thinking in his unconscious mind about the meaning of fluidity. About flowing. I forced him into that by confessing my own tone deafness and my own absolute ignorance of music. My inability to even touch a piano key. He had to do a lot of thinking; and yet I described this matter of angular movement, with his fingers and hands over the keyboard. I forced him into an analysis of that. What fluidity there was. So he was doing something.

H: The doing was thinking?

E: The doing was thinking. Because sometimes you assign a task with the patient knowing it's an assignment, and sometimes you assign a task without the patient knowing it's being assigned. But you know that there's no way for them to escape doing it.

H: You've managed to require it of them.

E: You're required it of them. I can think of Tom, who said, "I just can't find anything of interest. I just sit in my room and waste time. The days go by, and they're so long and dreary and depressing, and I do nothing. I just waste my time." I asked him, "Well, do you *have* to waste time sitting in your room? Can't you waste time elsewhere? You're lonesome, you're miserable, you have no contact with people. Why can't you waste your time where you have no contact with people because it's externally forbidden? Go down to the library and sit there and waste your time. There's silence in the library."

What did Tom do? He was a curious person. He was intellectually hungry. He was socially hungry. He just couldn't stand it to sit there in the library just staring, so he idled away his time picking up magazines. Got to reading an article on speleology. Someone happened to notice what he was reading. "Oh, are you interested in that?" I don't know how many caves Tom has explored. And he also took up skiing. Because he went, what do you call it, spelunking. In the group was someone who also did skiing. Tom turned out to be an enthusiastic spelunker. (Laughter) The other spelunker was also a skier and took Tom up to Flagstaff for skiing.

The world changed. That social thing of an unsocial atmosphere of the library. Silence. Everybody's there for reading books; that's not a place to make friendships. But when you stop to think about it, it's a very nice place to meet people and to form friendships. Some of my timid, inhibited patients who can't make friends, I send them down to the library. It's so nice to see someone else read something you're interested in. While my patients can't make the advances, I know that other people can.

H: You seem to assume that if you get somebody out into the world at all, somebody is going to make contact with them.

E: Well, isn't that true?

APPENDICES

Except for the recordings of him talking with groups in his old age, there are few interviews extant of Dr. Erickson doing therapy with patients. The following are two interviews. The first one is a demonstration interview. The second was an interview in his office where he introduced me to a patient and talked with him about his therapy.

INTERVIEW 1

A Depressed Man

The demonstration interview occurred in 1963 in an Eastern city. A group of therapists brought to him cases they were having difficulty with, and he talked with the patients in front of the small group. The therapist involved is listed here as Therapist 1, because at this time I do not recall the name.

Therapist 1: The man I will bring in is a Ph.D. an engineer. I'm not sure whether he still is, but at least until recently he has been the president and organizer of a firm. He's 32 years old, pretty striking appearance — he's about 6'8" tall and a movie star appearance. He's married to a second wife who is quite striking in appearance too, and also very tall. I've been seeing them as a couple, sometimes seeing them together and quite often seeing the two of them separately.

E: And her education?

T: She has an M.A. in psychology. He's an only child, and just recently I saw his parents with him in an attempt to try and get things going. This is a person who hasn't responded to analysis. He was in analysis for four years before I saw him. I've been seeing him and his wife for about a year. He's had ups and downs, sometimes feeling quite elated and expansive, particularly when things were going well early in the business, when he was first organizing the thing and getting things going. During these periods he tended to overextend himself and do too much, take over too much control, and then feel that he was stuck with a lot of responsibility after he did it. When he feels expansive he evidently gets bound up in a lot of power struggles with other people in the business, with his wife, and concerned about control over the least little issue.

When I first saw him he had been sort of catapulted into a manic period after having seen Don Jackson on a consultation basis. He had been sort of discouraged about his analysis, and the analyst suggested that he go see Don Jackson. Don had referred him to me. Well, you know, just one visit with Don just shot him sky high. He was really feeling good. He felt that here somebody had listened to him for a change and an important person had validated his opinion.

He came to see me. The wife was eager to get started in some sort of marital therapy. She's a very controlling person. I think underneath she is very insecure and dependent, but she really tests everybody, especially men, to the limit. She attacks him on the slightest pretext and just tears him to ribbons. When he gets depressed she'll call him a wet noodle, a seven-foot noodle, and just really devastate him. She's turned on me a time or two in therapy, and she really can be pretty melting in the way she handles you.

This is her first marriage, and she didn't marry until she was about 29, I think. They've been married about two years. When she met him, she felt that he was sort of a godlike figure, a superman, and really the ideal.

Well, he felt pretty good for a couple of months, and during this time he was expanding more and more, and one thing he did was to buy an expensive house which is, at this point, pretty much beyond him, I think, although they can barely scrape by. Once they moved into the house he got quite depressed, just crashed out almost as suddenly as he went up. He's been pretty much this same way for about eight or nine months now.

During this, when he's depressed, he's really impossible in therapy, and elsewhere too, I guess. He keeps just saying the same kind of thing over and over again about how he's so depressed that he can't make any decisions and he feels that life holds nothing for him. He particularly holds on to the idea that there's something wrong with his thinking. He can't concentrate, he can't remember things at all; there's something wrong with his memory. He almost talks about it as if it's an organic defect of some kind. He also has a tendency to find fault with everything. He's discouraged about therapy, he feels he's lost confidence in me, discouraged about his marriage, about himself and the business. Just anything you can think of. The slightest detail he can just pick apart. Any suggestion you make to him he can resist in some way. He'll say he wants to do something, and then, if you agree to do it, he says he's changed his mind and resists it.

E: Let's see him now.

T: Okay. (Patient enters) This is Dr. Erickson over here at the end of the table.

E: How do you do. Sit down here, please. This gentleman wants me to interview you.

P: Hmmm.

E: You're a college grad.

P: Right.

E: And an engineer.

P: That is correct.

E: You get depressed?

P: Very much so.

E: Mmmm.

P: It's my specialty.

E: And in your depression you feel you don't want very much, and you're incapable of a lot of things?

P: That's right.

E: Yes. You're a college graduate.

P: Right.

E: Are you right or left handed?

P: I'm right handed.

E: And you know that there's two sides to your body?

P: Right.

E: Do you think you know them both?

P: Well, I think I can distinguish them. I can distinguish my right leg from my left leg.

E: Are you right or left footed?

P: I've never thought about that.

E: Well, are you right or left eyed?

P: Oh, I guess I'm right eyed. I choose the right eye if I want to do something with one eye.

E: How would you find out if you're right or left eyed? You're an engineer.

P: Well, I suppose if I were trying to see something in the distance, or trying to study something in detail, and it had to be done with one eye, I would choose one or the other.

E: You'd choose one or the other.

P: Experiment.

E: Do you know Jay Haley?

P: No.

E: He's the gentleman there with the smile. Keep both eyes open. Now take this watch in your hand and hold it like this, or like this, and look at Jay Haley through it (the circle of the band).

P: Through—I'm sorry, I didn't follow you, through one eye first?

E: Through one eye. With both open. Which is he using Jay, right or left eye?

H: Right eyed.
P: Well, okay, I started off that way intentionally.
E: Mmmm. Will you put your hands up like this over your head and clasp them and bring them down tightly.
P: Tightly, okay.
E: Are you right or left thumbed?
P: Well, I guess I'm right thumbed.
E: Look. I'm right thumbed, and the dominant thumb is on top.
P: Okay, I guess.
E: How many years has your body known that, and you didn't know it, and you went through college? Your hands just went along with you to college.
P: Yeah.
E: It's your brain that went to college, but your hands learned more about right and left thumbness than you did.
P: Uh huh.
E: Do you suppose there's a lot of other things about yourself you don't know?
P: Very likely. Things about my body, and probably some positive things about my mind that I don't know.
E: And positive things about your functioning.
P: Yes.
E: Do you suppose you know those things about functioning in your depressed states?
P: Well, okay, I'm confused by your question.
E: Well, you're left thumbed no matter how depressed you are. Isn't that right?
P: All right, yes.
E: No matter how depressed you are, you're left thumbed. Your body knows that all the time. It's a function of the body. It's a function of the nerve cells in your brain. Now, no matter how depressed you are, you'll always be left thumbed, and you can't lose that learning, or that ability, or that function, in the left thumb.
P: Mmmm hmmm.

E: Now a friend of mine is making a study of the laterality of the body. The right and left sidedness of the body. He's utterly fascinated. Eventually football coaches are going to make use of it, because there's nothing more horrible than 6′6″ of brawn and brain and agility and speed, quick thinking, and right eyed, and right shouldered, and right handed, and right legged, and *left* hipped. Because he's a tragedy for the coach.

P: Most of the strength is on one side, but there ...

E: Most of the dominance.

P: Yes.

E: Because you can't make a man into a good football player if he's right legged and right footed and right handed and right armed and right shouldered and right eyed and left hipped.

P: Would it be better if he were right hipped also?

E: If he's dominantly right or left sided, yes. In football, which requires the body itself functioning as a totality. But in certain minor things, such as clasping one's hands ... there's a tremendous number of things.

P: Well, would you like me to ask you questions?

E: Mmmm hmmm.

P: Well, left hipped would mean that a man's left hip is stronger than his right hip?

E: No, that when he should be using his right hip, he's going to be using his left hip.

P: Okay, I guess.

E: And in interference, or running the field, when he should be using his right hip to knock the other guy out of his pathway, he uses his left hip. And he misses. (Laughs) And the tackle is good for the opposing team. You see?

P: Well, the mental picture I get is somebody running into somebody with his left hip out, and I guess what's going on is that you're saying that most of the coordination is in the right side of his body.

E: Yes, but it's broken at the middle. And so he never is really, fully coordinated. It's like breaking step when you're marching. There's that awkward pause when you break step. That's why he doesn't make a good football player. Now, when you get depressed, what happens to *you*?

P: Well, I'm not good for much of anything. I seem to specialize in dwelling on mistakes I've made, or present inadequacies. Or the current vogue with me seems to be dwelling on what would have happened if when I graduated from college I'd taken a job and had to take responsibility, instead of . . .

E: What do you mean, "inadequacies"?

P: Well, I'm presently aware that when I try to grasp an involved concept, or a complicated concept, well enough to understand it, that either I don't have the capability, or I don't want to have the capability. I have got some kind of a block. And then I think back to the fact that in undergraduate engineering courses, and a good many graduate courses, I did well. I could grasp moderately complex concepts. So, that's an inadequacy. Then the fact that I don't stand up to people enough, to assert myself, and I seem to be afraid to express how I feel. I have a wife who is very good at expressing how she feels.

E: Is she?

P: Yes. Well, okay.

E: What's "okay"?

P: Well, "okay" means, you said, "Is she?" and perhaps if one goes beneath the surface, you see that when she's angry, she's really saying she's hurt. So maybe I'm suspicious.

E: Where do you want to look, on the surface or underneath? As an engineer, if I wanted to know tensile strength of a steel beam, I'd want to know about the crystalization within the steel beam.

P: Okay.

E: Isn't that right?

P: That's true.

E: So why would I bother to look at the outside to see if it were smoothly polished?

P: Well, you might start with the outside, and you can tell something about the material from an examination of the surface.

E: Yes, you might. But you never stop there, do you?

P: That's true.

E: I think so. Let's see, inadequacy or incompleteness of functioning; you said inadequacy.

P: Yes.

E: Is it inadequacy? Or incompleteness? I think you're adequate to walk across this room, but I know you'd walk incompletely across it.

P: Yes.

E: Now, I'll give you a nice little question. It sounds like a riddle, and it can be used as a riddle. But I know you know the answer.

P: Hmmm.

E: There's a family of nine children, and the first one is named *One*. The second one is named *Two*. The third one is named *Three*. What are the last three names?

P: Well, possibly *Seven*, *Eight*, and *Nine*. You said a family of nine children.

E: Mmmm hmmm. And I said that the first three were named — *One*, *Two*, *Three*. Now what are the last three named? I'm not mentioning the middle three. It must be for some curious reason. So what's the last three names? I had a friend of mine working on that for a couple of weeks.

P: Well, through inadequacy or incompleteness I stop at the obvious at this point.

E: Is it inadequacy when the last three were named *Thirteen*, *Seventeen*, and *Nineteen*? What was the name of the family?

P: The last name?

E: What was the name of that family? I've given you six numbers, haven't I?

P: Yes, *One Two* and *Three, Thirteen, Seventeen* and *Nineteen.*

E: What *are* those numbers?

P: Well, they're prime numbers.

E: Well, certainly.

P: Yeah.

E: That's right. They're prime numbers. You knew that all the time. Were you inadequate to answer that question, or did you know about prime numbers all the time?

P: Well, all right, I know about prime numbers.

E: That's right, but you couldn't answer the question.

P: Yeah.

E: Why? Because I planted an even number into it.

P: You did?

E: One, two, three. And that even number throws anybody and everybody off.

P: Well, you went one, two, three. I thought an obvious extension of this is . . .

E: Is a sequence of counting?

P: That's right. This is one . . .

E: I said it was a family. Not a sequence.

P: Yeah.

E: And you know the difference between a sequence and a family.

P: Is there anything that rules out a family being a sequence?

E: No, there isn't. But I pointed out that I had deliberately omitted the three intervening numbers.

P: Yeah.

E: So I said it isn't a sequence, it's the family.

P: Oh, all right. Okay, I'm confused, and I'm in a state that I'm frequently in, which is that I feel there is something I don't understand.

E: That's right.

P: But it's not going to do me any good to try and understand it. Because there's something in me that doesn't
want to learn, and when I get in this state, one of the
things that goes on in my depression is I look long-
ingly back to being a student, or an engineer in earlier
days, when I wanted to know something and I'd go
to somebody and ask. My mind cooperated in the process of understanding, and then I took the understanding and went and did something.
E: Fine, and you described exactly what I wanted you to.
No matter how depressed you are, your mind can take
the backward trail. Back to those days in college.
P: Yeah?
E: Why don't you turn around and back up into the future?
P: Well, it would be a good thing to do. For some reason
I feel a little bit like crying now. It's the first time I've
felt that way in a long time, but anyway . . .
E: Isn't that a delightful experience – to suddenly come to
that, for the first time in a long period of time?
P: Yeah.
E: Is it? You can change, can't you?
P: Yeah. Okay. There's some part of me that's violently
protesting and saying I won't change or, you know.
I don't know. I visualize my messy office and all the
problems at work that I feel I can't cope with.
E: Well, it's much easier to visualize your office than it
would be something that's really painful, isn't it?
P: That's true.
E: Mmmm hmmm. Therefore, in the matter of therapy,
well, why stop at visualizing your messy office? I think
that you ought to be awfully curious when I say to
you, "Turn around and back into the future." Then
you don't have to *look* at the thing you're afraid of.
Until you've backed far enough into the future so that
it's ahead of you. But actually then, in reality, behind
you. Even though it's ahead of you, because you're
backing up. Can you get any more confused?

P: I feel a little confused.

E: That's right.

P: And I, okay, all right. Some of what you were saying, I wasn't listening to. Just the last 30 seconds or so, I was, I guess, trying to piece together what you said before.

E: Is anything wrong with that?

P: Well, it's a crippling pattern in that a lot of things go on that — around me that it would be to my advantage to be attentive to, and to recall, remember.

E: Well, there's a deuce of a lot of things going on all the time, but are you going to give your attention to *all* of those things or to selected things?

P: All right, to selected things.

E: That's right. How's your crying feeling?

P: Oh, it's going away.

E: How far?

P: Oh, you can probably bring it back.

E: What other things could I bring back?

P: Oh, possibly a conviction that I'll . . . that I *will* succeed.

E: How soon should I do that? Right now, today, tomorrow, next week, next month? I don't see there is very much of a hurry about it. Do you?

P: No.

E: What *do* you need to see? That's another confusing question.

P: Mmmm hmmm.

E: All you need to see is the fact that you *can* look forward with confidence. Not all the time, for heaven's sakes, no. I think you're entitled to what Longfellow said, "Some days are dark and dreary, and into each life some rain must fall."

P: Mmmm hmmm.

E: I think you ought to look forward to those. But I think you'd better also look forward to the sunny days too.

P: Okay.

E: How afraid are you of shedding tears?

P: Not afraid of it. I think I did too much of it when I was younger.

E: You mean you're caught up on it? Had more than your share?

P: No, I think I have turned against what I was, which was somebody who liked to emote, and in a way I blame myself and blame my wife. I guess they're emotional patterns, and things that I went through that once brought me satisfaction, that I now feel I mustn't do, or that are not valid.

E: Well, you know, many children can eat that cheap glucose candy with starry-eyed looks.

P: Yeah.

E: I don't want it.

P: But you don't want any?

E: No, I'm too old to eat it.

P: Yeah, yeah.

E: And I can think of the time at Christmas, when my grown-up sons came to visit me. I was out in the kitchen preparing steaks. And a seven- or eight-year-old boy came up and said, "What are we going to have for dinner tonight?" I said, "steak," and he said, "Oh, can't we have hot dogs?" The older boy said, "Same old story, isn't it, Dad?" Because they remember when they used to want hot dogs, when mother and I ate steak.

P: Mmmm hmmm.

E: But now they've learned to look back with pleasure and satisfaction upon those emotional wants of the past, and enjoy today's steak.

P: Well, okay.

E: When you first married your wife, you wanted a certain satisfaction, but that was three years ago, or thereabouts. And when she married you, she wanted certain emotional satisfactions. That was three years ago. Now I wonder how analytic you are in your thinking about who you are today and what your tastes are today: hot dog or steak, cheap candy or bittersweet chocolate?

P: I don't think I'm very analytical. I think I feel out of step with life.

E: Mmmm. You feel out of step with life.

P: Yeah. People my age are having families and are plugged in on their jobs. I'm sort of a quivering bundle of fear, and fairly convinced that I don't have what it takes to be a parent. That I don't have enough self-respect, you know.

E: How much does it take to be a parent?

P: Well, I think you have to like yourself enough that you're tolerant of other people. And I think you have to have some principles that you believe in, that you can stick to and not easily be talked out of. There has to be something consistent that you believe in.

E: Well, on the whole I would say that, in many, many ways, you are far superior to the feeble-minded citizen who's happily married, has an insecure job, and happy kids.

P: Yeah?

E: By the way, what makes you think you're inadequate?

P: Well, I can't look to very many jobs that I've done where I didn't lean on other people for help, or I . . .

E: Or did you give them the privilege of being supportive?

P: All right, I did that.

E: How would this world get along without the people we lean on? This is a community world, you know.

P: Mmmm hmmm.

E: And how willing are you to *lean* on your strengths?

P: Well, I don't know. I guess I'm not very willing. What you describe, at one time was very . . .

E: I think fair play is an important thing.

P: Fair play? Okay.

E: You should focus on your weaknesses a certain amount, and your strengths a certain amount.

P: Yeah.

E: If your wife has faults, for heaven's sake, recognize them. If she has virtues, for heaven's sake, recognize them. She'll have superiorities and inferiorities. Well, you're a good engineer; you ought to be able to recognize all manner of things, isn't that right?

P: Yeah, if you're a good engineer, and I don't feel I am.

E: Well, if you're not a good engineer, are you a fair engineer?

P: Well, I guess I feel that I'm a bizarre engineer, that there are some important things I've been able to do, and some things that I haven't done. To get ideas, for novel ideas, I've done pretty well. But to pursue in detail an analysis of something to understand why it doesn't work, or to be thorough in the design of something, this is something I have difficulty doing, and in recent times have resisted doing.

E: Is that wrong?

P: Well, it's wrong in the sense that it's either being unable to do something or refusing to do something that people are counting on me to do. If I don't do, I'm not pulling my share of the load.

E: I know that the first violinist is an excellent musician. Would you trust him with a bassoon?

P: Probably not.

E: No. Would a good violinist want to be trusted with a bassoon?

P: Okay, probably not.

E: Should he ever desire that? You say you're bizarre, and good in certain ways; for heaven's sakes, what more do you want? The bizarre musician plays the bassoon in the orchestra. Because it takes a special type of personality to play a bassoon. I think the bassoon adds great timbre to the orchestra. So does the first violinist. Violinists are a dime a dozen . . .

P: The violinists are what?

E: Violinists are a dime a dozen in the musical world. I

think of a friend of mine. She said, "I want to get into the California Symphony Orchestra. I play a violin
beautifully. I'm going to have an awful lot of competition, I'm going to play a viola. I learned to play this
as well as I do a violin." She auditioned for the California Youth Symphony and got in.

P: Very good.

E: Yes. And she is going to avoid playing the violin. She
wants to be in that symphony orchestra. Your bizarre-
ness can bring about certain desirable results. I don't
think you can forget the confusions I've inflicted on
you — because you cannot keep them in mind without
the need to drop one and go to another. To drop that
to go to another. And to drop that and go to another.

P: So you're saying you don't think I'll forget these confusions.

E: You'll go from one to another to another to another.
Now suppose I would give you confusing directions
in how to go to Chicago. If you definitely wanted to
go to Chicago, I could explain how you go from San
Francisco to Tokyo, to London, to New York. I can
explain to you how you go from San Francisco to
Phoenix to El Paso to Dallas to Forth Worth. And explain to you how you would go from San Francisco
to Portland to Seattle to St. Paul to Chicago. And as
surely as you start going from one confusion to another, somehow or another you're going to wind up
at Oklahoma City. (Laughs)

P: At the right point?

E: At the right place.

P: Yeah?

E: And why should you be afraid of which route you take?
Now Toyko, London and Paris, Madrid, Canary Is-
lands, Miami, Florida might be an awfully confusing
way of getting from San Francisco to Chicago. It
ought to be delightful.

P: Mmmm hmmm.

E: If you want to go by way of Anchorage, London, Buenos Aires, that ought to be delightful too.

P: Mmmm hmmm.

E: I wonder what you'll pick up on the way, jumping from one confusion to another?

P: Well . . . (Pause)

E: And what are the particular values in each depression that you have? Because I suspect you have the mistaken idea that depression is wrong.

P: Well, when I'm depressed I'm, I think, less productive.

E: Mmmm hmmm. And when you get the rear wheels of your car caught in a ditch, and you can't go ahead in first gear or second gear, third gear, well, I think it's awfully nice to shift into reverse, and then into first, and reverse, and first, and reverse, and first, and rock yourself out of the ditch.

P: Mmmm hmmm.

E: And I think you ought to enjoy it and really rock yourself out of it. And not regret going into reverse. You've learned an awful lot about driving, handling a car.

P: Mmmm hmmm.

E: When I teach my kids to drive a car, I deliberately do that. Tell them to get out of the ditch. When they catch on to the fact that's further into the ditch, then they'll really learn something about driving the car.

P: Okay, so I'm in a ditch, and you want me to be willing to back up to get out.

E: Get another head start.

P: Okay. Well, what's backing up for me? Going back to school? Or taking simpler tasks, or . . . ?

E: You can examine into your own feelings, your own thoughts, your own attitudes, your *own* self-defined disappointments. I think the next person is coming to pick me up at this hour.

T: That's right.

E: You know, it's been a pleasure for me.

P: Well, thank you.

E: And I'm interested to see what you do about these alternative routes.

P: Okay. So am I.

E: And you know what? What color kleenex do you like best?

P: Oh, I guess pink.

E: Pink? When you feel like crying, are you going to use pink or white for this?

P: Well, I'll probably . . .

E: You know, at Christmastime I always furnish my patients with green kleenex. I tell them to cry in the Christmas spirit. (Laughs)

Q1: Okay. (Patient exits)

*   *   *

H: That was a rapid half hour.

E: The manuevering of him. What kind of personal contact did I make with him?

T: Confusional? Confusional coach. (Laughs)

E: Mmmm hmmm. And what kind of kleenex will he have around the house at Christmastime? (Laughter)

T: So one of the things was to take away, in a sense, the gain of his – I mean, he says, "It's my specialty, you know, the depression is," as though there's almost a positive value in it. So this is one of the things that you were doing, sort of redefining depression.

E: It's a ditch. You can get in a ditch. How do you get out of a ditch? You work in the ditch. But it isn't threatening. My 18-year-old son had a very vital experience the other night. He was in a dark street, and two hoodlums came toward him. He recognized them as hoodlums. They said, "Buddy, can you loan us a dime?" They wanted to see that automatic movement of his hand toward his pocket. My son knew he was in a tight spot. Why not put the hoodlums in a tight spot? What do you do to put somebody in a tight spot? Robert looked straight ahead and kept on walking. The two hoodlums kept looking at him. "What in the hell was that?" (Laughter) Robert came home and said, "You know, I was a block away and they were still standing looking at me." (Laughter) It's such a simple procedure. What could he do? Well, let's do something that nobody on earth would ever expect. Now this man, I wouldn't attempt to hypnotize him under any circumstances.

T: One thing I forgot to mention was that he almost falls into a trance by himself in therapy.

E: Not today.

T: He'll sometimes get very sleepy, and if you say, "Well, don't fight it, just relax," he just goes over and starts having all sorts of hypnogogic imagery, and this sort of thing. Why wouldn't you hypnotize him?

E: That guy was too much on the alert, watching me.

T: You meant that more today, but you might after a number of sessions.

E: Maybe next time, yes.

*   *   *

(The next day)

E: Now that engineer. When I asked him that ridiculous question about the nine children named *One*, *Two*, and *Three*, and the names of the last three. Well, you could really struggle with that kind of question. But you know the thinking that's all going on in his mind. And while he was trying to solve that question, how much attention was he giving you, or you, or you? Very little. Because that was an intriguing question.

It's a confusion technique where you ask the patient, in some way, to get uncertain and confused in his mind so that he's very, very pleased to accept some reasonably intelligent reply to a statement made by him and replace that doggone annoying question. But you've only built up a situation in which he's literally, unwittingly begging you to say something he may understand. Well, that's the situation you want your patient in. He comes to you for therapy, and he should be open to the idea of receiving something from you. So you have him set the pace. And after I watched that engineer walk in here and sit down, I thought, "All right, now let's create a situation wherein he's going to be very glad to hear something intelligent from me." And he did take a great deal of pleasure in the prime numbers.

T: He called me a few hours later and wanted to know if he could come back today. (Laughter)

E: What did I do when I used that prime number thing? When did he first learn prime numbers? That simple little thing reminded him and vivified for him the relatively remote, remote past. I opened wide the possibility of getting from him, easily and readily, grade school memories, and I never mentioned grade school. I wouldn't have needed to mention grade school; prime numbers were all that was needed. It seemed to be such a silly little wisecrack on my part, a foolish little riddle, but an amusing thing. Then I pointed out that he was justified in not being able to answer because of that confusing thing, an even number. One, two, three. Two odd and one even, and that directed his thinking into two categories about numbers, odd and even. And took it far, far away from such a thing as prime numbers.

Now there are innumerable techniques. They're all essentially the same thing. The clenched fist technique. If you're right handed, that's really your good hand. Your good hand writes and your good hand feeds your face. His good hand shakes hands and, oh, any number of things; and therefore a state of tension means a bad thing. You know it, and I know it; and how do you get a state of tension? And that's unpleasant, horribly unpleasant. You'd much rather have the relaxation of the good hand. What have you taught him? The clenched fist technique brings on tension, and you yourself relieve it. So, if you want to, you can associate that clenched fist tension with any unhappy thing you want to, and you can associate the nice and good feelings with the goodness of your right hand. What happens? The tension disappears. But you've asked him to associate the tension of the thoughts of his mother-in-law with this (clenched fist), and the goodness of getting along in life and facing reality and enjoying life with a nice, comfortable relaxation over here. The conditioning process that even dogs can learn in the laboratory. Well, I've used up my three-quarters of an hour.

INTERVIEW 2

A Phantom
Limb Pain

In 1968, when Dr. Erickson was older and more limited physically, he allowed me to sit in on an interview with a patient who was quite old and, like Erickson, had experienced a great deal of pain. Before the man came in, Dr. Erickson described the problem as one of a severe pain in a "phantom" limb, an arm that the man still felt was across his lower chest in a cast. The man was 72 years old and had been a floor layer all his life, so he had other aches and pains as a residue of that work. Dr. Erickson was interested in the man's awareness of his other physical difficulties as the phantom limb pain disappeared.

The patient arrived in Dr. Erickson's small office.

E: You haven't met Mr. Haley, have you?

H: How do you do.

P: How do you do, sir.

E: He's the one who wrote this book.

P: I was very much interested in the piece you put here on the front. I don't know anything about the writings, but "a unique approach of psychotherapy" – that is a unique approach.

H: I would agree. (Laughs)

P: I think that the first day that I came here, when Dr.

Erickson started to talk to me, he gave me some confidence because he was confident he could do something for me. And I have confidence in him. I think between us we make a good pair, don't we Doctor?

E: Well, in therapy. (Laughs)

P: We're getting along better anyway.

E: What's happened since yesterday?

P: I think I've been very comfortable, all day yesterday. I've got a little pain this morning, but I kind of got rid of it.

E: What about your restless legs?

P: Beg your pardon?

E: What about your restless legs?

P: Oh my. We won't mention that.

E: Why?

P: Well, you know, Doctor, it isn't my legs so much, it's my rectal area. It is just really something. It's just like my leg; it jitters and shakes too.

E: Well, I know that. (Laughs)

P: Of course, my foot doesn't.

E: Why didn't you mention *that* yesterday?

P: I never thought of it. I just, I was thinking about my leg more than anything, but my leg doesn't bother me much until late in the evening. Seems like maybe when I get a little tired or something.

E: All right. You have several *other* things you haven't yet mentioned to me.

P: Since yesterday?

E: No. Concerning the results of your wood laying, your floor laying.

P: Oh, the results of it.

E: Well, restless legs came from that.

P: Oh, yes.

E: The cramps.

P: Yes, the cramps that . . .

E: And the muscle losses.

P: Yes it is. I've had . . .

E: Now, today you mentioned the rectal difficulties. Now there are some other things that came from working in that position.

P: Yes, I had tremendous back trouble over the years.

E: That's right.

P: And I've had sciatic nerve trouble. I was in traction one time 41 days from it.

E: Yes.

P: In fact, in 53 years It about wore me out all over.

(Dr. Erickson asked him to stand up and demonstrate for me how a floor layer works and the difficult physical effort involved. He did so, describing the work in some detail.)

P: Ordinarily, they say, a man in that business only lasts about 15 years, but my legs really held together 37 years in a row, and about 16 years before that, just off and on, not constant. All together, pretty near 53 years.

E: And now you've had freedom from pain today, or some pain.

P: I have a little, not very much. If it never got any worse than this, I wouldn't complain.

E: What about . . . you do know you'll trip again? Don't you?

P: Pardon?

E: You do know that you will fall down again?

P: Oh yes, I do. I know that, Doctor.

E: But you'll pick yourself up faster.

P: Yes.

E: And you won't fall down quite so hard.

P: Maybe not quite so often.

E: (Laughs) That's right. And are there any particular changes in the pain today?

P: No. Just normal. You mean in the arm itself? Where the arm should be, mostly just below the elbow, and not just from here down to my hand. Just to the edge of my fingers. But my shoulder isn't hurting today.

E: Now, do you want any suggestion from me today about your pain?

P: No. I think I'm getting along pretty good.

E: I think so too. All right. Give me an appointment form.

P: You gave me an appointment for 11 on Monday, Doctor.

E: That's right. All right now. If you want to watch the TV here, it would be all right.

P: Oh, I'll just watch it. And I'm also interested in the San Francisco Giants baseball game. That's home, where I live.

E: It may be on one of the stations.

P: Oh yes, it's on there now. But there's a lot more ball-games.

E: Well, what questions do you want to put to him?

H: I can't think of any at the moment.

P: Does Mr. Haley know we're going to Flagstaff Thursday?

E: I haven't had a chance to tell him that.

P: Oh.

E: I've used him as a subject in the class there. I thought you would want to get acquainted with him.

H: I gather he's a good subject?

P: Well, you know, Mr. Haley, at almost 72 I do have a ... I have a fairly good mind. It's active. And I have a fairly good memory. But if I could sort in my mind all the things that Dr. Erickson taught me, then I could say I do have a memory. I can sort some of them, most of them. But what I should have done – I wrote and told my brother, I said I regret now one thing – that when I first went to see Dr. Erickson, that when I got back to my hotel I hadn't made notes on what I learned, which would have been a big help.

H: How many times have you seen him?

P: Not too many, about 12 or 13, something like that. You should have seen me when I got here.

E: That's what he's interested in knowing.

H: How were you when you got here?

P: Pardon?

H: How were you when you got here?

P: I was just pretty near out of my mind. I don't know how much you know about this thing, this pain, but there's only one person who can tell you, and that's somebody who's had it. When I came here it just felt as if I had fallen down and a truck had run over my arm. Just right down across it, you know? When I had this accident and they took me to the hospital and performed the preliminary surgery, the two bones came sticking through my shirt out into the open air. I raised my head up and I was laying with my left hand like that. The two bones in my arm were sticking right out into the palm of my hand. I had four broken ribs right under. They put me in the hospital, and the next day my arm started to swell up. The circulation stopped, and the next day it started to turn dark, and the next day, of course, I had gas gangrene. The next day they took it off. They decided to take it off at 25 minutes to 9, and at 10 minutes to 9 I was on the operating table. No preparations, no nothing. Nothing like a tranquilizer for pain. So as I lay down on the operating table, I was really looking at my hand. And my arm was laying just like here where it is now (showing missing arm). Here is my arm, here is my elbow, and here is my hand. That's the exact position I was laying in on that operating table.

Well, they gave me an anesthetic and took my arm off, and the minute I came out of the anesthetic there was my arm. It's been there ever since. It's just embedded in my brain so deep that it's something that's hard to get out. It caused just quite a shock.

They've done everything for it. They took me over

to the University of California Medical Center to Dr.
J. A., supposed to be one of the finest neurosurgeons
in America. He's head of the Neurosurgery Department at the University of California Medical School.
He severed a nerve in my spinal cord up here, to dead-
en the pain in my left arm. And it got too much, and
that's why I had . . . one thing, I'm just numb. Right
down through my face, the side of my face. I can't
even tell when I use an electric razor on my face there.
This side over here is just as normal as can be. That
didn't help.

Two weeks later the pain—it stopped the pain for
two weeks. But it gave me one of the most violent
headaches a human ever had for a month. They put
me in a convalescent hospital and kept me there about
three weeks until I got rid of my headache. By that
time the pain had come back in my arm worse than
I'd ever had it before. I'd just about given up when
I came over here. But we did take—oh, a week, maybe
ten days—before I began to get kind of discouraged
because I didn't seem to be getting any better. Excuse me, but, I don't know, it was a week ago today.
I told you, Doctor, I went out of here walking on air
or something like that. I've been getting better ever
since.

H: Where did you hear of Dr. Erickson?

(The patient discussed various doctors he visited,
including a hypnotist who said he had a mental
block and referred him to Dr. Erickson.)

P: . . . So then Dr. B. told me about Dr. Erickson, and he
called up and made an appointment. So that's how I
came to be here. It's just something that fell out of
the clear sky. And I'm very, very glad I came.

E: What happened the first morning?

P: Pardon?

E: What happened the first morning, April 11th?

P: Well, I remember very distinctly. I told you what happened to me, about my wife dying, and you told me I resented it. I resented getting hurt. I was afraid of dying, but if I died I would get rid of this pain and, oh my, you said so many things since then. But you did take the pain away.

E: I what?

P: You took most of the pain away while I saw you. And then it came back though.

E: How did I take it away?

P: My eye on the corner of that, I looked through that, and I think you just talked me out of it.

E: Mr. Haley saw me do that to a woman this morning.

P: Oh. Well, it works. "A unique approach," the way you described it. I think the thing that impressed me most, Dr. Erickson, of anything—you told me to say what I thought, didn't you? Well, I think that the secret to the Doctor—his secret—he sits here, and I come in here sometimes feeling just miserable, you know. I tell him how I'm feeling, and he sits there for a few minutes, and taking my case in relation with an anecdote, happening, things that have happened to other patients, and the things that have happened to his friends, to his family, to himself. You know, he winds them all up together, and the first thing you know, lo and behold, I find out he's talking about me all the time. (Laughter)

You know, my brother wrote and asked me if Dr. Erickson put me in a trance. I said, "No." I said, "The answer is yes and no." I said, "But if you want the truth of the matter, Dr. Erickson puts himself in a trance." And I said, "The first thing you know I'm in there with him." (Laughter) But he has done me a world of good. At least he's given me some confidence, and I just know that someday it won't bother me at all because he's told me so.

E: You're getting the know-how.

P: Yes. I do know how to help myself.

E: You just make this movement.

P: This hand out there like that, that never quivers, or nervousness or nothing, the thing comes up, you know, and the first thing you know it's turned over, and it's just like you're getting manna from heaven or something. Unique method.

E: And your thumbnail.

P: Thumbnail, yes, a thumbnail.

H: You're staying in Phoenix for the treatment. Do you plan to go back to San Francisco afterwards?

P: Oh yes. I must. I have a . . . you see, my wife just died the 15th of June. I don't have any people up there, there's no reason on earth why I should go up there, but I have a house full of my furniture that my wife and I had. I have a five-room house I rent when I'm there. I rent out my back bedroom. You need company, you know. Sometimes some fellow, you know? I've gotten a dog, and I belong to the Los Gatos Senior Citizens Club. I've got quite a lot of friends. I got a card from them this morning, there's almost 400 signatures on it. Glad that I was feeling better. I write to them, and they write to me. I don't know where else I would go. I think my brother – I have a brother, two brothers, that's all the family I have left. My immediate family. They both live in Los Angeles. I think I may move down there but, oh, I don't know, I was down there a couple of times visiting, and that terrific smog there just . . . I lived there long years ago in '41 and the smog was unheard of and unknown. It was beautiful, clear.

E: Well, are you comfortable enough to leave?

P: Oh yes, Doctor, I'm very comfortable.

E: And if you've got too much competition on the TV at the hotel, you can see the games on one of the two TVs here.

P: Thank you. I'm glad to have met you.

H: Thank you for letting me sit in on this.

P: I'll see you Monday at 11, Doctor.

(Patient leaves)

H: Well now, what did you do with this man in the first session?

E: I had him fixate his eye on the corner of the clock, levitate his hand.

H: The real one?

E: Yes. I knew better than to touch that arm with all that pain and the bone sticking out.

H: And he still feels it with the bone just like it was? Sticking out?

E: Yes. And I can free him of the pain. He didn't know whether he was in a trance or not. He thought it was necessary for *me* to go into a trance. His unconscious mind could listen to me and his conscious mind could wander around, and I think I took a couple of phone calls during his hour without his noticing it. I suggested to him that he shouldn't try too hard to get rid of all of it, but it might be a good idea to get rid of some of it. He might let it flow all through his hand, through his hands and to his fingers. But as far as specific instruction, his own unconscious mind would decide on the right thing and it would decide if he wanted at least temporary relief. So that he could build up his confidence, and it was *his* confidence that needed building up, not mine. But I was absolutely positive that his unconscious could do all that was necessary, and I would be agreeable in working with his unconscious mind. To let him go at his own pace, based on his unconscious mind—but since I knew more about working with the unconscious mind, from time to time I might alter the direction or the course of his pain. A baby learning to walk doesn't happen to stand up and walk without ever once slipping and falling down. And sometimes I might even push him so he would fall down, but it would be because he might be going in the wrong direction. And I would like to have him be interrupted in walking toward freedom from pain. I might have to push him rather hard and suddenly in order to swing him around because he had his eye on the wrong goal.

H: Can you explain when you use that approach? What I mean by "that approach"—I mean that distinction between a conscious and an unconscious mind, and how he can do consciously one thing while his unconscious does another, and yet you're going to influence his unconscious? It's a very complex thing you're doing there.

E: I know it's complex. I'm doing it that way because, in the first place, I don't want to build any obligation of arguing it out with the conscious mind. You heard him say today his hand is so steady, doesn't shake or anything, and it turns over so smoothly.

H: He said, "Like manna from heaven."

E: Well, of course you recognize why he turned the hand over.

H: No, why did he turn the hand over?

E: You just explained it.

H: Like manna from heaven?

E: Like manna from heaven in his right hand. What I was saying, the gift I was giving him, dealing with his open extended palm. You see, you speak of yourself as a communications expert. Words can be words, or they can be symbols, and the open palm means what? It's put out for receiving, and the outstretched hand is what? One is offering aid. Aid for the poor and the needy. In helping the person to accomplish something. Put the open palm out for the reception of aid. Now, all through our lives, all through our lifetime of experience, we learn that sort of symbolic language.

*   *   *

H: This man, I thought, said that in that first session you talked to him about how he was afraid of dying. He phrased it in an odd way—he was afraid of dying to get rid of the pain.

E: Because when he died he would get rid of the pain.

H: And you say that you didn't discuss this with him?

E: Oh no. A patient never gives you an orderly account of his life experiences. He jumbles similar things from various periods of his life in the same paragraph, and that way you have to sort out the different times and places and you can't really be certain. And with all that it is very symbolic communication. I expect he may have been told by some doctor that he might get rid of his pain when he died.

H: Well now, he described you as being very explicit, and explaining the situation to him in the first session— that his wife died and he was angry about this and lonely and that he was in pain and was thinking about dying himself and so on. Now this is just not the way it was at all?

E: No. Because he can think of Dr. B. in terms of me. And when he says, "doctor," well, who led him to the reception of hypnotic relief of pain? Dr. B. directed the course of action that resulted in the loss of pain. But I'm a doctor too. Things equal to the same thing are equal to each other. B. is a doctor; Erickson is a doctor. Therefore, B. equals Erickson.

H: Well, do you recall when you first saw him whether you were concerned about his being suicidal?

E: No. (Pause) No, I don't. As he phrased it, it might be

so interpreted. You see, I'm still not certain whether he's been married twice. But I think he has been. And I have, in his presence, told a class he was alone in this world, no relatives, just friends.

H: And it wasn't until now that he mentioned his brothers then?

E: I've learned he had *two* brothers.

H: Well, this raises interesting problems about how you describe therapy. Because if you took that man's description of what you did with him you would look like a very different sort of a therapist.

E: That's right. Have you seen marble cake?

H: Yes.

E: If you saw the baker preparing marble cake, the finished product looks entirely different.

H: Oh yes, I'm sure patients have to make some sense out of what's happened to them, so they put it together in some framework that is reasonable to them.

E: It's a framework that depends upon *their* understandings, and my statements are all studded with a wealth of phrases and sentences that can be interpreted in terms of his own life. As he mentioned this morning, I told him about this person, another patient, this gentleman himself, and, "You find out he's just been talking about *you*." (Laughs)

In the anecdote approach the patient has long had the experiences of listening to you tell a story and wanting to tell you *his* story. And if I want to find out in ordinary social conversation if so-and-so has a brother, I'll say something about mine. It won't be long before he starts talking about his.

H: Okay. I would agree with that. I don't see what that has to do with the relief of pain in the situation.

E: All right. Now I talk about other patients who have had pain, who get relief from pain. Now he has had the experience, in the past, of having had pain and having

had relief from pain. I hope you remember two particular statements he made. He said he was suffering un-
bearable pain, came in, sat down, and I levitated his
hand. I turned it over and then he said, "It's like the
manna from heaven." Then I told him I had levitated
his hand, and I turned it over so his hand was in a *receiving* position. It was several sessions later I remarked to him that relief from pain was like manna
from heaven. When he demonstrated that to you, with
his palm extended, he said it was like manna from
heaven, putting it together. (Phone call)
Mrs. E: Mrs. F. (On the telephone)
E: Hello, Mrs. F. Yes. Mmmm hmm. I noticed in your voice
that you have pain. All right. Now take a good position in your chair, look at something, and recall what
I said, and nobody needs to speak to you. Recall how
I told you to look at the corner of the clock, keep your
head still, and close your eyes. And I would say spend
about 15, 20 minutes with increasing comfort, and in
about 15 or 20 minutes, take your time and awaken
and be free of pain. Yes, about 10 o'clock. Goodbye."
(Hangs up telephone)

Mr. Smith remarked that I told anecdotes about
former patients, people in general, my family, and
after a while he knew that I wasn't talking about any
of those people. I was just talking about *him*. And he
said that after stating, separately, that I went into
a trance first, and he later joined me. I think that's
a very pertinent summary.

The thing I want to take up with you today is this:
You know about the ways of communication; you
know Ray Birdwhistell. We learn those nonverbal
ways of communication. We think of the nonverbal
as *not* spoken communication, but nonverbal communication also includes any casual conversation that
does not mention it, but which *does* bring forth memo-

ries and understanding, such as the outstretched hand
and the receiving palm. And whatever you say may
not necessariliy be related to a verbalization of receiving manna from heaven, but the outstretched palm,
or rather the receiving palm, and the subsequent mention that relief from pain is like manna from heaven.

H: This analogy business again. Now you must have some
timing which you're watching, and if they begin to
connect it with themselves, do you then shift it further away from them?

E: I'm very likely to shift it over to them as soon as I see
them doing it. Mr. Smith said, "First Dr. Erickson
goes into a trance, then he tells me things, and I join
him in the trance because he wasn't talking about all
of those other people. You suddenly realize he was
talking about you all the time."

H: Well, when you tell a particular anecdote, would you
rather the patient at that moment didn't know it was
about them, or would you rather they did?

E: They shouldn't know it's about them.

H: So if it begins to look like they're relating this to themselves, you drift away, making it further from them?

E: I drift away at first to make it further from them, thereby eliciting a further effort to understand. Then when
I see them beginning to apply it to themselves, and
when I see them stepping over and joining me, then
I can shift explicitly to them. Sometimes without even
completing the anecdote. Because we all have so many,
many memories that we don't recall, are unaware of.
Now if I really wanted to find out about Mr. Smith's
background, then I might describe driving across the
desert, camping out, roaming at a high point, and seeing there a lonesome ironwood tree. Apparently one
of the branches got broken by the wind smashing
around the corner. Now the anecdote doesn't have to
be true. But you phrase it correctly. An ironwood tree

— most people can't last more than 15 years laying floors. But he lasted 37 years. Ironwood tree. Broken branch, probably the wind smashing around the corner.

H: Wait a minute. The wind smashing, I don't understand that. Having the wind smash around the corner of the tree?

E: Of this high place.

H: Oh.

E: That had obscured any view of that tree until you got to the tree, or rather got the tree *within* your view, and saw the broken branch caused by the wind smashing around the corner. Broken branch, broken wind, the smash.

H: Mmmm hmm. And that would bring forth what from him do you think?

E: If I wanted to know how many relatives, I'd start looking around the ironwood tree for mesquite bushes. And I would learn about his relatives, because a tree doesn't stand alone. "If I should be the last leaf upon the tree."

H: Why do you prefer to do it that way rather than asking about his relatives?

E: If I don't know anything at all about his relatives, and he specified that date in June, which means he will be in this *alone*, and I see that one ironwood tree with a broken branch. Wind that swept around that high rise. Broken branch, broken limb, smashing wind. I would look around for a small sage bush, higher mesquite bushes, any old-timer out in the desert, and the tall tree.

H: Well, granted that you can do it that way and get this information, why is this, to you, a better way than asking them about it?

E: Because when I ask you about your sister, brother, parents, then you put them into a social frame befitting your education. When I do it in this indirect way, there's that broken branch, smashed, and I'm looking around for small sage bushes, taller mesquite — grand-children, relatives that are taller than grandchildren.

INDEX